MAHAN
ON NAVAL WARFARE

Selections from the Writings of
Rear Admiral Alfred T. Mahan

Edited by

Allan Westcott

DOVER PUBLICATIONS, INC.
Mineola, New York

Published in Canada by General Publishing Company, Ltd., 30 Lesmill Road, Don Mills, Toronto, Ontario.

Bibliographical Note

This Dover edition, first published in 1999, is an unabridged reprint of the 1941 edition, edited by Allan Westcott and published by Little, Brown and Company, Boston.

Library of Congress Cataloging-in-Publication Data

Mahan, A. T. (Alfred Thayer), 1840–1914.
    Mahan on naval warfare : selections from the writings of Rear Admiral Alfred Thayer Mahan / edited by Allan Westcott.
        p.   cm.
    Originally published: Boston : Little, Brown and Co., 1941.
    ISBN 0-486-40729-2 (pbk.)
    1. Sea-power. 2. Naval strategy. 3. Naval art and science. I. Westcott, Allan. II. Title.
V25.M3723   1999
359—dc21   99-30216
                                                                    CIP

Manufactured in the United States of America
Dover Publications, Inc., 31 East 2nd Street, Mineola, N.Y. 11501

ALFRED THAYER MAHAN

A HUNDRED years or more after his birth, the name of Rear Admiral Mahan is unquestionably more widely known, both at home and abroad, than that of any other American naval officer. Yet his fame rests, not on his achievements as a ship or fleet commander, but on his writings as a great naval historian and student of naval warfare.

In this turn of fortune, some justification may be found for the opinion of Mahan's father, as related in the Admiral's delightful volume of reminiscences, "From Sail to Steam," regarding the son's choice of the navy as a lifework. "My father told me," writes Mahan, "that he thought me less fit for a military than for a civil profession, having watched me carefully. I think myself now that he was right; for though I have no cause to complain of unsuccess, I believe I should have done better elsewhere." [1] The father, Dennis Hart Mahan, was a graduate of West Point, in later life a distinguished professor of engineering at the Military Academy, and thus well qualified to weigh his son's character and the requirements of a military career.

Whatever the apparent wisdom of the choice at the time, it was in the event fortunate both for himself and for the naval profession. His long and varied service as an officer afloat and ashore gave him an invaluable background for the study of

[1] "From Sail to Steam," p. xiv.

naval history and international affairs. On the other hand, his writings have brought home to every maritime nation the importance of sea power, and have stimulated in his own profession an interest in naval history and naval science which has helped to keep it abreast the progress of the age. This direct bearing of his professional experience upon his writings adds significance to the details of his life in the navy.

Alfred Thayer Mahan entered the Naval Academy at Annapolis, Maryland, September 30, 1856. Born at West Point, September 27, 1840, he was at the time of his entrance but three days above sixteen. Like many another candidate for the navy, he solicited his own appointment, obtaining it finally through the influence of Jefferson Davis, who had studied under his father at West Point, and was at this time Secretary of War. Having attended Columbia College for two years preceding, the boy was permitted — by a concession of which this is believed to be the only instance in the annals of the Academy — to omit the first year's work and enter with the "Youngster" class, or "class of '55 date," according to the nomenclature then used. Up to the year 1851 the midshipmen's course had consisted of five years at sea followed by one at the Academy. Mahan entered in the autumn after the graduation of the last class under the old scheme; and it was to the more mature, "sea-going" character of former classes that he attributes the total absence of hazing in his day. The practice was "not so much reprobated as ignored." It came in later, when the Academy was moved to Newport during the Civil War, and "new ideals were evolved by a mass of schoolboys, severed from those elder associates with the influence of whom no professors nor officers can vie." [1]

In the dusty files of Academy registers for that period one may read the names of boys famous in later years. George Dewey was a class ahead of Mahan; Schley and Sampson were respectively one class and two classes behind. On graduation, Dewey stood fifth in a class of fifteen; Mahan second in a class of twenty, with a record apparently very close to the leader's; and Sampson stood first. In his last year the future historian was first in seamanship, physics, political science, and moral science, third in naval tactics and gunnery, fourth in "steam engine," and fifth in astronomy and navigation. The year before he had excelled in physics, rhetoric, and Spanish. The details are noteworthy chiefly as they show the subjects of the old-time curriculum, in which so-called practical branches were less predominant than they are today. Of Mahan's class, which numbered forty-nine at the time of entrance, twenty-nine had dropped back or resigned before the end of the course.

After a cruise in South American waters in the old frigate *Congress,* Mahan at once received his commission as lieutenant, August 31, 1861, and soon afterward an appointment as second in command of the steam corvette *Pocahontas,* then in the Potomac flotilla. It illustrates the rapid promotion

[1] "From Sail to Steam," p. 55.

of those war-time days that each member of his class received similar advancement in the first year of the war. In the *Pocahontas* he came under fire in the attack on Port Royal, and afterward spent many weary months in blockade duty, first in the *Pocahontas* off the south Atlantic coast, and later in the *Seminole* off Sabine Pass, Texas. This latter station, Mahan remarks, "was a jumping-off place, the end of nowhere." "Day after day we lay inactive — roll, roll." The monotony was broken by a pleasant eight months at the Naval Academy in Newport and a "practice cruise" to England in the *Macedonian;* and in the last year of the war he saw more varied service on the staff of Rear Admiral Dahlgren, again on the Atlantic coast blockade.

Commissioned lieutenant commander in 1865, Mahan passed the ensuing twenty years in the customary routine of alternate sea and shore duty. In 1867–1869, a long cruise in the steam frigate *Iroquois* to Japan, via Guadeloupe, Rio, Cape Town, Madagascar, Aden, and Bombay, gave opportunity, unusual even in the navy, to see the world, and brought him to Kobe in time to witness the opening of new treaty ports and the last days of medieval Japan.

In 1885, when he had reached the rank of captain and was forty-five years of age, he had yet had little opportunity to display the distinctive talents which were to win him permanent fame. Partly, perhaps, in consequence of a book by his pen entitled "The Gulf and Inland Waters" and published two years before, but more likely as a result of the shrewd

estimate which naval officers form regarding their
fellows in the service, he was requested at this time
to give a series of lectures on naval history and
tactics at the Naval War College, then just established at Newport, Rhode Island. His acceptance
of this duty marks a turning point in his career.

The call reached him in the *Wachusett* off the
west coast of South America. It was nearly two
years later, in August, 1886, when he took up his
residence at the college, succeeding Rear Admiral
Luce as president. A change of political administration in the meantime had brought about a less
favorable policy toward this new departure in naval
education, with the result that, to quote Mahan
again, the college "was reefed close down, looking
out for squalls at any moment from any quarter,"
for the next four or five years. It bears evidence
of his tact and tenacity, and it was not the least of
his accomplishments for the navy, that he piloted
the institution safely through this crucial period,
with scant appropriations or none at all, in the face
of a hostile Secretary of the Navy and a lukewarm
service.

After seven years devoted chiefly to the War
College, Mahan went to sea for the last time as
commander of the cruiser *Chicago* in the European
squadron. At this time "The Influence of Sea
Power upon History" had already been published,
and the volume on the French Revolution and
Empire was nearly ready for the press. Upon re-
questing postponement of sea duty until its completion, he was informed by his superior in the

Bureau of Navigation that it was "not the business
of a naval officer to write books." The remark
was narrow, for the naval or any other profession
would soon stagnate without the stimulus of free
discussion and study, which finds its best outlet
through the press; and it showed slight recognition
of the immense value of Mahan's writings to the
navy and the nation. Still it was well for the
author that he made this last cruise — his only experience with a ship of the new fleet. If the importance of his first book was not realized at home —
and it is stated that he had great difficulty in finding
a publisher — it was fully recognized abroad. His
arrival in England was taken as an opportunity to
pay a national tribute of appreciation, of which the
degrees conferred by both Oxford and Cambridge
were but one expression. There is a slightly
humorous aspect to the competition of American
universities to award similar honors upon his return.

Retiring in 1896 after forty years of service, he
was recalled to act as a member of the Naval War
Board from May 9, 1898, until the close of the
War with Spain. His fellow members were Rear
Admiral Montgomery Sicard and Captain A. S.
Crowninshield. This board practically controlled
the naval strategy of the war. Some of its more
important decisions were made before Mahan joined;
but throughout the war its naval dispositions were
effective, and, aside from the location of the "Flying
Squadron" at Hampton Roads as a concession to
the fears of coast cities, they are fully approved in
his writings.

His choice a year later as one of the American delegates to the first Peace Conference at The Hague was eminently fitting in view of his thorough knowledge of international relations and the rules governing naval warfare. In determining the attitude of the American delegation, he took a strong stand against any agreement that would contract our freedom of action with regard to the Monroe Doctrine, and against immunity of private property at sea. The arguments against this latter policy he afterward stated effectively in print[1] and in a memorandum to the Navy Department. With the fulfillment of this duty, his public services, aside from his work as a writer, came to a close.

In the navy, as in other walks of life, an incompatibility is often assumed — and often unjustly — between mastery of theory and skill in practice, between the thoughtful student and the capable man of action; and there is no denying that among his contemporaries this assumption was current with regard to Mahan. While a conclusion is difficult in such a matter, the case may well rest on the following statement by a friend and fellow officer: "Duty, in whatever form it came, was sacred. Invariably he gave to its performance the best that was in him. That he distinguished himself pre-eminently on shipboard cannot be claimed. Luck or circumstances denied him the opportunity of doing things heroic, and his modesty those purely spectacular. As a subordinate or as captain of a single ship, what he did was well done. No further proof of his qualities

[1] See pp. 328–341.

in this respect is needed than the fact that, at the outbreak of the Civil War, when finishing his midshipman's cruise, he was asked by a shipmate, an officer who expected a command, to go with him as 'first lieutenant.' To his colleagues of the old navy this invitation was the highest form of professional approval. The fates decreed that the wider field should not be his wherein, as commander-in-chief of a fleet in war time, he could have exhibited the mastery he surely possessed of that art with which his name will forever be indissolubly linked." [1]

From the same source may be taken a passage of more intimate portrayal. "In person Mahan was tall, spare, erect, with blue eyes, fair complexion, hair and beard originally sandy. He respected the body as the temple of his soul, and he paid it the homage of abstemious living, of outdoor games and abundant exercise. In manner he was modest to excess, dignified, courteous. Reticent in speech with people in general, those who enjoyed the rare privilege of his intimacy knew him to be possessed of a keen sense of humor and a fund of delightful anecdotes. To such friends he was a most charming companion, so different from the grave, self-contained philosopher he appeared to the rest and less favored of his acquaintance. His home life was ideal."

The lectures delivered at the Naval War College were the basis of "The Influence of Sea Power

[1] Rear Admiral Bradley A. Fiske, *U. S. Naval Institute*, January–February, 1915, p. 2.

upon History." The author tells us how the central idea came to him in the library of the English Club at Lima, Peru, while reading Momsen's "History of Rome." "It suddenly struck me . . . how different things might have been could Hannibal have invaded Italy by sea, as the Romans often had Africa, instead of by the long land route." A year later, when he returned to the United States, the plan of the lectures was already formed: "I would investigate coincidently the general history and the naval history of the past two centuries with a view to demonstrating the influence of the events of the one upon the other." Written between May and September of 1886, and delivered as lectures during the next four years, the book was carefully revised before its publication in the spring of 1890.

This book exerted at the time, and has continued to exert, a widespread influence; and while its author's reputation was increased by his later writings, it remains his best known and greatest work. One reason for this is that it states his fundamental teaching, and in a form easy to grasp. The preface and the first chapter, which cover but eighty-nine pages, survey rapidly the rise and decline of great sea powers and the national characteristics affecting maritime development. The rest of the book, treating in detail the period between 1660 and 1783, reinforces the conclusions already stated.

Timeliness also contributed to its success. The book furnished authoritative guidance in a period of transition and new departures in international affairs. For nearly twenty years, under Bismarck,

Germany had been consolidating the empire established in 1871. When William II ascended the throne in 1888, the ambitions of both ruler and nation were already turned toward colonial expansion and world power. A German Admiralty separate from the War Office was established in 1889; Heligoland was secured a year later; the Kiel Canal was nearing completion. In England, the Naval Defense Act of 1889 provided an increase of seventy ships during the next four years. The rivals against whom she measured her naval strength were still France and Russia. In the United States, Congress in 1890 authorized three battleships, the first vessels of this class to be added to the American navy. During the following ten years the rivalry of nations was chiefly in commercial and colonial aggrandizement, marked by the final downfall of Spain's colonial empire and a greatly increased importance attached to control of the sea.

For the nations taking part in this expansion, Mahan was a kind of gospel, furnishing texts for every discussion of naval policy. "After his first book," says a French writer, "and especially from 1895 on, Mahan supplied the sound basis for all thought on naval and maritime affairs; it was seen clearly that sea power was the principle which, adhered to or departed from, would determine whether empires should stand or fall." [1]

To Great Britain in particular the book came as

[1] "La Maîtrise de la Mer," Auguste Moireau, *Revue des Deux Mondes*, October, 1902.

a timely analysis of the means by which she had grown in wealth and dominion. This was indeed no discovery. Nearly three centuries earlier Francis Bacon had written, "To be master of the sea is an abridgment [epitome] of monarchy . . . he that commands the sea is at great liberty, and may take as much and as little of the war as he will." [1] Before and after Bacon, England had acted upon this principle. But it remained for Mahan to give the thesis full expression, to demonstrate it by concrete illustration, and to apply it to modern conditions. "For the first time," writes the British naval historian Sir Julian Corbett, "naval history was placed on a philosophical basis. From the mass of facts which had hitherto done duty for naval history, broad generalizations were possible. The ears of statesmen and publicists were opened, and a new note began to sound in world politics. Regarded as a political pamphlet in the higher sense — for that is how the famous book is best characterized — it has few equals in the sudden and far-reaching effect it produced on political thought and action." [2]

Germany was not slow to take to heart this interpretation of the vital dependence of world empire on sea power. The Kaiser read the book, annotated its pages, and placed copies in every ship of the German fleet.[3] It was soon translated not

[1] "Of Kingdoms and Estates."

[2] "The Revival of Naval History," *Contemporary Review*, November, 1917. While the term "political pamphlet" suggests the influence of the book abroad, it is obviously inappropriate in describing its purpose and method of treatment.

[3] See Captain W. D. Puleston, "The Life and Work of Captain Alfred Thayer Mahan, U.S.N." (1939).

only into German but into French, Japanese, Russian, Italian, and Spanish. This and later works by the same author were perhaps most diligently studied by officers of the Japanese navy, then rising rapidly to the strength manifested in the Russian war. "As far as known to myself," writes Mahan, "more of my works have been done into Japanese than into any other one tongue." [1] The debt of all students of naval warfare is well expressed by a noted Italian officer and writer, — "Mahan, who is the great teacher of us all." [2]

What has been said of "The Influence of Sea Power upon History" applies in varying degrees to the sixteen historical works and collections of essays which appeared in the ensuing twenty-five years. While extending the field covered by the earlier book, they maintained in general its high qualities. The most important of these, "The Influence of Sea Power upon the French Revolution and Empire," covers the period from 1793 to 1812. This and the studies of the American Revolution and the War of 1812 form with his first book a continuous historical series from 1660 to 1815. The "Life of Nelson" and "Life of Farragut" are standard professional biographies of these two commanders, who, if we accept Mahan's opinion, rank respectively first and second among naval leaders. The best of his thought on contemporary naval warfare is gathered up in his "Naval Strategy," published in 1911. Based on lectures

[1] "From Sail to Steam," p. 303.
[2] "Captain Romeo Bernotti," letter to the editor, April 25, 1918.

first delivered in 1887, and afterward frequently expanded and modified to meet changing conditions, this book, while invaluable to the professional student, lacks something of the continuity and clearness of structure of the historical works.

The authoritativeness of these writings, it may be repeated, was strengthened by the author's technical equipment and long years of practical experience. Moreover, as his friend Theodore Roosevelt remarked of him, "Mahan was the only great naval writer who also possessed the mind of a statesman of the first class."[1] His concern always was not merely with the facts of history but with the "logic of events" and their lessons for today.

Following his retirement, Admiral Mahan wrote more frequently and freely on problems of the present and future. Of the subjects treated, some were distinctly professional — the speed and size of battleships, the size, composition, and disposition of fleets, modifications in the international codes affecting naval warfare, naval events in contemporary wars. Others entered the wider field of world politics, voicing the author's sincere belief in American colonial expansion and active participation in world affairs, in the need of a navy sufficient to make our influence felt, in the limitations as well as the usefulness of arbitration, in the continuance of force as an important factor in international relations.

Many of these later essays bore directly upon American naval and national problems; and in fact,

[1] "A Great Public Servant," *The Outlook*, January 13, 1915.

though Mahan's influence made its first great impact abroad, in England and on the continent, it was also powerfully exerted in his native land. As has only recently been fully recognized,[1] it was his writings that supplied the philosophical groundwork and strongest arguments for the American expansionist movement centering about the Spanish–American War. Up to the late 1880's Mahan himself had been an anti-imperialist, but was converted to the opposite view by his own studies, which found in world trade, expansion, and sea power the keys to national greatness. The America of his time, extended now to its continental frontiers and awakened to a sense of its vastly increased wealth and power, was ripe for these new ideas. In his first magazine article, "The United States Looking Outward" (1890), Mahan stressed the larger part which he felt his country should play in world affairs; and in subsequent articles, such as "Hawaii and Our Future Sea Power" and "The Isthmus and Sea Power," both published in 1893, he emphasized vigorously our need of naval bases in the Caribbean and Pacific to guard our coasts and commerce on two oceans, and our need to control and strongly defend any passageway constructed between the two. Like the teachings of his first books, these were ideas which his warm friends Theodore Roosevelt and Henry Cabot Lodge received with enthusiasm, and which they well knew how to apply in a practical way. Unquestionably, though the details are too long for elaboration here, the historian of sea power had much

[1] See Julius W. Pratt, "Expansionists of 1898" (1936).

to do with the emergence of the United States in 1898 as a world power, with possessions and new interests in distant seas. And no one believed more sincerely than he that this would be good for the United States and the rest of the world.

In this country his influence was also strong in the more strictly naval field. By prevision and warm advocacy he did much to secure professional and public acceptance of such policies as the peace-time concentration of fleets in preparation for war, the abandonment of a passive defensive in naval strategy, the systematic professional study of the art of war, and in general the maintenance of a strong and efficient fleet, as against the constant national tendency toward the opposite extreme. His writings on such subjects avoided jingoism and sensation-mongering; and only a fanatical advocate of immediate disarmament and peace at any price could have denied the steadying and sobering effect of his opposition, with its firm grip on realities and steadfast respect for truth. As Andrew D. White said of his colleague Mahan's antagonistic views at the First Hague Conference: "They were an excellent tonic . . . When he speaks the millennium fades, and this stern, severe, actual world appears."

Mahan's style naturally varied somewhat with the audience and the theme. His historical writings have been justly described as burdened with qualifications, and marked by a laborious fullness of statement, which strains the attention, while it adds weight and dignity to the presentation. This in general is true of the histories; but there are many passages in these where the subject inspires him to genuine eloquence. In the "Life of Nelson" and "Types of Naval Officers" there is little of the defect mentioned, and there are few more entertaining volumes of naval reminiscence than "From Sail to Steam." "The besetting anxiety of my soul," writes the author himself, "was to be exact and lucid. I might not succeed, but my wish was indisputable. To be accurate in facts and correct in conclusions, both as to application and expression, dominated all other motives." [1] One might dispense with reams of "fine writing" for a page of prose guided by these standards.

On December 1, 1914, Rear Admiral Mahan died suddenly of heart failure. A month before, he had left his home at Quogue, Long Island, and come to Washington to pursue investigations for a history of American expansion and its bearing on sea power. His death, occurring four months after the outbreak of hostilities in Europe, was perhaps hastened by constant study of the diplomatic and military events of the war, the approach of which he had clearly foreseen, as well as America's vital interest in the Allied cause. It was unfortunate that his political and professional wisdom should have been lost at that time.

The World War of 1914–1918, illustrating once more the slow, constrictive pressure of sea power, may be said to have vindicated Mahan's theories, though it might be argued on the other side that commerce destruction, ruthlessly applied by the

[1] "From Sail to Steam," p. 288.

weaker naval belligerent, very nearly won the war for Germany.

Since that time, the view has not infrequently been advanced that changes in weapons and changed conditions of warfare have lessened the value of his teaching, and the value which he attached to naval armaments. It may be admitted, indeed, that, writing from a naval standpoint, Mahan did not always recognize fully the limitations of sea power against a nation supreme and self-sufficient on land, or the important contribution to Britain's victories which was rendered by the land forces of her allies. On the other hand, it can hardly be said that changes in weapons have seriously altered the importance to be attached to control of the great avenues of sea communication, whether such control is exercised upon, or beneath, or above, the surface of the sea. Certainly, were he alive today, Mahan would be among the first to study eagerly the effect of changes in weapons upon sea control. Interpreting his teachings in these broader terms, few Britons and few Americans, a quarter century after his death, would question the continued importance of sea power.

ALLAN WESTCOTT.

UNITED STATES NAVAL ACADEMY,
January, 1941.

CONTENTS

Contents

LIST OF MAPS AND PLANS

PART I

NAVAL PRINCIPLES

MAHAN
ON NAVAL WARFARE

PART I: NAVAL PRINCIPLES

1. THE VALUE OF HISTORICAL STUDY [1]

THE history of Sea Power is largely, though by
no means solely, a narrative of contests between
nations, of mutual rivalries, of violence frequently
culminating in war. The profound influence of sea
commerce upon the wealth and strength of countries
was clearly seen long before the true principles which
governed its growth and prosperity were detected.
To secure to one's own people a disproportionate
share of such benefits, every effort was made to
exclude others, either by the peaceful legislative
methods of monopoly or prohibitory regulations, or,
when these failed, by direct violence. The clash of
interests, the angry feelings roused by conflicting
attempts thus to appropriate the larger share, if not
the whole, of the advantages of commerce, and of
distant unsettled commercial regions, led to wars.
On the other hand, wars arising from other causes
have been greatly modified in their conduct and issue
by the control of the sea. Therefore the history of
sea power, while embracing in its broad sweep all

[1] "The Influence of Sea Power upon History," pp. 1-2, 8-10.

that tends to make a people great upon the sea or by the sea, is largely a military history; and it is in this aspect that it will be mainly, though not exclusively, regarded in the following pages.

A study of the military history of the past, such as this, is enjoined by great military leaders as essential to correct ideas and to the skillful conduct of war in the future. Napoleon names among the campaigns to be studied by the aspiring soldier, those of Alexander, Hannibal, and Cæsar, to whom gunpowder was unknown; and there is a substantial agreement among professional writers that, while many of the conditions of war vary from age to age with the progress of weapons, there are certain teachings in the school of history which remain constant, and being, therefore, of universal application, can be elevated to the rank of general principles. For the same reason the study of the sea history of the past will be found instructive, by its illustration of the general principles of maritime war, notwithstanding the great changes that have been brought about in naval weapons by the scientific advances of the past half century, and by the introduction of steam as the motive power. [The pages omitted point out lessons to be drawn from galley and sailing-ship warfare. — EDITOR.]

Before hostile armies or fleets are brought into con*tact* (a word which perhaps better than any other indicates the dividing line between tactics and strategy), there are a number of questions to be decided, covering the whole plan of operations throughout the theater of war. Among these are the proper

function of the navy in the war; its true objective;
the point or points upon which it should be concentrated; the establishment of depots of coal and supplies; the maintenance of communications between
these depots and the home base; the military value
of commerce-destroying as a decisive or a secondary
operation of war; the system upon which commerce-
destroying can be most efficiently conducted, whether
by scattered cruisers or by holding in force some
vital center through which commercial shipping must
pass. All these are strategic questions, and upon all
these history has a great deal to say. There has
been of late a valuable discussion in English naval
circles as to the comparative merits of the policies
of two great English admirals, Lord Howe and Lord
St. Vincent, in the disposition of the English navy
when at war with France. The question is purely
strategic, and is not of mere historical interest; it is
of vital importance now, and the principles upon
which its decision rests are the same now as then.
St. Vincent's policy saved England from invasion,
and in the hands of Nelson and his brother admirals
led straight up to Trafalgar.

It is then particularly in the field of naval strategy
that the teachings of the past have a value which is
in no degree lessened. They are there useful not
only as illustrative of principles, but also as prece-
dents, owing to the comparative permanence of the
conditions. This is less obviously true as to tactics,
when the fleets come into collision at the point to
which strategic considerations have brought them.
The unresting progress of mankind causes continual

change in the weapons; and with that must come a
continual change in the manner of fighting, — in the
handling and disposition of troops or ships on the
battlefield. Hence arises a tendency on the part of
many connected with maritime matters to think that
no advantage is to be gained from the study of
former experiences; that time so used is wasted.
This view, though natural, not only leaves wholly out
of sight those broad strategic considerations which
lead nations to put fleets afloat, which direct the
sphere of their action, and so have modified and will
continue to modify the history of the world, but is
one-sided and narrow even as to tactics. The battles
of the past succeeded or failed according as they
were fought in conformity with the principles of
war; and the seaman who carefully studies the causes
of success or failure will not only detect and gradually assimilate these principles, but will also acquire
increased aptitude in applying them to the tactical
use of the ships and weapons of his own day. He
will observe also that changes of tactics have not
only taken place *after* changes in weapons, which
necessarily is the case, but that the interval between
such changes has been unduly long. This doubtless
arises from the fact that an improvement of weapons
is due to the energy of one or two men, while changes
in tactics have to overcome the inertia of a conserva-
tive class; but it is a great evil. It can be remedied
only by a candid recognition of each change, by careful study of the powers and limitations of the new
ship or weapon, and by a consequent adaptation of
the method of using it to the qualities it possesses,

which will constitute its tactics. History shows that it is vain to hope that military men generally will be at the pains to do this, but that the one who does will go into battle with a great advantage, — a lesson in itself of no mean value.

2. " Theoretical " versus " Practical " Training [1]

A Historical Instance

THERE have long been two conflicting opinions as to the best way to fit naval officers, and indeed all men called to active pursuits, for the discharge of their duties. The one, of the so-called practical man, would find in early beginning and constant remaining afloat *all* that is requisite; the other will find the best result in study, in elaborate mental preparation. I have no hesitation in avowing that personally I think that the United States Navy is erring on the latter side; but, be that as it may, there seems little doubt that the mental activity which exists so widely is not directed toward the management of ships in battle, to the planning of naval campaigns, to the study of strategic and tactical problems, nor even to the secondary matters connected with the maintenance of warlike operations at sea.[2] Now we have had the results of the two opinions as to the training of naval officers pretty well tested by the experience of two great maritime nations, France and England, each of which, not so much by formulated purpose as by national bias, committed itself unduly to the one or

---

[1] "Naval Administration and Warfare," Objects of the Naval War College (1888), pp. 193–194, 233–240.
[2] In a preceding passage the author shows that American naval thought has been preoccupied with problems of material. — Editor.

the other. The results were manifested in our War of Independence, which gave rise to the only well-contested, wide-spread maritime war between nearly equal forces that modern history records. There remains in my own mind no doubt, after reading the naval history on both sides, that the English brought to this struggle much superior seamanship, learned by the constant practice of shipboard; while the French officers, most of whom had been debarred from similar experience by the decadence of their navy in the middle of the century, had devoted themselves to the careful study of their profession. In short, what are commonly called the practical and the theoretical man were pitted against each other, and the result showed how mischievous is any plan which neglects either theory or practice, or which ignores the fact that correct theoretical ideas are essential to successful practical work. The practical seamanship and experience of the English were continually foiled by the want of correct tactical conceptions on the part of their own chiefs, and the superior science of the French, acquired mainly by study.   It is true that the latter were guided by a false policy on the part of their government and a false professional tradition. The navy, by its mobility, is pre-eminently fitted for offensive war, and the French deliberately and constantly subordinated it to defensive action.   But, though the system was faulty, they had a system; they had ideas; they had plans familiar to their officers, while the English usually had none — and a poor system is better than none at all. . . .

What is Practical?

It was said to me by some one: " If you want
to attract officers to the College, give them something that will help them pass their next examination." But the test of war, when it comes, will
be found a more searching trial of what is in a
man than the verdict of several amiable gentlemen, disposed to give the benefit of every doubt.
Then you will encounter men straining every
faculty and every means to injure you. Shall we
then, who prepare so anxiously for an examination, view as a " practical " proceeding, worthy of
" practical " men, the postponing to the very moment of imperative action the consideration of *how*
to act, *how* to do our fighting, either in the broader
domain of strategy, or in the more limited field of
tactics, whether of the single ship or of the fleet?
Navies exist for war; and the question presses for
an answer: " Is this neglect to master the experience
of the past, to elicit, formulate, and absorb its principles, is it *practical?* " Is it " practical " to wait
till the squall strikes you before shortening sail?
If the object and aim of the College is to promote
such study, to facilitate such results, to foster and
disseminate such ideas, can it be reproached that its
purpose is not " practical," even though at first its
methods be tentative and its results imperfect?
    The word " practical " has suffered and been de-
based by a misapprehension of that other word
" theoretical," to which it is accurately and logically

opposed. Theory is properly defined as a scheme
of things which *terminates in speculation, or con-
templation,* without a view to practice. The idea
was amusingly expressed in the toast, said to have
been drunk at a meeting of mathematicians, " Eternal perdition to the man who would degrade pure
mathematics by applying it to any useful purpose."
The word " theoretical," therefore, is applied
rightly and legitimately only to mental processes
that end in themselves, that have no result in action;
but by a natural, yet most unfortunate, confusion of
thought, it has come to be applied to all mental
processes whatsoever, whether fruitful or not, and
has transferred its stigma to them, while " practical " has walked off with all the honors of a
utilitarian age.

If therefore the line of thought, study and reflection, which the War College seeks to promote, is
really liable to the reproach that it leads to no useful end, can result in no effective action, it falls
justly under the condemnation of being not " practical." But it must be said frankly and fearlessly
that the man who is prepared to apply this stigma
to the line of the College effort must also be prepared to class as not " practical " men like Napoleon, like his distinguished opponent, the Austrian
Archduke Charles, and like Jomini, the profuse
writer on military art and military history, whose
works, if somewhat supplanted by newer digests,
have lost little or none of their prestige as a profound study and exposition of the principles of
warfare.

Jomini was not merely a military theorist, who saw war from the outside; he was a distinguished and thoughtful soldier, in the prime of life during the Napoleonic wars, and of a contemporary reputation such that, when he deserted the cause of the emperor, he was taken at once into a high position as a confidential adviser of the allied sovereigns. Yet what does he say of strategy? Strategy is to him the queen of military sciences; it underlies the fortunes of every campaign. As in a building, which, however fair and beautiful the superstructure, is radically marred and imperfect if the foundation be insecure — so, if the strategy be wrong, the skill of the general on the battlefield, the valor of the soldier, the brilliancy of victory, however otherwise decisive, fail of their effect. Yet how does he define strategy, the effects of which, if thus far-reaching, must surely be esteemed " practical "? " Strategy," he said, " is the art of making war upon the map. It precedes the operations of the campaign, the clash of arms on the field. It is done in the cabinet, it is the work of the student, with his dividers in his hand and his information lying beside him." In other words, it originates in a mental process, but it does not end there; therefore it is practical.

Most of us have heard an anecdote of the great Napoleon, which is nevertheless so apt to my purpose that I must risk the repetition. Having had no time to verify my reference, I must quote from memory, but of substantial accuracy I am sure. A few weeks before one of his early and most decisive campaigns, his secretary, Bourrienne, entered the office and found the First Consul, as he then was, stretched on the floor with a large map before him. Pricked over the map, in what to Bourrienne was confusion, were a number of red and black pins. After a short silence the secretary, who was an old friend of school days, asked him what it all meant. The Consul laughed goodnaturedly, called him a fool, and said: " This set of pins represents the Austrians and this the French. On such a day I shall leave Paris. My troops will then be in such positions. On a certain day," naming it, " I shall be here," pointing, " and my troops will have moved there. At such a time I shall cross the mountains, a few days later my army will be here, the Austrians will have done thus and so; and at a certain date I will beat them here," placing a pin. Bourrienne said nothing, perhaps he may have thought the matter not " practical; " but a few weeks later, after the battle (Marengo, I think) had been fought, he was seated with the general in his military traveling carriage. The programme had been carried out, and he recalled the incident to Bonaparte's mind. The latter himself smiled at the singular accuracy of his predictions in the particular instance.

In the light of such an incident, the question I would like to pose will receive of course but one answer. Was the work on which the general was engaged in his private office, this work of a student, was it " practical "? Or can it by any reasonable method be so divorced from what followed, that

the word " practical " only applies farther on. Did
he only begin to be practical when he got into his
carriage to drive from the Tuileries, or did the
practical begin when he joined the army, or when
the first gun of the campaign was fired? Or, on
the other hand, if he had passed that time, given to
studying the campaign, in arranging for a new
development of the material of war, and so had
gone with his plans undeveloped, would he not
have done a thing very far from " practical " ?

But we must push our inquiry a little farther
back to get the full significance of Bourrienne's
story. Whence came the facility and precision
with which Bonaparte planned the great campaign
of Marengo? Partly, unquestionably, from a native genius rarely paralleled; partly, but not by any
means wholly. Hear his own prescription: " If
any man will be a great general, let him study."
Study what? " Study history. Study the campaigns
of the great generals — Alexander, Hannibal,
Cæsar " (who never smelt gunpowder, nor dreamed
of ironclads) " as well as those of Turenne, Frederick, and myself, Napoleon." Had Bonaparte
entered his cabinet to plan the campaign of Marengo, with no other preparation than his genius,
without the mental equipment and the ripened experience that came from knowledge of the past,
acquired by study, he would have come unprepared.
Were, then, his previous study and reflection, for
which the time of action had not come, were they
not " practical," because they did not result in immediate action? Would they even have been " not

practical " if the time for action had never come to him?

As the wise man said, " There is a time for every-thing under the sun," and the time for one thing cannot be used as the time for another. That there is time for action, all concede; few consider duly that there is also a time for preparation. To use the time of preparation for preparation is practical, whatever the method; to postpone preparation to the time for action is not practical. Our new navy is preparing now; it can scarcely be said, as regards its material, to be yet ready. The day of grace is still with us — or with those who shall be the future captains and admirals. There is time yet for study; there is time to imbibe the experience of the past, to become imbued, steeped, in the eternal principles of war, by the study of its history and of the maxims of its masters. But the time of preparation will pass; some day the time of action will come. Can an admiral then sit down and re-enforce his intel-lectual grasp of the problem before him by a study of history, which is simply a study of past experi-ence? Not so; the time of action is upon him, and he must trust to his horse sense.

3. ELEMENTS OF SEA POWER [1]

THE first and most obvious light in which the sea presents itself from the political and social point of view is that of a great highway; or better, perhaps, of a wide common, over which men may pass in all directions, but on which some well-worn paths show that controlling reasons have led them to choose certain lines of travel rather than others. These lines of travel are called trade routes; and the reasons which have determined them are to be sought in the history of the world.

Notwithstanding all the familiar and unfamiliar dangers of the sea, both travel and traffic by water have always been easier and cheaper than by land. The commercial greatness of Holland was due not only to her shipping at sea, but also to the numerous tranquil water-ways which gave such cheap and easy access to her own interior and to that of Germany. This advantage of carriage by water over that by land was yet more marked in a period when roads were few and very bad, wars frequent and society unsettled, as was the case two hundred years ago. Sea traffic then went in peril of robbers, but was

---

[1] "The Influence of Sea Power upon History," pp. 25–59. Mr. S. G. W. Benjamin has pointed out (N. Y. *Times* Book Review, Feb. 2, 1902) that it was in the preface and opening chapter of this book, "comprising only eighty-nine pages, that Captain Mahan brought forward his famous presentation of the theory about the influence of sea power on empire." The present selection includes the major part of the first chapter. — EDITOR.

nevertheless safer and quicker than that by land. A Dutch writer of that time, estimating the chances of his country in a war with England, notices among other things that the water-ways of England failed to penetrate the country sufficiently; therefore, the roads being bad, goods from one part of the kingdom to the other must go by sea, and be exposed to capture by the way. As regards purely internal trade, this danger has generally disappeared at the present day. In most civilized countries, now, the destruction or disappearance of the coasting trade would only be an inconvenience, although water transit is still the cheaper. Nevertheless, as late as the wars of the French Republic and the First Empire, those who are familiar with the history of the period, and the light naval literature that has grown up around it, know how constant is the mention of convoys stealing from point to point along the French coast, although the sea swarmed with English cruisers and there were good inland roads.

Under modern conditions, however, home trade is but a part of the business of a country bordering on the sea. Foreign necessaries or luxuries must be brought to its ports, either in its own or in foreign ships, which will return, bearing in exchange the products of the country, whether they be the fruits of the earth or the works of men's hands; and it is the wish of every nation that this shipping business should be done by its own vessels. The ships that thus sail to and fro must have secure ports to which to return, and must, as far as possible, be followed by the protection of their country throughout the voyage.

This protection in time of war must be extended by armed shipping. The necessity of a navy, in the restricted sense of the word, springs, therefore, from the existence of a peaceful shipping, and disappears with it,[1] except in the case of a nation which has aggressive tendencies, and keeps up a navy merely as a branch of the military establishment. As the United States has at present no agressive purposes, and as its merchant service has disappeared, the dwindling of the armed fleet and general lack of interest in it are strictly logical consequences. When for any reason sea trade is again found to pay, a large enough shipping interest will reappear to compel the revival of the war fleet. It is possible that when a canal route through the Central-American Isthmus is seen to be a near certainty, the aggressive impulse may be strong enough to lead to the same result. This is doubtful, however, because a peaceful, gain-loving nation is not far-sighted, and far-sightedness is needed for adequate military preparation, especially in these days.

As a nation, with its unarmed and armed shipping, launches forth from its own shores, the need is soon felt of points upon which the ships can rely for peaceful trading, for refuge and supplies. In the present day friendly, though foreign, ports are to be found all over the world; and their shelter is

---

[1] For the author's later opinion on the need of a navy, see pp. 355–357. — EDITOR.

enough while peace prevails. It was not always so, nor does peace always endure, though the United States have been favored by so long a continuance of it. In earlier times the merchant seaman, seeking for trade in new and unexplored regions, made his gains at risk of life and liberty from suspicious or hostile nations, and was under great delays in collecting a full and profitable freight. He therefore intuitively sought at the far end of his trade route one or more stations, to be given to him by force or favor, where he could fix himself or his agents in reasonable security, where his ships could lie in safety, and where the merchantable products of the land could be continually collecting, awaiting the arrival of the home fleet, which should carry them to the mother-country. As there was immense gain, as well as much risk, in these early voyages, such establishments naturally multiplied and grew until they became colonies; whose ultimate development and success depended upon the genius and policy of the nation from which they sprang, and form a very great part of the history, and particularly of the sea history, of the world. All colonies had not the simple and natural birth and growth above described. Many were more formal, and purely political, in their conception and founding, the act of the rulers of the people rather than of private individuals; but the trading-station with its after expansion, the work simply of the adventurer seeking gain, was in its reasons and essence the same as the elaborately organized and chartered colony. In both cases the mother-country had won a foothold in a foreign land, seeking a new outlet for what it had to sell, a new sphere for its shipping, more employment for its people, more comfort and wealth for itself.

The needs of commerce, however, were not all provided for when safety had been secured at the far end of the road. The voyages were long and dangerous, the seas often beset with enemies. In the most active days of colonizing there prevailed on the sea a lawlessness the very memory of which is now almost lost, and the days of settled peace between maritime nations were few and far between. Thus arose the demand for stations along the road, like the Cape of Good Hope, St. Helena, and Mauritius, not primarily for trade, but for defense and war; the demand for the possession of posts like Gibraltar, Malta, Louisburg, at the entrance of the Gulf of St. Lawrence, — posts whose value was chiefly strategic, though not necessarily wholly so. Colonies and colonial posts were sometimes commercial, sometimes military in their character; and it was exceptional that the same position was equally important in both points of view, as New York was.

In these three things — production, with the necessity of exchanging products, shipping, whereby the exchange is carried on, and colonies, which facilitate and enlarge the operations of shipping and tend to protect it by multiplying points of safety — is to be found the key to much of the history, as well as of the policy, of nations bordering upon the sea. The policy has varied both with the spirit of the age and with the character and clear-sightedness of the rulers; but the history of the seaboard nations has been less determined by the shrewdness and foresight of governments than by conditions of position, extent, configuration, number and character of their people, — by what are called, in a word, natural conditions. It must however be admitted, and will be seen, that the wise or unwise action of individual men has at certain periods had a great modifying influence upon the growth of sea power in the broad sense, which includes not only the military strength afloat, that rules the sea or any part of it by force of arms, but also the peaceful commerce and shipping from which alone a military fleet naturally and healthfully springs, and on which it securely rests.

The principal conditions affecting the sea power of nations may be enumerated as follows: I. Geographical Position. II. Physical Conformation, including, as connected therewith, natural productions and climate. III. Extent of Territory. IV. Number of Population. V. Character of the People. VI. Character of the Government, including therein the national institutions.

I. *Geographical Position.* — It may be pointed out, in the first place, that if a nation be so situated that it is neither forced to defend itself by land nor induced to seek extension of its territory by way of the land, it has, by the very unity of its aim directed upon the sea, an advantage as compared with a people one of whose boundaries is continental. This has been a great advantage to England over both

France and Holland as a sea power. The strength
of the latter was early exhausted by the necessity
of keeping up a large army and carying on expensive
wars to preserve her independence; while the policy
of France was constantly diverted, sometimes wisely
and sometimes most foolishly, from the sea to projects of continental extension. These military efforts
expended wealth; whereas a wiser and consistent
use of her geographical position would have added
to it.

The geographical position may be such as of itself to promote a concentration, or to necessitate
a dispersion, of the naval forces. Here again the
British Islands have an advantage over France.
The position of the latter, touching the Mediterranean as well as the ocean, while it has its advantages, is on the whole a source of military weakness
at sea. The eastern and western French fleets have
only been able to unite after passing through the
Straits of Gibraltar, in attempting which they have
often risked and sometimes suffered loss. The position of the United States upon the two oceans would
be either a source of great weakness or a cause of
enormous expense, had it a large sea commerce on
both coasts.[1]

England, by her immense colonial empire, has
sacrificed much of this advantage of concentration
of force around her own shores; but the sacrifice
was wisely made, for the gain was greater than the
loss, as the event proved. With the growth of her
colonial system her war fleets also grew, but her

[1] Written before 1890. — Editor.

merchant shipping and wealth grew yet faster. Still, in the wars of the American Revolution, and of the French Republic and Empire, to use the strong expression of a French author, "England, despite the immense development of her navy, seemed ever, in the midst of riches, to feel all the embarrassment of poverty." The might of England was sufficient to keep alive the heart and the members; whereas the equally extensive colonial empire of Spain, through her maritime weakness, but offered so many points for insult and injury.

The geographical position of a country may not only favor the concentration of its forces, but give the further strategic advantage of a central position and a good base for hostile operations against its probable enemies. This again is the case with England; on the one hand she faces Holland and the northern powers, on the other France and the Atlantic. When threatened with a coalition between France and the naval powers of the North Sea and the Baltic, as she at times was, her fleets in the Downs and in the Channel, and even that off Brest, occupied interior positions, and thus were readily able to interpose their united force against either one of the enemies which should seek to pass through the Channel to effect a junction with its ally. On either side, also, Nature gave her better ports and a safer coast to approach. Formerly this was a very serious element in the passage through the Channel; but of late, steam and the improvement of her harbors have lessened the disadvantage under which France once labored. In the days of sailing-ships, the English fleet operated against Brest, making its base at Torbay and Plymouth. The plan was simply this: in easterly or moderate weather the blockading fleet kept its position without difficulty; but in westerly gales, when too severe, they bore up for English ports, knowing that the French fleet could not get out till the wind shifted, which equally served to bring them back to their station.

The advantage of geographical nearness to an enemy, or to the object of attack, is nowhere more apparent than in that form of warfare which has lately received the name of commerce-destroying, which the French call *guerre de course*. This operation of war, being directed against peaceful merchant vessels which are usually defenseless, calls for ships of small military force. Such ships, having little power to defend themselves, need a refuge or point of support near at hand; which will be found either in certain parts of the sea controlled by the fighting ships of their country, or in friendly harbors. The latter give the strongest support, because they are always in the same place, and the approaches to them are more familiar to the commerce-destroyer than to his enemy. The nearness of France to England has thus greatly facilitated her *guerre de course* directed against the latter. Having ports on the North Sea, on the Channel, and on the Atlantic, her cruisers started from points near the focus of English trade, both coming and going. The distance of these ports from each other, disadvantageous for regular military combinations, is an advantage for this irregular secondary operation; for the essence of the one is concentration of effort, whereas for commerce-destroying diffusion of effort is the rule. Commerce-destroyers scatter, that they may see and seize more prey. These truths receive illustration from the history of the great French privateers, whose bases and scenes of action were largely on the Channel and North Sea, or else were found in distant colonial regions, where islands like Guadaloupe and Martinique afforded similar near refuge. The necessity of renewing coal makes the cruiser of the present day even more dependent than of old on his port. Public opinion in the United States has great faith in war directed against an enemy's commerce; but it must be remembered that the Republic has no ports very near the great centers of trade abroad. Her geographical position is therefore singularly disadvantageous for carrying on successful commerce-destroying, unless she find bases in the ports of an ally.

If, in addition to facility for offense, Nature has so placed a country that it has easy access to the high sea itself, while at the same time it controls one of the great thoroughfares of the world's traffic, it is evident that the strategic value of its position is very high. Such again is, and to a greater degree was, the position of England. The trade of Holland, Sweden, Russia, Denmark, and that which went up the great rivers to the interior of Germany, had to pass through the Channel close by her doors; for sailing-ships hugged the English coast. This northern trade had, moreover, a peculiar bearing upon sea power; for naval stores, as they are commonly called, were mainly drawn from the Baltic countries.

But for the loss of Gibraltar, the position of Spain would have been closely analogous to that of England. Looking at once upon the Atlantic and the Mediterranean, with Cadiz on the one side and Cartagena on the other, the trade to the Levant must have passed under her hands, and that round the Cape of Good Hope not far from her doors. But Gibraltar not only deprived her of the control of the Straits, it also imposed an obstacle to the easy junction of the two divisions of her fleet.

At the present day, looking only at the geographical position of Italy, and not at the other conditions affecting her sea power, it would seem that with her extensive sea-coast and good ports she is very well placed for exerting a decisive influence on the trade route to the Levant and by the Isthmus of Suez. This is true in a degree, and would be much more so did Italy now hold all the islands naturally Italian; but with Malta in the hands of England, and Corsica in those of France, the advantages of her geographical position are largely neutralized. From race affinities and situation those two islands are as legitimately objects of desire to Italy as Gibraltar is to Spain. If the Adriatic were a great highway of commerce, Italy's position would be still more influential. These defects in her geographical completeness, combined with other causes injurious to a full and secure development of sea power, make it more than doubtful whether Italy can for some time be in the front rank among the sea nations.

As the aim here is not an exhaustive discussion, but merely an attempt to show, by illustration, how vitally the situation of a country may affect its career upon the sea, this division of the subject may be dismissed for the present; the more so as instances which will further bring out its importance will continually recur in the historical treatment. Two remarks, however, are here appropriate.

Circumstances have caused the Mediterranean Sea to play a greater part in the history of the world, both in a commercial and a military point of view, than any other sheet of water of the same size. Nation after nation has striven to control it, and the strife still goes on. Therefore a study of the conditions upon which preponderance in its waters has rested, and now rests, and of the relative military values of different points upon its coasts, will be more instructive than the same amount of effort expended in another field. Furthermore, it has at the present time a very marked analogy in many respects to the Caribbean Sea, — an analogy which will be still closer if a Panama canal-route ever be completed. A study of the strategic conditions of the Mediterranean, which have received ample illustration, will be an excellent prelude to a similar study of the Caribbean, which has comparatively little history.

The second remark bears upon the geographical position of the United States relatively to a Central-American canal. If one be made, and fulfil the

hopes of its builders, the Caribbean will be changed
from a terminus, and place of local traffic, or at
best a broken and imperfect line of travel, as it now
is, into one of the great highways of the world.
Along this path a great commerce will travel, bringing the interests of the other great nations, the
European nations, close along our shores, as they
have never been before. With this it will not be so
easy as heretofore to stand aloof from international
complications. The position of the United States
with reference to this route will resemble that of
England to the Channel, and of the Mediterranean
countries to the Suez route. As regards influence
and control over it, depending upon geographical
position, it is of course plain that the center of the
national power, the permanent base,[1] is much nearer
than that of other great nations. The positions now
or hereafter occupied by them on island or mainland, however strong, will be but outposts of their
power; while in all the raw materials of military
strength no nation is superior to the United States.
She is, however, weak in a confessed unpreparedness
for war; and her geographical nearness to the point
of contention loses some of its value by the character
of the Gulf coast, which is deficient in ports com-
bining security from an enemy with facility for repairing warships of the first class, without which
ships no country can pretend to control any part of
the sea. In case of a contest for supremacy in the

---

[1] By a base of permanent operations "is understood a country
whence come all the resources, where are united the great lines of communication by land and water, where are the arsenals and armed posts."

Caribbean, it seems evident from the depth of the South Pass of the Mississippi, the nearness of New Orleans, and the advantages of the Mississippi Valley for water transit, that the main effort of the country must pour down that valley, and its permanent base of operations be found there. The defense of the entrance to the Mississippi, however, presents peculiar difficulties; while the only two rival ports, Key West and Pensacola, have too little depth of water, and are much less advantageously placed with reference to the resources of the country. To get the full benefit of superior geographical position, these defects must be overcome. Furthermore, as her distance from the Isthmus, though relatively less, is still considerable, the United States will have to obtain in the Caribbean stations fit for contingent, or secondary, bases of operations; which by their natural advantages, susceptibility of defense, and nearness to the central strategic issue, will enable her fleets to remain as near the scene as any opponent. With ingress and egress from the Mississippi sufficiently protected, with such outposts in her hands, and with the communications between them and the home base secured, in short, with proper military preparation, for which she has all necessary means, the preponderance of the United States on this field follows, from her geographical position and her power, with mathematical certainty.

II. *Physical Conformation.* — The peculiar features of the Gulf coast, alluded to, come properly

under the head of Physical Conformation of a country, which is placed second for discussion among the
conditions which affect the development of sea power.
The seaboard of a country is one of its frontiers;
and the easier the access offered by the frontier to
the region beyond, in this case the sea, the greater
will be the tendency of a people toward intercourse
with the rest of the world by it. If a country be
imagined having a long seaboard, but entirely without a harbor, such a country can have no sea trade of
its own, no shipping, no navy. This was practically
the case with Belgium when it was a Spanish and an
Austrian province. The Dutch, in 1648, as a condition of peace after a successful war, exacted that
the Scheldt should be closed to sea commerce. This
closed the harbor of Antwerp and transferred the
sea trade of Belgium to Holland. The Spanish
Netherlands ceased to be a sea power.

Numerous and deep harbors are a source of
strength and wealth, and doubly so if they are the
outlets of navigable streams, which facilitate the
concentration in them of a country's internal trade;
but by their very accessibility they become a source
of weakness in war, if not properly defended. The
Dutch in 1667 found little difficulty in ascending the
Thames and burning a large fraction of the English
navy within sight of London; whereas a few years
later the combined fleets of England and France,
when attempting a landing in Holland, were foiled
by the difficulties of the coast as much as by the
valor of the Dutch fleet. In 1778 the harbor of
New York, and with it undisputed control of the

Hudson River, would have been lost to the English, who were caught at disadvantage, but for the hesitancy of the French admiral. With that control, New England would have been restored to close and safe communication with New York, New Jersey, and Pennsylvania; and this blow, following so closely on Burgoyne's disaster of the year before, would probably have led the English to make an earlier peace. The Mississippi is a mighty source of wealth and strength to the United States; but the feeble defenses of its mouth and the number of its subsidiary streams penetrating the country made it a weakness and source of disaster to the Southern Confederacy. And lastly, in 1814, the occupation of the Chesapeake and the destruction of Washington gave a sharp lesson of the dangers incurred through the noblest waterways, if their approaches be undefended; a lesson recent enough to be easily recalled, but which, from the present appearance of the coast defenses, seems to be yet more easily forgotten. Nor should it be thought that conditions have changed; circumstances and details of offense and defense have been modified, in these days as before, but the great conditions remain the same.

Before and during the great Napoleonic wars, France had no port for ships-of-the-line east of Brest. How great the advantage to England, which in the same stretch has two great arsenals, at Plymouth and at Portsmouth, besides other harbors of refuge and supply. This defect of conformation has since been remedied by the works at Cherbourg.

Besides the contour of the coast, involving easy

access to the sea, there are other physical conditions
which lead people to the sea or turn them from it.
Although France was deficient in military ports on
the Channel, she had both there and on the ocean,
as well as in the Mediterranean, excellent harbors,
favorably situated for trade abroad, and at the outlet of large rivers, which would foster internal
traffic. But when Richelieu had put an end to civil
war, Frenchmen did not take to the sea with the
eagerness and success of the English and Dutch. A
principal reason for this has been plausibly found in
the physical conditions which have made France a
pleasant land, with a delightful climate, producing
within itself more than its people needed. England,
on the other hand, received from Nature but little,
and, until her manufactures were developed, had
little to export. Their many wants, combined with
their restless activity and other conditions that
favored maritime enterprise, led her people abroad;
and they there found lands more pleasant and richer
than their own. Their needs and genius made them
merchants and colonists, then manufacturers and
producers; and between products and colonies shipping is the inevitable link. So their sea power grew.
But if England was drawn to the sea, Holland was
driven to it; without the sea England languished, but
Holland died. In the height of her greatness, when
she was one of the chief factors in European politics,
a competent native authority estimated that the soil
of Holland could not support more than one eighth
of her inhabitants. The manufactures of the country were then numerous and important, but they had

been much later in their growth than the shipping interest. The poverty of the soil and the exposed nature of the coast drove the Dutch first to fishing. Then the discovery of the process of curing the fish gave them material for export as well as home consumption, and so laid the corner-stone of their wealth. Thus they had become traders at the time that the Italian republics, under the pressure of Turkish power and the discovery of the passage round the Cape of Good Hope, were beginning to decline, and they fell heirs to the great Italian trade of the Levant. Further favored by their geographical position, intermediate between the Baltic, France, and the Mediterranean, and at the mouth of the German rivers, they quickly absorbed nearly all the carrying-trade of Europe. The wheat and naval stores of the Baltic, the trade of Spain with her colonies in the New World, the wines of France, and the French coasting-trade were, little more than two hundred years ago, transported in Dutch shipping. Much of the carrying-trade of England, even, was then done in Dutch bottoms. It will not be pretended that all this prosperity proceeded only from the poverty of Holland's natural resources. Something does not grow from nothing. What is true, is, that by the necessitous condition of her people they were driven to the sea, and were, from their mastery of the shipping business and the size of their fleets, in a position to profit by the sudden expansion of commerce and the spirit of exploration which followed on the discovery of America and of the passage round the Cape. Other causes concurred,

but their whole prosperity stood on the sea power
to which their poverty gave birth. Their food, their
clothing, the raw material for their manufactures,
the very timber and hemp with which they built and
rigged their ships (and they built nearly as many as
all Europe besides), were imported; and when a
disastrous war with England in 1653 and 1654 had
lasted eighteen months, and their shipping business
was stopped, it is said "the sources of revenue
which had always maintained the riches of the State,
such as fisheries and commerce, were almost dry.
Workshops were closed, work was suspended. The
Zuyder Zee became a forest of masts; the country
was full of beggars; grass grew in the streets, and
in Amsterdam fifteen hundred houses were un-
tenanted." A humiliating peace alone saved them
from ruin.

This sorrowful result shows the weakness of a
country depending wholly upon sources external to
itself for the part it is playing in the world. With
large deductions, owing to differences of conditions
which need not here be spoken of, the case of Holland then has strong points of resemblance to that
of Great Britain now; and they are true prophets,
though they seem to be having small honor in their
own country, who warn her that the continuance of
her prosperity at home depends primarily upon
maintaining her power abroad. Men may be discontented at the lack of political privilege; they will
be yet more uneasy if they come to lack bread. It
is of more interest to Americans to note that the
result to France, regarded as a power of the sea,

caused by the extent, delightfulness, and richness of the land, has been reproduced in the United States. In the beginning, their forefathers held a narrow strip of land upon the sea, fertile in parts though little developed, abounding in harbors and near rich fishing grounds. These physical conditions combined with an inborn love of the sea, the pulse of that English blood which still beat in their veins, to keep alive all those tendencies and pursuits upon which a healthy sea power depends. Almost every one of the original colonies was on the sea or on one of its great tributaries. All export and import tended toward one coast. Interest in the sea and an intelligent appreciation of the part it played in the public welfare were easily and widely spread; and a motive more influential than care for the public interest was also active, for the abundance of ship-building materials and a relative fewness of other investments made shipping a profitable private interest. How changed the present condition is, all know. The center of power is no longer on the seaboard. Books and newspapers vie with one another in describing the wonderful growth, and the still undeveloped riches, of the interior. Capital there finds its best investments, labor its largest opportunities. The frontiers are neglected and politically weak; the Gulf and Pacific coasts actually so, the Atlantic coast relatively to the central Mississippi Valley. When the day comes that shipping again pays, when the three sea frontiers find that they are not only militarily weak, but poorer for lack of national shipping, their united efforts may avail to lay again the foundations of our sea power. Till then, those who follow the limitations which lack of sea power placed upon the career of France may mourn that their own country is being led, by a like redundancy of home wealth, into the same neglect of that great instrument.

Among modifying physical conditions may be noted a form like that of Italy, — a long peninsula, with a central range of mountains dividing it into two narrow strips, along which the roads connecting the different ports necessarily run. Only an absolute control of the sea can wholly secure such communications, since it is impossible to know at what point an enemy coming from beyond the visible horizon may strike; but still, with an adequate naval force centrally posted, there will be good hope of attacking his fleet, which is at once his base and line of communications, before serious damage has been done. The long, narrow peninsula of Florida, with Key West at its extremity, though flat and thinly populated, presents at first sight conditions like those of Italy. The resemblance may be only superficial, but it seems probable that if the chief scene of a naval war were the Gulf of Mexico, the communications by land to the end of the peninsula might be a matter of consequence, and open to attack.

When the sea not only borders, or surrounds, but also separates a country into two or more parts, the control of it becomes not only desirable, but vitally necesary. Such a physical condition either gives birth and strength to sea power, or makes the country powerless. Such is the condition of the present kingdom of Italy, with its islands of Sardinia and Sicily; and hence in its youth and still existing financial weakness it is seen to put forth such vigorous and intelligent efforts to create a military navy. It has even been argued that, with a navy decidedly superior to her enemy's, Italy could better base her power upon her islands than upon her mainland; for the insecurity of the lines of communication in the peninsula, already pointed out, would most seriously embarrass an invading army surrounded by a hostile people and threatened from the sea.

The Irish Sea, separating the British Islands, rather resembles an estuary than an actual division; but history has shown the danger from it to the United Kingdom. In the days of Louis XIV, when the French navy nearly equalled the combined English and Dutch, the gravest complications existed in Ireland, which passed almost wholly under the control of the natives and the French. Nevertheless, the Irish Sea was rather a danger to the English — a weak point in their communications — than an advantage to the French. The latter did not venture their ships-of-the-line in its narrow waters, and expeditions intending to land were directed upon the ocean ports in the south and west. At the supreme moment the great French fleet was sent upon the south coast of England, where it decisively defeated the allies, and at the same time twenty-five frigates were sent to St. George's Channel, against the English communications. In the midst of a hostile people, the English army in Ireland was seriously imperiled, but was saved by the battle of the Boyne and flight of James II. This movement against the enemy's communications was strictly strategic, and would be as dangerous to England now as in 1690.

Spain, in the same century, afforded an impressive lesson of the weakness caused by such separation when the parts are not knit together by a strong sea power. She then still retained, as remnants of her past greatness, the Netherlands (now Belgium), Sicily, and other Italian possessions, not to speak of her vast colonies in the New World. Yet so low had the Spanish sea power fallen, that a well-informed and sober-minded Hollander of the day could claim that " in Spain all the coast is navigated by a few Dutch ships; and since the peace of 1648 their ships and seamen are so few that they have publicly begun to hire our ships to sail to the Indies, whereas they were formerly careful to exclude all foreigners from there. . . . It is manifest," he goes on, " that the West Indies, being as the stomach to Spain (for from it nearly all the revenue is drawn), must be joined to the Spanish head by a sea force; and that Naples and the Netherlands, being like two arms, they cannot lay out their strength for Spain, nor receive anything thence but by shipping, — all which may easily be done by our shipping in peace, and by it obstructed in war." Half a century before, Sully, the great minister of Henry IV, had characterized Spain " as one of those States whose legs and arms are strong and powerful, but the heart infinitely weak and feeble." Since his day the Spanish navy had suffered not only disaster, but annihilation; not only humiliation, but degradation.

The consequences briefly were that shipping was destroyed; manufactures perished with it. The government depended for its support, not upon a widespread healthy commerce and industry that could survive many a staggering blow, but upon a narrow stream of silver trickling through a few treasure-ships from America, easily and frequently intercepted by an enemy's cruisers. The loss of half a dozen galleons more than once paralyzed its movements for a year. While the war in the Netherlands lasted, the Dutch control of the sea forced Spain to send her troops by a long and costly journey overland instead of by sea; and the same cause reduced her to such straits for necessaries that, by a mutual arrangement which seems very odd to modern ideas, her wants were supplied by Dutch ships, which thus maintained the enemies of their country, but received in return specie which was welcome in the Amsterdam exchange. In America, the Spanish protected themselves as best they might behind masonry, unaided from home; while in the Mediterranean they escaped insult and injury mainly through the indifference of the Dutch, for the French and English had not yet begun to contend for mastery there. In the course of history the Netherlands, Naples, Sicily, Minorca, Havana, Manila, and Jamaica were wrenched away, at one time or another, from this empire without a shipping. In short, while Spain's maritime impotence may have been primarily a symptom of her general decay, it became a marked factor in precipitating her into the abyss from which she has not yet wholly emerged.

Except Alaska, the United States has no outlying
possession, — no foot of ground inaccessible by land.
Its contour is such as to present few points specially
weak from their saliency, and all important parts of
the frontiers can be readily attained, — cheaply by
water, rapidly by rail. The weakest frontier, the
Pacific, is far removed from the most dangerous
of possible enemies. The internal resources are
boundless as compared with present needs; we can
live off ourselves indefinitely in " our little corner,"
to use the expression of a French officer to the
author. Yet should that little corner be invaded by
a new commercial route through the Isthmus, the
United States in her turn may have the rude awaken-
ing of those who have abandoned their share in the
common birthright of all people, the sea.

III. *Extent of Territory.* — The last of the conditions affecting the development of a nation as a
sea power, and touching the country itself as distinguished from the people who dwell there, is Extent of Territory. This may be dismissed with
comparatively few words.

As regards the development of sea power, it is
not the total number of square miles which a country
contains, but the length of its coast-line and the
character of its harbors that are to be considered.
As to these it is to be said that, the geographical and
physical conditions being the same, extent of sea-
coast is a source of strength or weakness according
as the population is large or small. A country is in
this like a fortress; the garrison must be propor-

tioned to the *enceinte*. A recent familiar instance is found in the American War of Secession. Had the South had a people as numerous as it was warlike, and a navy commensurate to its other resources as a sea power, the great extent of its sea-coast and its numerous inlets would have been elements of great strength. The people of the United States and the Government of that day justly prided themselves on the effectiveness of the blockade of the whole Southern coast. It was a great feat, a very great feat; but it would have been an impossible feat had the Southerners been more numerous, and a nation of seamen. What was there shown was not, as has been said, how such a blockade can be maintained, but that such a blockade is possible in the face of a population not only unused to the sea, but also scanty in numbers. Those who recall how the blockade was maintained, and the class of ships that blockaded during great part of the war, know that the plan, correct under the circumstances, could not have been carried out in the face of a real navy. Scattered unsupported along the coast, the United States ships kept their places, singly or in small detachments, in face of an extensive network of inland water communications which favored secret concentration of the enemy. Behind the first line of water communications were long estuaries, and here and there strong fortresses, upon either of which the enemy's ships could always fall back to elude pursuit or to receive protection. Had there been a Southern navy to profit by such advantages, or by the scattered condition of the United States ships, the latter could not have been distributed as they were; and being forced to concentrate for mutual support, many small but useful approaches would have been left open to commerce. But as the Southern coast, from its extent and many inlets, might have been a source of strength, so, from those very characteristics, it became a fruitful source of injury. The great story of the opening of the Mississippi is but the most striking illustration of an action that was going on incessantly all over the South. At every breach of the sea frontier, war-ships were entering. The streams that had carried the wealth and supported the trade of the seceding States turned against them, and admitted their enemies to their hearts. Dismay, insecurity, paralysis, prevailed in regions that might, under happier auspices, have kept a nation alive through the most exhausting war. Never did sea power play a greater or a more decisive part than in the contest which determined that the course of the world's history would be modified by the existence of one great nation, instead of several rival States, in the North American continent. But while just pride is felt in the well-earned glory of those days, and the greatness of the results due to naval preponderance is admitted, Americans who understand the facts should never fail to remind the over-confidence of their countrymen that the South not only had no navy, not only was not a seafaring people, but that also its population was not proportioned to the extent of the sea-coast which it had to defend.

IV. *Number of Population.* — After the consideration of the natural conditions of a country should follow an examination of the characteristics of its population as affecting the development of sea power; and first among these will be taken, because of its relations to the extent of the territory, which has just been discussed, the number of the people who live in it. It has been said that in respect of dimensions it is not merely the number of square miles, but the extent and character of the sea-coast that is to be considered with reference to sea power; and so, in point of population, it is not only the grand total, but the number following the sea, or at least readily available for employment on shipboard and for the creation of naval material, that must be counted.

For example, formerly and up to the end of the great wars following the French Revolution, the population of France was much greater than that of England; but in respect of sea power in general, peaceful commerce as well as military efficiency, France was much inferior to England. In the matter of military efficiency this fact is the more remarkable because at times, in point of military preparation at the outbreak of war, France had the advantage; but she was not able to keep it. Thus in 1778, when war broke out, France, through her maritime inscription, was able to man at once fifty ships-of-the-line. England, on the contrary, by reason of the dispersal over the globe of that very shipping on which her naval strength so securely rested, had much trouble in manning forty at home;

but in 1782 she had one hundred and twenty in commission or ready for commission, while France had never been able to exceed seventy-one.

[The need is further shown, not only of a large seafaring population, but of skilled mechanics and artisans to facilitate ship construction and repair and supply capable recruits for the navy. — EDITOR.]

. . . That our own country is open to the same reproach is patent to all the world. The United States has not that shield of defensive power behind which time can be gained to develop its reserve of strength. As for a seafaring population adequate to her possible needs, where is it? Such a resource, proportionate to her coast-line and population, is to be found only in a national merchant shipping and its related industries, which at present scarcely exist. It will matter little whether the crews of such ships are native or foreign born, provided they are attached to the flag, and her power at sea is sufficient to enable the most of them to get back in case of war. When foreigners by thousands are admitted to the ballot, it is of little moment that they are given fighting-room on board ship.

Though the treatment of the subject has been somewhat discursive, it may be admitted that a great population following callings related to the sea is, now as formerly, a great element of sea power; that the United States is deficient in that element; and that its foundations can be laid only in a large commerce under her own flag.

V. *National Character.* — The effect of national character and aptitudes upon the development of sea power will next be considered.

If sea power be really based upon a peaceful and extensive commerce, aptitude for commercial pursuits must be a distinguishing feature of the nations that have at one time or another been great upon the sea. History almost without exception affirms that this is true. Save the Romans, there is no marked instance to the contrary.

[Here follows a survey, covering several pages, of the commercial history and colonial policies of Spain, Holland, and Great Britain. — EDITOR.]

. . . The fact of England's unique and wonderful success as a great colonizing nation is too evident to be dwelt upon; and the reason for it appears to lie chiefly in two traits of the national character. The English colonist naturally and readily settles down in his new country, identifies his interest with it, and though keeping an affectionate remembrance of the home from which he came, has no restless eagerness to return. In the second place, the Englishman at once and instinctively seeks to develop the resources of the new country in the broadest sense. In the former particular he differs from the French, who were ever longingly looking back to the delights of their pleasant land; in the latter, from the Spaniards, whose range of interest and ambition was too narrow for the full evolution of the possibilities of a new country.

The character and the necessities of the Dutch led them naturally to plant colonies; and by the year

1650 they had in the East Indies, in Africa, and in America a large number, only to name which would be tedious. They were then far ahead of England in this matter. But though the origin of these colonies, purely commercial in its character, was natural, there seems to have been lacking to them a principle of growth. " In planting them they never sought an extension of empire, but merely an acquisition of trade and commerce. They attempted conquest only when forced by the pressure of circumstances. Generally they were content to trade under the protection of the sovereign of the country." This placid satisfaction with gain alone, unaccompanied by political ambition, tended, like the despotism of France and Spain, to keep the colonies mere commercial dependencies upon the mother-country, and so killed the natural principle of growth.

Before quitting this head of the inquiry, it is well to ask how far the national character of Americans is fitted to develop a great sea power, should other circumstances become favorable.

It seems scarcely necessary, however, to do more than appeal to a not very distant past to prove that, if legislative hindrances be removed, and more remunerative fields of enterprise filled up, the sea power will not long delay its appearance. The instinct for commerce, bold enterprise in pursuit of gain, and a keen scent for trails that lead to it, all exist; and if there be in the future any fields calling for colonization, it cannot be doubted that Americans will carry to them all their inherited aptitude for self-government and independent growth.

VI. *Character of the Government.* — In discussing the effects upon the development of a nation's sea power exerted by its government and institutions, it will be necessary to avoid a tendency to over-philosophizing, to confine attention to obvious and immediate causes and their plain results, without prying too far beneath the surface for remote and ultimate influences.

Nevertheless, it must be noted that particular forms of government with their accompanying institutions, and the character of rulers at one time or another, have exercised a very marked influence upon the development of sea power. The various traits of a country and its people which have so far been considered constitute the natural characteristics with which a nation, like a man, begins its career; the conduct of the government in turn corresponds to the exercise of the intelligent will-power, which, according as it is wise, energetic and persevering, or the reverse, causes success or failure in a man's life or a nation's history.

It would seem probable that a government in full accord with the natural bias of its people would most successfully advance its growth in every respect; and, in the matter of sea power, the most brilliant successes have followed where there has been intelligent direction by a government fully imbued with the spirit of the people and conscious of its true general bent. Such a government is most certainly secured when the will of the people, or of their best natural exponents, has some large share in making it; but such free governments have sometimes fallen short, while on the other hand despotic power, wielded with judgment and consistency, has created at times a great sea commerce and a brilliant navy with greater directness than can be reached by the slower processes of a free people. The difficulty in the latter case is to insure perseverance after the death of a particular despot.

England having undoubtedly reached the greatest height of sea power of any modern nation, the action of her government first claims attention. In general direction this action has been consistent, though often far from praiseworthy. It has aimed steadily at the control of the sea.

[The remainder of the chapter, quoted in part on pp. 141–146, outlines the extension of Great Britain's trade and sea power during the seventeenth and eighteenth centuries. — EDITOR.]

4. Definition of Terms [1]

Strategy, Tactics, Logistics

"STRATEGY," says Jomini, speaking of the art of war on land, " is the art of making war upon the map, and comprehends the whole theater of warlike operations. Grand tactics is the art of posting troops upon the battle-field, according to the accidents of the ground; of bringing them into action; and the art of fighting upon the ground in contradistinction to planning upon a map. Its operations may extend over a field of ten or twelve miles in extent. Strategy decides where to act. Grand tactics decides the manner of execution and the employment of troops," when, by the combinations of strategy, they have been assembled at the point of action.

. . . Between Strategy and Grand Tactics comes logically Logistics. Strategy decides where to act; Logistics is the act of moving armies; it brings the troops to the point of action and controls questions of supply; Grand Tactics decides the methods of giving battle.

[1] "Naval Administration and Warfare," pp. 199, 206. For the distinction drawn, see also pp. 4, 12. — EDITOR.

5. FUNDAMENTAL PRINCIPLES [1]

Central Position, Interior Lines, Communications

THE situation here used in illustration is taken from the Thirty Years' War, 1618–1648, in which the French House of Bourbon opposed the House of Austria, the latter controlling Spain, Austria, and parts of Germany. France lay between Spain and Austria; but if Spain commanded the sea, her forces could reach the field of conflict in central Europe either by way of Belgium or by way of the Duchy of Milan in northern Italy, both of which were under her rule.

The upper course of the Danube between Ulm and Ratisbon is also employed to illustrate central position, dominating the great European theater of war north of the Alps and east of the Rhine. — EDITOR.]

The situation of France relatively to her two opponents of this period — Spain and Austria — illustrates three elements of strategy, of frequent mention, which it is well here to name and to define, as well as to illustrate by the instance before you.

1. There is central position, illustrated by France; her national power and control interposing by land between her enemies. Yet not by land only, provided the coast supports an adequate navy; for, if

[1] "Naval Strategy," pp. 31–53.

that be the case, the French fleet also interposes between Spanish and Italian ports. The Danube is similarly an instance of central position.

2. Interior lines. The characteristic of interior lines is that of the central position prolonged in one or more directions, thus favoring sustained interposition between separate bodies of an enemy; with the consequent power to concentrate against either, while holding the other in check with a force possibly distinctly inferior. An interior line may be conceived as the extension of a central position, or as a series of central positions connected with one another, as a geometrical line is a continuous series of geometrical points. The expression " Interior Lines " conveys the meaning that from a central position one can assemble more rapidly on either of two opposite fronts than the enemy can, and therefore can utilize force more effectively. Particular examples of maritime interior lines are found in the route by Suez as compared with that by the Cape of Good Hope, and in Panama contrasted with Magellan. The Kiel Canal similarly affords an interior line between the Baltic and North Sea, as against the natural channels passing round Denmark, or between the Danish Islands, — the Sound and the two Belts.[1] These instances of " Interior "

[1] An interesting instance of the method and forethought which cause German naval development of all kinds to progress abreast, on parallel lines, is found in the fact that by the time the three Dreadnoughts laid down in 1911 are completed, and with them two complete Dreadnought squadrons of eight each, which probably will be in 1914, the Kiel Canal will have been enlarged to permit their passage. There will then be a fleet of thirty-eight battleships; including these sixteen, which will be stationed, eight in the North Sea, eight in the Baltic, linked for mutual support by the central canal. The programme contemplates a contin-

will recall one of your boyhood's geometrical
theorems, demonstrating that, from a point interior
to a triangle, lines drawn to two angles are shorter
than the corresponding sides of the triangle itself.
Briefly, interior lines are lines shorter in time than
those the enemy can use. France, for instance, in
the case before us, could march twenty thousand men
to the Rhine, or to the Pyrenees, or could send necessary supplies to either, sooner than Spain could send
the same number to the Rhine, or Austria to the
Pyrenees, granting even that the sea were open to
their ships.

3. The position of France relatively to Germany
and Spain illustrates also the question of communications. " Communications " is a general term, desig-
nating the lines of movement by which a military
body, army or fleet, is kept in living connection with
the national power. This being the leading characteristic of communications, they may be considered
essentially lines of defensive action; while interior
lines are rather offensive in character, enabling the
belligerent favored by them to attack in force one
part of the hostile line sooner than the enemy can
reinforce it, because the assailant is nearer than the
friend. As a concrete instance, the disastrous attempt already mentioned, of Spain in 1639 to send
reinforcements by the Channel, followed the route
from Corunna to the Straits of Dover. It did so
because at that particular moment the successes of
France had given her control of part of the valley

uous prearranged replacing of the present pre-Dreadnoughts by Dreadnoughts.

of the Rhine, closing it to the Spaniards from Milan; while the more eastern route through Germany was barred by the Swedes, who in the Thirty Years' War were allies of France. The Channel therefore at that moment remained the only road open from Spain to the Netherlands, between which it became the line of communications. Granting the attempt had been successful, the line followed is exterior; for, assuming equal rapidity of movement, ten thousand men starting from central France should reach the field sooner.

The central position of France, therefore, gave both defensive and offensive advantage. In consequence of the position she had interior lines, shorter lines, by which to attack, and also her communications to either front lay behind the front, were covered by the army at the front; in other words, had good defense, besides being shorter than those by which the enemy on one front could send help to the other front. Further, by virtue of her position, the French ports on the Atlantic and Channel flanked the Spanish sea communications.

At the present moment, Germany and Austria-Hungary, as members of the Triple Alliance, have the same advantage of central and concentrated position against the Triple *Entente,* Russia, France, and Great Britain.

Transfer now your attention back to the Danube when the scene of war is in that region; as it was in 1796, and also frequently was during the period of which we are now speaking. . . . You have seen before, that, if there be war between Austria and

France, as there so often was, the one who held
the Danube had a central position in the region.
Holding means possession by military power, which
power can be used to the full against the North

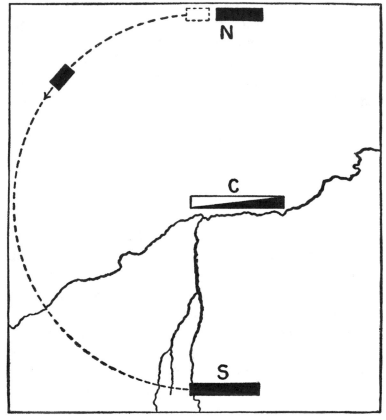

or against the South — offensive power — far more
easily than the South and North can combine against
him; because he is nearer to each than either is to
the other. (See map.)   Should North wish to send
a big reinforcement to South, it cannot march across
the part of the Danube held, but must march around

it above or below; exactly as, in 1640, reinforcements from Spain to the Rhine had, so to say, to march around France. In such a march, on land, the reinforcement making it is necessarily in a long column, because roads do not allow a great many men to walk abreast. The road followed designates in fact the alignment of the reinforcement from day to day; and because its advance continually turns the side to the enemy, around whom it is moving, the enemy's position is said to flank the movement, constituting a recognized danger. It makes no difference whether the line of march is straight or curved; it is extension upon it that constitutes the danger, because the line itself, being thin, is everywhere weak, liable to an attack in force upon a relatively small part of its whole. Communications are exposed, and the enemy has the interior line. . . .

This is an illustration of the force of Napoleon's saying, that "War is a business of positions." All this discussion turns on position; the ordinary, semipermanent, positions of Center, North, and South; or the succession of positions occupied by the detachment on that line of communications along which it moves. This illustrates the importance of positions in a single instance, but is by no means exhaustive of that importance. Fully to comprehend, it is necessary to study military and naval history; bearing steadily in mind Napoleon's saying, and the definitions of central position, interior lines, and communications.

Take, for example, an instance so recent as to have been contemporary with men not yet old, —

the Turkish position at Plevna in 1877. This
stopped the Russian advance on Constantinople for
almost five months. Why? Because, if they had
gone on, Plevna would have been close to their line
of communications, and in a central position relatively to their forces at the front and those in the
rear, or behind the Danube. It was also so near,
that, if the enemy advanced far, the garrison of
Plevna could reach the only bridge across the Danube, at Sistova, and might destroy it, before help
could come; that is, Plevna possessed an interior
line towards a point of the utmost importance.
Under these circumstances, Plevna alone arrested
the whole Russian movement. In the recent war
between Japan and Russia,[1] the Port Arthur fleet
similarly threatened the Japanese line of communications from Japan to Manchuria, and so affected the
whole conduct of the war. It was central, as regards
Japan and Liao-Yang, or Mukden. Study of such
conditions reinforces knowledge, by affording numerous illustrations of the effect of position under
very differing circumstances.

Let us now go back from the Danube with its
Center, North, and South, to the communications
between the Spanish coast and the Austrian army in
Germany. Should the House of Austria in Spain
desire to send large reinforcements to the Danube,
or to the Rhine, by way of Italy, it can do so, provided it controls the sea; and provided also that
France has not shaken its hold upon North Italy.
Such a condition constitutes open and safe com-

[1] See map on page 278.

munications. If, however, command of the sea is not assured, if the French navy, say at Toulon, is equal to the Spanish navy in the neighborhood, there is danger of a reverse; while if the French navy is superior locally, there is great danger not merely of a reverse but of a serious disaster. In such a case the French navy, or the port of Toulon, flanks the Spanish line of communication; again an instance of position. As to position, Toulon would correspond to Plevna and Port Arthur. This instance illustrates, however, as Port Arthur conspicuously did, that the value of a position is not in the bare position, but in the use you make of it. This, it is pertinent to note, is just the value of anything a man possesses, his brains or his fortune — the use he makes of either. Should the French navy be decisively inferior locally to the Spanish, Toulon loses its importance. As position it is still good, but it cannot be used. It is an unavailable asset. So at Plevna, had the garrison been so small that it could not take the field, the place either would have been captured, or could have been watched by a detachment, while the main Russian body moved on. At Port Arthur, the inefficiency of the Russian navy permitted this course to the Japanese. They watched the place by navy and army, and went on with their march in Manchuria. Even so, the threat inherent in the position compelled an immense detachment of troops necessary for the siege, and so greatly weakened the main army in its action.

Note that it is the nearness of Toulon, as of Plevna, which constitutes the menace to the line of

communication; the line from the port to that of
the communications is thus an interior line, short,
enabling an attack by surprise, or in force. It is
the same consideration that has made Cadiz at one
time, Gibraltar now, Malta, Jamaica, Guantanamo
Bay, all threatening positions; the ones to vessels
bound up or down the Mediterranean to or from
Suez, the others to vessels going to or from the
Isthmus of Panama. If it had been feasible for
Spain to carry her reinforcements south of Sardinia
and thence north, Toulon would so far have lost
much of this value. As the line drew near Genoa,
it would have regained control only in some measure;
that is, to a less degree and for a shorter time. As
a matter of fact such roundabout lines, *fausses routes*
as Napoleon called them, have played a notable
part in the strategy of a weaker party. The most
convenient commercial route is not necessarily the
most significant to strategy. Napoleon, for example, when bound to Egypt from Malta in 1798,
did not go direct, but first sighted Crete and then
bore away for Egypt. Owing to this, Nelson in
pursuit missed the French because he naturally went
direct.

The same beneficial effect — the same amount of
protection as a roundabout line would give — might
have been obtained if the Spanish navy on the
Atlantic coast threatened French ports and commerce, and thus induced France to keep her navy,
in whole or in part, in that quarter, weakening her
Toulon force; so that, though favorably situated,
it was not strong enough to attack. This was

actually the case up to 1634, in which year the defeat of the allies of France at Nordlingen, due to Spanish troops from Italy reinforcing the Imperial armies in Germany, compelled France to declare open war against Spain and to transfer her fleet to the Mediterranean. This effect was produced also in 1898 on the United States; not by the Spanish navy, which was innoxious in everything but talk, but by the fears of the American people, which prompted the American Government to keep the so-called Flying Squadron in Hampton Roads, instead of close to the probable scene of war. Owing to this distribution, if Cervera's squadron had been efficient, it could have got into Cienfuegos instead of Santiago; a very much harder nut to crack, because in close railroad communication with Havana and with the great mass of the Spanish army in Cuba. It is the same sort of unintelligent fear which prompts the demand now to send half the battle-fleet to the Pacific. No course could be more entirely satisfactory to an enemy, or more paralyzing to the United States fleet, than just this. All or none; the battle-fleet concentrated, whether in the Pacific or the Atlantic.

You will remember that in the war with Spain the United States navy had reproduced for it the situation I have depicted, of a detachment trying to pass round the Danube from North to South. The "Oregon" was the detachment, and she had to join the American fleet in the West Indies, in spite of the Spanish squadron. She reached Barbados May 18; the day before Cervera entered Santiago, and six days after he left Martinique, which is only one hundred miles from Barbados. The utter inefficiency of the Spanish navy has caused us to lose sight of the risk to the " Oregon," which was keenly felt by her commander, and concerning which at the moment two former secretaries of the navy expressed to me their anxiety. Despite this experience, there are those now who would reconstitute it for us, half the fleet in the Pacific and half in the Atlantic. Should then war arise with a European state, or with Japan, it would be open to either enemy to take the Danube position between our two divisions, as Togo did between the Port Arthur and the Baltic squadrons. . . .

Concentration

The general war against the House of Austria, as conducted by Richelieu, appears to have suffered from the same cause that saps the vigor of many wars; he attempted too many things at once, instead of concentrating for decided superiority in some one or two localities. For such concentration he had good opportunities, owing to the central position and interior lines possessed by France. It was open to him to act in great force either in Belgium, or on the Rhine, or in Italy, or towards Spain. Moreover, he had the initial advantage of a natural concentration: one nation against two, and those separated in space. The proverbial weakness of alliances is due to inferior power of concentration. Granting the same aggregate of force, it is never as great in two hands as in one, because it is not perfectly concentrated. Each party to an alliance usually has its particular aim, which divides action. In any military scheme that comes before you, let your first question to yourself be, Is this consistent with the requirement of concentration? Never attempt to straddle, to do two things at the same time, unless your force is evidently so supreme that you have clearly more than enough for each.

Our profession has never produced a man more daring in enterprise, nor more skillful in management, than Nelson. Remember, therefore, and always, that, when he sent off two frigates on some expedition, he charged their captains:

"If you meet two enemies, do not each attack one. Combine both on one of the enemy; you will make sure of that one, and you may also get the other afterwards; but, whether the second escape or not, your country will have won a victory, and gained a ship."

The same consideration applies to ship design. You cannot have everything. If you attempt it, you will lose everything; by which I mean that in no one quality will your vessel be as efficient as if you had concentrated purpose on that one. On a given tonnage, — which in ship-building corresponds to a given size of army or of fleet, — there cannot be had the highest speed, *and* the heaviest battery, *and* the thickest armor, *and* the longest coal endurance, which the tonnage would allow to any one of these objects by itself. If you try, you will be repeating

Richelieu's mistake when he tried to carry on offensive war on four frontiers.

The fighting order of navies still continues a line; which is called more properly a column, because the ships are ranged one behind the other. Nevertheless, if the arrangement of the guns, from van to rear, is regarded, it will be seen that they really are deployed on a line fronting the enemy. As a rule, in instructed naval warfare, attack has been on one flank of that line. It is commonly spoken of as an attack on van or rear, because of the columnar formation of the ships, but it is really a flank attack; and, whichever flank is chosen, the attack on the other is essentially refused, because the numbers devoted to it are not sufficient to press an attack home. The culmination of the sail era — Trafalgar — was fought exactly on these lines. Nelson concentrated the bulk of his fleet, a superior force, on the left flank of the enemy, which happened to be the rear; against the right flank he sent a smaller number. He did not indeed give specific orders to the smaller body not to attack, or to refuse themselves. That was not his way. Moreover, he intended himself to take charge of this attack in smaller force, and to be governed by circumstances as to the development of it; but the result was shown in the fact that the larger part of the enemy's right flank escaped, and all probably would if they had maneuvered well. The hostile loss fell on the other flank and on the center; and not only was this the case in result, but also Nelson in form and in his orders purposed just this. He put the concentrated attack in the hands of his second; " I," said he, in effect, " will see that the other flank of the enemy does not interfere." Conditions modified his action; but that was his plan, and although, from the particular conditions, he actually pierced the enemy's center, still, having done so, the subsequent attack fell upon the flank originally intended, while the other flank was kept in check by the rear ships of Nelson's own division. These, as they advanced in column, lay athwart the line by which the enemy's van, if it tacked, would approach the rear, or other flank; and they thus prevented its approach by that route until too late to be effective.

Nelson, who was a thoughtful as well as a daring tactician, expressed reasons for attacking one flank rather than another, under differing conditions in which the fleets presented themselves; but, speaking generally, the rear was the better to attack, because the van could not, and cannot, come as soon to help the rear as the rear can the van. It has to turn round, to begin with; and, before turning round, its commander has to make up his mind, which few men do quickly, unless they have reached conclusions beforehand. All this means time. Besides, the assailant can more easily place himself in the way of such new movement of the van, than he can of the rear coming up on the line of advance it already has. Still, there are some reasons in favor of the van. Nelson in 1801 said that in case of encountering a Russian fleet he would attack the van; because injury to it would throw the enemy's order into confusion, from which the Russians were not good enough maneuverers to recover. That is a special reason, not a general. It takes account of a particular circumstance, as a general on shore does of a particular locality. When Farragut passed the Mobile forts his van was thrown into confusion, and all know what a critical moment that was. It matters little what the incident is, if the confusion is produced.

In the Battle of the Japan Sea the attack again was on a flank, and that the van. Whether this was due to previous purpose of the Japanese, or merely arose from the conditions as they presented themselves, I do not know; but its tendency certainly would be to cause confusion. I do not wish, however, to argue here a question of tactics. My subject is strategy, and I am using tactics simply to illustrate the predominance, everywhere, under all conditions and from the nature of things, of the one great principle of concentration; and that, too, in the specific method of so distributing your own force as to be superior to the enemy in one quarter, while in the other you hold him in check long enough to permit your main attack to reach its full result. That necessary time may be half an hour on a field of battle; in a campaign it may be days, weeks, perhaps more.

. . . In any frontier line, or any strategic front of operations, or any line of battle, offensive effort may, and therefore should, be concentrated in one part, not distributed along the whole. This possibility, and a convenient way of conceiving it, Jomini expresses in an aphorism which may be commended to memory, because it sums up one important consideration concerning any military disposition whatever; whether it be the strategic front of operations in a campaign, or a tactical order of battle, or a frontier. Every such situation, Jomini says, may be properly regarded as a line; and every line divides, logically and actually, into three parts, — the center, and the two extremes, or flanks.

Guard yourselves, of course, from imagining three *equal* parts. We are not dealing here with mathematics, but with military conceptions. For practical results, let us apply at once to the United States of to-day. The United States has a long ocean frontier, broken at Mexico by the interposition of land, as the French maritime frontier is broken at the Pyrenees; yet the coast lines, like the French, possess a certain maritime continuity, in that ships can pass from end to end by sea. In such cases, it may be said without exaggeration that an ocean frontier is continuous. At present, the United States has one frontier which is strictly continuous, by land as by water, from the coast of Maine to the Rio Grande. There are in it, by natural division, three principal parts: the Atlantic, the Gulf, and the Straits of Florida. I do not deny that for purposes of study further convenient subdivisions may be made; but it may fairly be claimed that these three are clear, are primary, and are principal. They are very unequal in length, and, from the military standpoint, in importance; for while the peninsula of Florida does not rank very high in the industrial interests of the nation, a superior hostile fleet securely based in the Straits of Florida could effectively control intercourse by water between the two flanks. It would possess central position; and in virtue of that central position, its superiority need not be over the whole United States navy, should that be divided on each side of the central position. The supposed enemy, in such position, would need only to be decisively superior to each of the divisions lying on either side; whereas, were they united, superiority would require to be over the whole. It was this condition which made Cuba for the first century of our national existence a consideration of the first importance in our international relations. It flanked national communications, commercial and military. We know that there exists in our country an element of wisdom which would treat such a situation, which geography has constituted for us, as two boys do an apple. This would divide the fleet between the two coasts, and call it fair to both; because, so it is reasoned, — or rather argued, — defending both. It certainly, however, would not be concentration, nor effective.

Before passing on, note the striking resemblance between the Florida peninsula and that of Korea. Togo, at Masampo, was to Rozhestvensky and the Russians at Vladivostok just as a hostile fleet in the Straits of Florida would be to American divisions in the Gulf and at Hampton Roads. In like manner at an earlier period Togo and Kamimura, working apart but on interior lines, separated the three fine fighting ships in Vladivostok from the Port Arthur division.

The United States, however, has an even more urgent situation as to frontier in its Atlantic and Pacific coasts. If my claim is correct, in the instance of France, that a water frontier is continuous when passage from end to end by water is practicable, this is also continuous; and the battle-fleet has demonstrated the fact within the past few years. The United States, then, has a maritime frontier line from Eastport, Maine, to Puget Sound; and, like other military lines, it divides into three principal parts immediately obvious, — the Atlantic Coast, the Pacific Coast, and the line between. This summary will not be any more true, nor any more useful for reflection, when the line passes by Panama instead of the Straits of Magellan; but it certainly will be more obvious. It then will be seen easily, as now may be seen certainly, that the important part of the long line in the present case, as in the future, is the center, because that insures or prevents passage in force from side to side; the transfer of force; in short, the communications. This reproduces again the Danube position, and also the chain of Spanish positions from Genoa to Belgium. It is once more the central position, which we have met before in such varying localities and periods; but the central position of Panama has over that now open to us, by Magellan, the advantage of interior lines, of which class of lines indeed the contrast between the existing and the future of routes offers a notable illustration.

6. STRATEGIC POSITIONS [1]

THE strategic value of any place depends upon three principal conditions:

1. Its position, or more exactly its situation. A place may have great strength, but be so situated with regard to the strategic lines as not to be worth occupying.

2. Its military strength, offensive and defensive. A place may be well situated and have large resources and yet possess little strategic value, because weak. It may, on the other hand, while not naturally strong, be given artificial strength for defense. The word "fortify" means simply to make strong.

3. The resources, of the place itself and of the surrounding country. . . . Where all three conditions, situation, intrinsic strength, and abundant resources, are found in the same place, it becomes of great consequence strategically and may be of the very first importance, though not always. For it must be remarked that there are other considerations, lesser in the purely military point of view, which enhance the consequence of a seaport even strategically; such as its being a great mart of trade, a blow to which would cripple the prosperity of the country; or the capital,

---

[1] "Naval Strategy," pp. 130–163.

the fall of which has a political effect additional to
its importance otherwise.

I. *Situation*

Of the three principal conditions, the first, situation, is the most indispensable; because strength and
resources can be artificially supplied or increased,
but it passes the power of man to change the situation of a port which lies outside the limits of
strategic effect.

Generally, value of situation depends upon nearness to a sea route; to those lines of trade which,
when drawn upon the ocean common, are as imaginary as the parallels of the chart, yet as really and
usefully exist. If the position be on two routes at
the same time, that is, near the crossing, the value
is enhanced. A cross-roads is essentially a central
position, facilitating action in as many directions as
there are roads. Those familiar with works on the
art of land war will recognize the analogies. The
value becomes yet more marked if, by the lay of
the land, the road to be followed becomes very
narrow; as at the Straits of Gibraltar, the English
Channel, and in a less degree the Florida Strait.
Perhaps narrowing should be applied to every inlet
of the sea, by which trade enters into and is distributed over a great extent of country; such as the
mouth of the Mississippi, of the Dutch and German
rivers, New York harbor, etc. As regards the sea,
however, harbors or the mouths of rivers are usually
termini or *entrepôts*, at which goods are trans-
shipped before going farther. If the road be nar-

rowed to a mere canal, or to the mouth of a river, the point to which vessels must come is reduced almost to the geometrical definition of a point and near-by positions have great command. Suez presents this condition now, and Panama soon will.

Analogously, positions in narrow seas are more important than those in the great ocean, because it is less possible to avoid them by a circuit. If these seas are not merely the ends — " *termini* " — of travel but " highways," parts of a continuous route; that is, if commerce not only comes to them but passes through to other fields beyond, the number of passing ships is increased and thereby the strategic value of the controlling points. . . .

[Illustrations are here employed to show that, owing to the freedom of movements on the open sea, dangerous positions when not located in narrow channels are more easily avoided than on land. Hence " *fausses routes et moments perdus*," in Napoleon's phrase, play an important part in naval operations, as shown by Napoleon's route to Egypt via Malta and Crete, and Rozhestvensky's choice of routes before Tsushima. On the other hand, obstacles when they exist are impassable. Only submarines can avoid danger by transit over land. — EDITOR.]

II. *Military Strength*

A. *Defensive Strength.* [Military strength is considered in two aspects, (A) defensive, and (B) offensive. Under defensive strength, it is first pointed out that, as illustrated by Port Arthur and

Santiago, coast bases are in chief danger of capture from the land side. While it is the business of the navy to prevent the landing of forces, its operations, though defensive in result, must be offensive in character, and not confined to the vicinity of the bases. — EDITOR.]

In the sphere of maritime war, the navy represents the army in the field; and the fortified strategic harbors, upon which it falls back as ports of refuge after battle or defeat, for repairs or for supplies, correspond precisely to strongholds, like Metz, Strasburg, Ulm, upon which, systematically occupied with reference to the strategic character of the theater of war, military writers agree the defense of a country must be founded. The foundation, however, must not be taken for the superstructure for which it exists. In war, the defensive exists mainly that the offensive may act more freely. In sea warfare, the offensive is assigned to the navy; and if the latter assumes to itself the defensive, it simply locks up a part of its trained men in garrisons, which could be filled as well by forces that have not their peculiar skill. To this main proposition I must add a corollary, that if the defense of ports, many in number, be attributed to the navy, experience shows that the navy will be subdivided among them to an extent that will paralyze its efficiency. I was amused, but at the same time instructed as to popular understanding of war, by the consternation aroused in Great Britain by one summer's maneuvers, already alluded to, and the remedy proposed in some papers. It appeared that several seaports

were open to bombardment and consequent exaction
of subsidies by a small squadron, and it was gravely
urged that the navy should be large enough to spare
a small detachment to each port. Of what use is a
navy, if it is to be thus whittled away? But a
popular outcry will drown the voice of military
experience.

. . . The strictly defensive strength of a seaport
depends therefore upon permanent works, the provision of which is not the business of naval officers.
The navy is interested in them because, when effective, they release it from any care about the port;
from defensive action to the offensive, which is its
proper sphere.

There is another sense in which a navy is regarded as defensive; namely, that the existence of
an adequate navy protects from invasion by commanding the sea. That is measurably and in very
large degree true, and is a strategic function of great
importance; but this is a wholly different question
from that of the defensive strength of seaports, of
strategic points, with which we are now dealing. It
therefore will be postponed, with a simple warning
against the opinion that because the navy thus de-
fends there is no need for local protection of the
strategic ports; no need, that is, for fortifications.
This view affirms that a military force can always,
under all circumstances, dispense with secure bases
of operations; in other words, that it can never be
evaded, nor know momentary mishap.

I have now put before you reasons for rejecting
the opinion that the navy is the proper instrument,

generally speaking, for coast defense in the narrow sense of the expression, which limits it to the defense of ports. The reasons given may be summed up, and reduced to four principles, as follows:

1. That for the same amount of offensive power, floating batteries, or vessels of very little mobility, are less strong defensively against naval attack than land works are.

2. That by employing able-bodied seafaring men to defend harbors you lock up offensive strength in an inferior, that is, in a defensive, effort.

3. That it is injurious to the *morale* and skill of seamen to keep them thus on the defensive and off the sea. This has received abundant historical proof in the past.

4. That in giving up the offensive the navy gives up its proper sphere, which is also the most effective.

B. *Offensive Strength.* — The offensive strength of a seaport, considered independently of its strategic situation and of its natural and acquired resources, consists in its capacity:

1. To assemble and hold a large military force, of both ships of war and transports.

2. To launch such force safely and easily into the deep.

3. To follow it with a continued support until the campaign is ended. In such support are always to be reckoned facilities for docking, as the most important of all supports.

[These points are discussed in detail. It is noted that a port with two outlets, like New York and Vladivostok, has a decided advantage. — EDITOR.]

III. *Resources*

The wants of a navy are so many and so varied that it would be time lost to name them separately. The resources which meet them may be usefully divided under two heads, natural and artificial. The latter, again, may be conveniently and accurately subdivided into resources developed by man in his peaceful occupation and use of a country, and those which are immediately and solely created for the maintenance of war.

Other things being equal, the most favorable condition is that where great natural resources, joined to a good position for trade, have drawn men to settle and develop the neighboring country. Where the existing resources are purely artificial and for war, the value of the port, in so far, is inferior to that of one where the ordinary occupations of the people supply the necessary resources. To use the phraseology of our subject, a seaport that has good strategic situation and great military strength, but to which all resources must be brought from a distance, is much inferior to a similar port having a rich and developed friendly region behind it. Gibraltar and ports on small islands, like Santa Lucia and Martinique, labor under this disadvantage, as compared with ports of England, France, the United States; or even of a big island like Cuba, if the latter be developed by an industrial and commercial people.

7. STRATEGIC LINES [1]

Communications

THE most important of strategic lines are those which concern the communications. Communications dominate war. This has peculiar force on shore, because an army is immediately dependent upon supplies frequently renewed. It can endure a brief interruption much less readily than a fleet can, because ships carry the substance of communications largely in their own bottoms. So long as the fleet is able to face the enemy at sea, communications mean essentially, not geographical lines, like the roads an army has to follow, but those necessaries, supplies of which the ships cannot carry in their own hulls beyond a limited amount. These are, first, fuel; second, ammunition; last of all, food. These necessaries, owing to the facility of water transportation as compared with land, can accompany the movements of a fleet in a way impossible to the train of an army. An army train follows rather than accompanies, by roads which may be difficult and must be narrow; whereas maritime roads are easy, and illimitably wide.

Nevertheless, all military organizations, land or sea, are ultimately dependent upon open communi-

---

[1] "Naval Strategy," pp. 166–167. For illustration and further discussion of strategic lines, see "General Strategy of the War of 1812," in this volume, pp. 229–240. — EDITOR.

cations with the basis of the national power; and the line of communications is doubly of value, because it usually represents also the line of retreat. Retreat is the extreme expression of dependence upon the home base. In the matter of communications, free supplies and open retreat are two essentials to the *safety* of an army or of a fleet. Napoleon at Marengo in 1800, and again at Ulm in 1805, succeeded in placing himself upon the Austrian line of communication and of retreat, in force sufficient to prevent supplies coming forward from the base, or the army moving backward to the base. At Marengo there was a battle, at Ulm none; but at each the results depended upon the same condition, — the line of communication controlled by the enemy. In the War of Secession the forts of the Mississippi were conquered as soon as Farragut's fleet, by passing above, held their line of communications. Mantua in 1796 was similarly conquered as soon as Napoleon had placed himself upon the line of retreat of its garrison. It held out for six months, very properly; but the rest of the campaign was simply an effort of the outside Austrians to drive the French off the line, and thus to reinforce the garrison or to enable it to retreat.

Importance of Sea Communications [1]

Except Russia and Japan, the nations actively concerned in this great problem [the problem of Asia] rest, for home bases, upon remote countries.

[1] "The Problem of Asia" (1900), pp. 124–127.

We find therefore two classes of powers: those whose communication is by land, and those who depend upon the sea. The sea lines are the most numerous and easy, and they will probably be determinative of the courses of trade. Among them there are two the advantages of which excel all others — for Europe by Suez, from America by way of the Pacific Ocean. The latter will doubtless receive further modification by an isthmian canal, extending the use of the route to the Atlantic seaboard of America, North and South.

Communications dominate war; broadly considered, they are the most important single element in strategy, political or military. In its control over them has lain the pre-eminence of sea power — as an influence upon the history of the past; and in this it will continue, for the attribute is inseparable from its existence. This is evident because, for reasons previously explained, transit in large quantities and for great distances is decisively more easy and copious by water than by land. The sea, therefore, is the great medium of communications — of commerce. The very sound, "commerce," brings with it a suggestion of the sea, for it is maritime commerce that has in all ages been most fruitful of wealth; and wealth is but the concrete expression of a nation's energy of life, material and mental. The power, therefore, to insure these communications to one's self, and to interrupt them for an adversary, affects the very root of a nation's vigor, as in military operations it does the existence of an army, or as the free access to rain and sun —

communication from without — does the life of a plant. This is the prerogative of the sea powers; and this chiefly — if not, indeed, this alone — they have to set off against the disadvantage of position and of numbers under which, with reference to land power, they labor in Asia. It is enough. Pressure afar off — diversion — is adequate to relieve that near at hand, as Napoleon expected to conquer Pondicherry on the banks of the Vistula. But if the sea powers embrace the proposition that has found favor in America, and, by the concession of immunity to an enemy's commerce in time of war, surrender their control of maritime communications, they will have abdicated the scepter of the sea, for they will have abandoned one chief means by which pressure in one quarter — the sea — balances pressure in a remote and otherwise inaccessible quarter. Never was moment for such abandonment less propitious than the present, when the determination of influence in Asia is at stake.

8. Offensive Operations [1]

[THE situation here considered is that of a fleet that has driven the enemy from a base in the theater of war, but has still to cope with the enemy fleet falling back on another base. — EDITOR.]

The case of further advance from your new base may not be complicated by the consideration of great distance. The next step requisite to be taken may be short, as from Cuba to Jamaica; or it may be that the enemy's fleet is still at sea, in which case it is the great objective, now as always. Its being at sea may be because retreating, from the position you have occupied, towards his remoter base; either because conscious of inferiority, or, perhaps, after a defeat more or less decisive. It will then be necessary to act with rapidity, in order to cut off the enemy from his port of destination. If there is reason to believe that you can overtake and pass him with superior force, every effort to do so must be made. The direction of his retreat is known or must be ascertained, and it will be borne in mind that the base to which he is retreating and his fleet are separated parts of one force, the union of which must be prevented. In such a case, the excuses frequently made for a sluggish pursuit ashore, such as fatigue of troops, heavy roads, etc., do not apply. Crippled battleships must be dropped, or ordered

"Naval Strategy," pp. 266–272.

to follow with the colliers.   Such a pursuit presumes
but one disadvantage to the chasing fleet, viz., that
it is leaving its coal base while the chase is approaching his; and this, if the calculations are close,
may give the pursuing admiral great anxiety.   Such
anxieties are the test and penalty of greatness.   In
such cases, excuses for failure attributed to short-
ness of coal will be closely scrutinized; and justly.
In all other respects, superiority must be assumed,
because on no other condition could such headlong
pursuit be made.   It aims at a great success, and
successes will usually be in proportion to superiority,
either original or acquired.   " What the country
needs," said Nelson, " is the annihilation of the
enemy.   Only numbers can annihilate."

If such a chase follow a battle, it can scarcely fail
that the weaker party — the retreating party — is
also distressed by crippled ships, which he may be
forced to abandon — or fight.   Strenuous, unrelax-
ing pursuit is therefore as imperative after a battle
as is courage during it.   Great political results often
flow from correct military action; a fact which no
military commander is at liberty to ignore.   He may
very well not know of those results; it is enough to
know that they may happen, and nothing can excuse
his losing a point which by exertion he might have
scored.   Napoleon, says Jomini, never forgave the
general who in 1796, by resting his troops a couple
of hours, failed to get between an Austrian division
and Mantua, in which it was seeking refuge, and by
his neglect found it.   The failure of Admiral de
Tourville to pursue vigorously the defeated Dutch

and English fleet, after the battle of Beachy Head, in 1690, caused that victory to be indecisive, and helped to fasten the crown of England on the head of a Dutch King, who was the soul of the alliance against France. Slackness in following up victory had thus a decisive influence upon the results of the whole war, both on the continent and the sea. I may add, it has proved injurious to the art of naval strategy, by the seeming confirmation it has given to the theory of the " fleet in being." It was not the beaten and crippled English and Dutch " fleet in being " that prevented an invasion of England. It was the weakness or inertness of Tourville, or the unreadiness of the French transports.

Similarly, the refusal of Admiral Hotham to pursue vigorously a beaten French fleet in 1795, unquestionably not only made that year's campaign indecisive, but made possible Napoleon's Italian campaign of 1796, from which flowed his whole career and its effects upon history. The same dazzling career received its sudden mortal stab when, in the height of his crushing advance in Spain, with its capital in his hands, at the very moment when his vast plans seemed on the eve of accomplishment, a more enterprising British leader, Sir John Moore, moved his petty army to Sahagun, on the flank of Napoleon's communications between France and Madrid. The blow recoiled upon Moore, who was swept as by a whirlwind to Coruña, and into the sea; but Spain was saved. The Emperor could not retrieve the lost time and opportunity. He could not return to Madrid in person, but had to entrust to several subordinates the task which only his own supreme genius could successfully supervise. From the military standpoint, his downfall dates from that day. The whole career of Wellington, to Waterloo, lay in the womb of Moore's daring conception. But for that, wrote Napier, the Peninsular War would not have required a chronicler.

An admiral may not be able to foresee such remote consequences of his action, but he can safely adopt the principle expressed by Nelson, in the instance just cited, after hearing his commander-in-chief say they had done well enough: " If ten ships out of eleven were taken, I would never call it well enough, if we were able to get at the eleventh."

The relations between the fleets of Admirals Rozhestvensky and Togo prior to their meeting off Tsushima bore no slight resemblance to those between a pursued and a pursuing fleet. The Russian fleet, which had started before the Port Arthur division succumbed, was placed by that event in the position of a fleet which has suffered defeat so severe that its first effort must be to escape into its own ports. This was so obvious that many felt a retreat upon the Baltic was the only course left open; but, failing that, Rozhestvensky argued that he should rush on to Vladivostok at once, before the Japanese should get again into the best condition to intercept him, by repairing their ships, cleaning the bottoms, and refreshing the ships' companies. Instead of so ordering, the Russian government decided to hold him at Nossi-Bé (the north end of Madagascar), pending a reinforcement to be sent under Admiral Nebogatoff. Something is to be said for both views, in the abstract; but considering that the reinforcement was heterogeneous and inferior in character, that the Russian first aim was not battle but escape to Vladivostok, and, especially, that the Japanese were particularly anxious to obtain the use of delay for the very purpose Rozhestvensky feared, it seems probable that he was right. In any event, he was delayed at Nossi-Bé from January 9 to March 16; and afterwards at Kamranh Bay in French Cochin-China, from April 14 to May 9, when Nebogatoff joined. Allowing time for coaling and refitting, this indicates a delay of sixty to seventy days; the actual time underway from Nossi-Bé to Tsushima being only forty-five days. Thus, but for the wait for Nebogatoff, the Russian division would have reached Tsushima two months before it did, or about March 20.

Togo did not have to get ahead of a flying fleet, for by the fortune of position he was already ahead of it; but he did have to select the best position for intercepting it, as well as to decide upon his general course of action: whether, for instance, he should advance to meet it; whether he should attempt embarrassment by his superior force of torpedo vessels, so as to cripple or destroy some of its units, thus reducing further a force already inferior; also the direction and activities of his available scouts. His action may be taken as expressing his opinions on these subjects. He did not advance; he did not attempt harassment prior to meeting; he concen-

trated his entire battle force on the line by which he
expected the enemy must advance; and he was so
far in ignorance of their movements that he received
information only on the very morning of the battle.
This was well enough; but it is scarcely unreason-
able to say it might have been bettered. The
Japanese, however, had behind them a large part
of a successful naval campaign, the chief points of
which it is relevant to our subject to note. They had
first by a surprise attack inflicted a marked injury
on the enemy's fleet, which obtained for them a time
of delay and opportunity during its enforced in-
activity. They had then reduced one of the enemy's
two naval bases, and destroyed the division sheltered
in it. By this they had begun to beat the enemy in
detail, and had left the approaching reinforcement
only one possible port of arrival.

If a flying fleet has been lost to sight and has but
one port of refuge, pursuit, of course, will be
directed upon that port; but if there are more, the
chasing admiral will have to decide upon what point
to direct his fleet, and will send out despatch vessels
in different directions to find the enemy and transmit
intelligence. Cruisers engaged in such duty should
be notified of the intended or possible movements
of the fleet, and when practicable should be sent in
couples; for although wireless telegraphy has now
superseded the necessity of sending one back with
information, while the other remains in touch with
the enemy, accidents may happen, and in so important a matter it seems expedient to double precautions. The case resembles duplicating important

correspondence; for wireless cannot act before it has news, and to obtain news objects must be seen. It is to be remembered, too, that wireless messages may be intercepted, to the serious disadvantage of the sender. It seems possible that conjunctures may arise when it will be safer to send a vessel with tidings rather than commit them to air waves.

Thus, in theory, and to make execution perfect, — to capture, so to say, Nelson's eleventh ship, — the aim must be to drive the enemy out of every foothold in the whole theater of war, and particularly to destroy or shut up his fleet. Having accomplished the great feature of the task by getting hold of the most decisive position, further effort must be directed towards, possibly not upon, those points which may serve him still for bases. In so doing, your fleet must not be divided, unless overwhelmingly strong, and must not extend its lines of communication beyond the power of protecting them, unless it be for a dash of limited duration.

If compelled to choose between fortified ports of the enemy and his fleet, the latter will be regarded as the true objective; but a blockade of the ports, or an attack upon them, may be the surest means of bringing the ships within reach. Thus, in the War of American Independence, the siege of Gibraltar compelled the British fleet on more than one occasion to come within fighting reach of the enemy's blockading fleet, in order to throw in supplies. That the allies did not attack, except on one occasion, does not invalidate the lesson. Corbett in his " Seven Years' War " points out very justly, in Byng's celebrated failure, which cost him his life, that if he had moved against the French transports, in a neighboring bay, the French admiral would have had to attack, and the result might have been more favorable to the British. Such movements are essentially blows at the communications of the enemy, and if aimed without unduly risking your own will be in thorough accord with the most assured principles of strategy. A militarily effective blockade of a base essential to the enemy will force his fleet either to fight or to abandon the theater of war. Thus, as has been pointed out elsewhere, in Suffren's campaign in Indian Seas, so long as Trincomalee was in possession of the British, a threat at it was sure to bring them out to fight, although it was not their principal base. The abandonment of the theater of war by the navy will cause the arsenal to fall in time, through failure of resources, as Gibraltar must have fallen if the British fleet had not returned and supplied it at intervals. Such a result, however, is less complete than a victory over the enemy's navy, which would lead to the same end, and so be a double success, ships *and* port.

9. THE VALUE OF THE DEFENSIVE [1]

IT is true that in certain respects the defensive has advantages, the possession of which may even justify an expression, which has been stated as a maxim of war, that "Defense is a stronger form of war than Offense is." I do not like the expression, for it seems to me misleading as to the determinative characteristics of a defensive attitude; but it may pass, if properly qualified. What is meant by it is that in a particular operation, or even in a general plan, the party on the defense, since he makes no forward movement for the time, can strengthen his preparations, make deliberate and permanent dispositions; while the party on the offensive, being in continual movement, is more liable to mistake, of which the defense may take advantage, and in any case has to accept as part of his problem the disadvantage, to him, of the accumulated preparations that the defense has been making while he has been marching. The extreme example of preparation is a fortified permanent post; but similar instances are found in a battle field carefully chosen for advantages of ground, where attack is awaited, and in a line of ships, which by the solidarity of its order, and deployment of broadside, awaits an enemy who has to approach in column with disadvantage as to train of guns. In so far, the *form*

1 "Naval Strategy," pp. 277–280.

taken by the defense is stronger than the *form* assumed for the moment by the offense.

If you will think clearly, you will recognize that at Tsushima the Japanese were on the defensive, for their object was to stop, to thwart, the Russian attempt. Essentially, whatever the tactical method they adopted, they were to spread their broadsides across the road to Vladivostok, and await. The Russians were on the offensive, little as we are accustomed so to regard them; they had to get through to Vladivostok — if they could. They had to hold their course to the place, and to break through the Japanese, — if they could. In short, they were on the offensive, and the form of their approach had to be in column, bows on, — a weaker form, — which they had to abandon, tactically, as soon as they came under fire.

In our hostilities with Spain, also, Cervera's movement before reaching Santiago was offensive in character, the attitude of the United States defensive; that is, he was trying to effect something which the American Navy was set to prevent. There being three principal Spanish ports, Havana, Cienfuegos, and Santiago, we could not be certain for which he would try, and should have been before two in such force that an attempt by him would have assured a battle. We were strong enough for such a disposition. The two ports thus to be barred were evidently Havana and Cienfuegos. The supposed necessity for defending our northern coast left Cienfuegos open. Had Cervera made for it, he would have reached it before the Flying Squadron did. The need for keeping the Flying Squadron in Hampton Roads was imaginary, but it none the less illustrates the effect of inadequate coast defenses upon the military plan of the nation.

The author whom I quote (Corbett, " Seven Years' War," Vol. I, p. 92), who himself quotes from one of the first of authorities, Clausewitz, has therefore immediately to qualify his maxim, thus:

" When we say that defense is a stronger form of war, *that is, that it requires a smaller force, if soundly designed,* we are speaking, of course, only of one certain line of operations. If we do not know the general line of operation on which the enemy intends to attack, and so cannot mass our force upon it, then defense is weak, because we are compelled to distribute our force so as to be strong enough to stop the enemy on any line of operations he may adopt."

Manifestly, however, a force capable of being strong enough on several lines of operation to stop an enemy possesses a superiority that should take the offensive. In the instance just cited, of Cervera's approach, the American true policy of concentration would have had to yield to distribution, between Cienfuegos and Havana. Instead of a decisive superiority on one position, there would have been a bare equality upon two. Granting an enemy of equal skill and training, the result might have been one way or the other; and the only compensation would have been that the enemy would have been so badly handled that, to use Nelson's phrase, he would give no more trouble that season, and the other American division would have controlled the seas, as Togo did after August 10, 1904. From the purely professional point of view it is greatly to be regretted that the Spaniards and Russians showed such poor professional aptitude. The radical disadvantage of the defensive is evident. It not only is the enforced attitude of a weaker party, but it labors under the further onerous uncertainty where the offensive may strike, when there is more than one line of operation open to him, as there usually is. This tends to entail dissemination of force. The advantages of the defensive have been sufficiently indicated; they are essentially those of deliberate preparation, shown in precautions of various kinds. In assuming the defensive you take for granted the impossibility of your own permanent advance and the ability of the enemy to present himself before your front in superior numbers; unless you can harass him on the way and cause loss enough to diminish the inequality. Unless such disparity exists, you should be on the offensive. On the other hand, in the defensive it has to be taken for granted that you have on your side a respectable though inferior battle fleet, and a sea frontier possessing a certain number of ports which cannot be reduced without regular operations, in which the armed shipping can be got ready for battle, and to which, as to a base, they can retire for refit. Without these two elements there can be no serious defense.

10. COMMERCE DESTROYING AND BLOCKADE [1]

IT is desirable to explain here what was, and is, the particular specific utility of operations directed toward the destruction of an enemy's commerce; what its bearing upon the issues of war; and how, also, it affects the relative interests of antagonists, unequally paired in the matter of sea power. Without attempting to determine precisely the relative importance of internal and external commerce, which varies with each country, and admitting that the length of transportation entails a distinct element of increased cost upon the articles transported, it is nevertheless safe to say that, to nations having free access to the sea, the export and import trade is a very large factor in national prosperity and comfort. At the very least, it increases by so much the aggregate of commercial transactions, while the ease and copiousness of water carriage go far to compensate for the increase of distance. Furthermore, the public revenue of maritime states is largely derived from duties on imports. Hence arises, therefore, a large source of wealth, of money; and money — ready money or substantial credit — is proverbially the sinews of war, as the War of 1812 was amply to demonstrate. Inconvertible assets, as business men know, are a very inefficacious form of

[1] "Sea Power in its Relations to the War of 1812," Vol. I, pp. 284–290.

wealth in tight times; and war is always a tight time for a country, a time in which its positive wealth, in the shape of every kind of produce, is of little use, unless by freedom of exchange it can be converted into cash for governmental expenses. To this sea-commerce greatly contributes, and the extreme embarrassment under which the United States as a nation labored in 1814 was mainly due to commercial exclusion from the sea. To attack the commerce of the enemy is therefore to cripple him, in the measure of success achieved, in the particular factor which is vital to the maintenance of war. Moreover, in the complicated conditions of mercantile activity no one branch can be seriously injured without involving others.

This may be called the financial and political effect of "commerce destroying," as the modern phrase runs. In military effect, it is strictly analogous to the impairing of an enemy's communications, of the line of supplies connecting an army with its base of operations, upon the maintenance of which the life of the army depends. Money, credit, is the life of war; lessen it, and vigor flags; destroy it, and resistance dies. No resource then remains except to "make war support war;" that is, to make the vanquished pay the bills for the maintenance of the army which has crushed him, or which is proceeding to crush whatever opposition is left alive. This, by the extraction of private money, and of supplies for the use of his troops, from the country in which he was fighting, was the method of Napoleon, than whom no man held more delicate views concerning the gross impropriety of capturing private property at sea, whither his power did not extend. Yet this, in effect, is simply another method of forcing the enemy to surrender a large part of his means, so weakening him, while transferring it to the victor for the better propagation of hostilities. The exaction of a pecuniary indemnity from the worsted party at the conclusion of a war, as is frequently done, differs from the seizure of property in transit afloat only in method, and as peace differs from war. In either case, money or money's worth is exacted; but when peace supervenes, the method of collection is left to the Government of the country, in pursuance of its powers of taxation, to distribute the burden among the people; whereas in war, the primary object being immediate injury to the enemy's fighting power, it is not only legitimate in principle, but particularly effective, to seek the disorganization of his financial system by a crushing attack upon one of its important factors, because effort thus is concentrated on a readily accessible, fundamental element of his general prosperity. That the loss falls directly on individuals, or a class, instead of upon the whole community, is but an incident of war, just as some men are killed and others not. Indirectly, but none the less surely, the whole community, and, what is more important, the organized government, are crippled; offensive powers impaired.

But while this is the absolute tendency of war against commerce, common to all cases, the relative value varies greatly with the countries having recourse to it. It is a species of hostilities easily extemporized by a great maritime nation; it therefore favors one whose policy is not to maintain a large naval establishment. It opens a field for a sea militia force, requiring little antecedent military training. Again, it is a logical military reply to commercial blockade, which is the most systematic, regularized, and extensive form of commerce-destruction known to war. Commercial blockade is not to be confounded with the military measure of confining a body of hostile ships of war to their harbor, by stationing before it a competent force. It is directed against merchant vessels, and is not a military operation in the narrowest sense, in that it does not necessarily involve fighting, nor propose the capture of the blockaded harbor. It is not usually directed against military ports, unless these happen to be also centers of commerce. Its object, which was the paramount function of the United States Navy during the Civil War, dealing probably the most decisive blow inflicted upon the Confederacy, is the destruction of commerce by closing the ports of egress and ingress. Incidental to that, all ships, neutrals included, attempting to enter or depart, after public notification through customary channels, are captured and confiscated as remorselessly as could be done by the most greedy privateer. Thus constituted, the operation receives far wider scope than commerce-destruction on the high seas; for this is confined to merchantmen of belligerents, while commercial blockade, by universal consent, subjects to capture neutrals who attempt to infringe it, because, by attempting to defeat the efforts of one belligerent, they make themselves parties to the war. In fact, commercial blockade, though most effective as a military measure in broad results, is so distinctly commerce-destructive in essence, that those who censure the one form must logically proceed to denounce the other. This, as has been seen, Napoleon did; alleging in his Berlin Decree, in 1806, that war cannot be extended to any private property whatever, and that the right of blockade is restricted to *fortified* places, actually invested by competent forces. This he had the face to assert, at the very moment when he was compelling every vanquished state to extract, from the private means of its subjects, coin running up to hundreds of millions to replenish his military chest for further extension of hostilities. Had this dictum been accepted international law in 1861, the United States could not have closed the ports of the Confederacy, the commerce of which would have proceeded unmolested; and hostile measures being consequently directed against men's persons instead of their trade, victory, if accomplished at all, would have cost three lives for every two actually lost.

It is apparent, immediately on statement, that against commerce-destruction by blockade, the recourse of the weaker maritime belligerent is commerce-destruction by cruisers on the high sea. Granting equal efficiency in the use of either measure, it is further plain that the latter is intrinsically far less efficacious. To cut off access to a city is much more certainly accomplished by holding the

gates than by scouring the country in search of
persons seeking to enter. Still, one can but do what
one can.   In 1861 to 1865, the Southern Confederacy, unable to shake off the death grip fastened on
its throat, attempted counteraction by means of the
" Alabama," " Sumter," and their less famous con-
sorts, with what disastrous influence upon the navigation — the shipping — of the Union it is needless
to insist.   But while the shipping of the opposite
belligerent was in this way not only crippled, but
indirectly was swept from the seas, the Confederate
cruisers, not being able to establish a blockade, could
not prevent neutral vessels from carrying on the
commerce of the Union.   This consequently suffered
no serious interruption; whereas the produce of the
South, its inconvertible wealth — cotton chiefly —
was practically useless to sustain the financial system
and credit of the people.   So, in 1812 and the two
years following, the United States flooded the seas
with privateers, producing an effect upon British
commerce which, though inconclusive singly, doubtless co-operated powerfully with other motives to
dispose the enemy to liberal terms of peace.   It was
the reply, and the only possible reply, to the commercial blockade, the grinding efficacy of which it
will be a principal object of these pages to depict.
The issue to us has been accurately characterized by
Mr. Henry Adams, in the single word " Exhaustion." [1]

Both parties to the War of 1812 being conspicuously maritime in disposition and occupation,

[1] "History of the United States," Vol. VIII, chap. VIII.

while separated by three thousand miles of ocean, the sea and its navigable approaches became necessarily the most extensive scene of operations. There being between them great inequality of organized naval strength and of pecuniary resources, they inevitably resorted, according to their respective force, to one or the other form of maritime hostilities against commerce which have been indicated. To this procedure combats on the high seas were merely incidental. Tradition, professional pride, and the combative spirit inherent in both peoples, compelled fighting when armed vessels of nearly equal strength met; but such contests, though wholly laudable from the naval standpoint, which under ordinary circumstances cannot afford to encourage retreat from an equal foe, were indecisive of general results, however meritorious in particular execution. They had no effect upon the issue, except so far as they inspired moral enthusiasm and confidence. Still more, in the sequel they have had a distinctly injurious effect upon national opinion in the United States. In the brilliant exhibition of enterprise, professional skill, and usual success, by its naval officers and seamen, the country has forgotten the precedent neglect of several administrations to constitute the navy as strong in proportion to the means of the country as it was excellent through the spirit and acquirements of its officers. Sight also has been lost of the actual conditions of repression, confinement, and isolation, enforced upon the maritime frontier during the greater part of the war, with the misery and mortification thence ensuing. It has been widely inferred that the maritime conditions in general were highly flattering to national pride, and that a future emergency could be confronted with the same supposed facility, and as little preparation, as the odds of 1812 are believed to have been encountered and overcome. This mental impression, this picture, is false throughout, alike in its grouping of incidents, in its disregard of proportion, and in its ignoring of facts. The truth of this assertion will appear in due course of this narrative, and it will be seen that, although relieved by many brilliant incidents, indicative of the real spirit and capacity of the nation, the record upon the whole is one of gloom, disaster, and governmental incompetence, resulting from lack of national preparation, due to the obstinate and blind prepossessions of the Government, and, in part, of the people.

Command of the Sea Decisive [1]

It is not the taking of individual ships or convoys, be they few or many, that strikes down the money power of a nation; it is the possession of that overbearing power on the sea which drives the enemy's flag from it, or allows it to appear only as a fugitive; and which, by controlling the great common, closes the highways by which commerce moves to and from the enemy's shores. This overbearing power can only be exercised by great navies, and by them (on the broad sea) less efficiently now than in the days when the neutral flag had not its present immunity.[2]

[1] "The Influence of Sea Power upon History," p. 138.
[2] This immunity of enemy property in neutral ships, guaranteed by

It is not unlikely that, in the event of a war between maritime nations, an attempt may be made by the one having a great sea power and wishing to break down its enemy's commerce, to interpret the phrase " effective blockade " in the manner that best suits its interests at the time; to assert that the speed and disposal of its ships make the blockade effective at much greater distances and with fewer ships than formerly. The determination of such a question will depend, not upon the weaker belligerent, but upon neutral powers; it will raise the issue between belligerent and neutral rights; and if the belligerent have a vastly overpowering navy he may carry his point, just as England, when possessing the mastery of the seas, long refused to admit the doctrine of the neutral flag covering the goods.

the Declaration of Paris in 1856, has been to a large extent nullified in recent practice by extension of the lists of contraband, to say nothing of the violations of all law in submarine warfare. — EDITOR.]

11. Strategic Features of the Gulf of Mexico and the Caribbean [1]

IN the special field proposed for our study, there are two principal points of such convergence — or divergence: the mouth of the Mississippi River, and the Central American Isthmus. At the time when these lectures were first written the opinion of the world was hesitating between Panama and Nicaragua as the best site for a canal through the Isthmus. This question having now been settled definitively in favor of Panama, the particular point of convergence for trade routes passing through the Caribbean for the Pacific will continue at Colon, whither it for so long has been determined because there is the terminus of the Panama Railroad.

These two meeting points or cross-roads have long been, and still are, points of supreme interest to all mankind. At the one all the highways of the Mississippi valley, all the tributaries and subtributaries of the great river, meet, and thence they part. At the other all highways between the Atlantic and Pacific focus and intersect. The advancing population and development of the Mississippi valley, and the completion of the Panama Canal, will work together to cause this international interest to grow proportionately in the future. Among the great Powers of the world, no one is concerned so vitally

[1] "Naval Strategy," pp. 303–304, 356–367, 381–382.

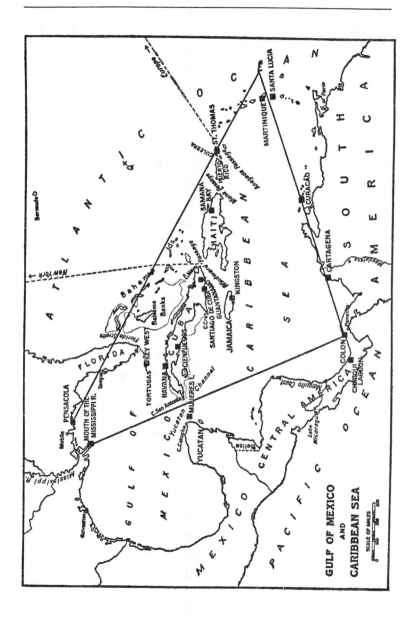

GULF OF MEXICO
AND
CARIBBEAN SEA

SCALE OF MILES

in this progress as is the United States; because of
her possession of one of these centers, the mouth of
the Mississippi with its huge back country, and because of her geographical nearness to the other.
This peculiar interest, which is natural and inevitable
in virtue of proximity, is emphasized by the national
policy known as the Monroe Doctrine; and still
more by the particular result of the Doctrine which
has involved the control, administration, and military protection of that belt of Isthmian territory
called the Panama Canal Zone.

[In the intervening pages, it is shown that the
triangle drawn on the map (p. 101) includes all
points of strategic importance, these being indicated
by black squares. Cuba is the key to the Gulf of
Mexico, and also controls three entrances to the
Caribbean — the Yucatan, Windward, and Mona
Passages. The entrances, the chief points of destination (Jamaica and the Isthmus), and the routes
thither, constitute the main objects of military control in the Caribbean. — EDITOR.]

. . . Taking all together, control over transit
depending upon situation only, other conditions
being equal, is greatest with Jamaica, next with
Cuba, least with the Lesser Antilles.

Accepting these conclusions as to control over
transit, we now revert to that question to which all
other inquiries are subsidiary, namely, Which of
the three bases of operations in the Caribbean —
one of the Lesser Antilles, Jamaica, or Cuba with
its sphere of influence — is most powerful for military control of the principal objective points in the

same sea? These principal objectives are Jamaica and the Isthmus; concerning the relative importance of which it may be remarked that, while the Isthmus intrinsically, and to the general interest of the world, is incomparably the more valuable, the situation of Jamaica gives such command over all the approaches to the Isthmus, as to make it in a military sense the predominant factor in the control of the Caribbean. Jamaica is a pre-eminent instance of central position, conferring the advantage of interior lines, for action in every direction within the field to which it belongs.

Military control depends chiefly upon two things, position and active military strength. As equal military strength has been assumed throughout, it is now necessary only to compare the positions held by other states in the field with that of the occupant of Cuba. This inquiry also is limited to the ability either to act offensively against these objective points, or, on the contrary, to defend them if already held by oneself or an ally; transit having been considered already.

Control by virtue of position, over a point external to your territory, depends upon nearness in point of time and upon the absence of obstacles capable of delaying or preventing your access to it.

Both Santiago (or Guantanamo) and Cienfuegos are nearer to the Isthmus than is any other one of the first-class strategic points that have been chosen on the *borders* of the Caribbean Sea, including Samana Bay and St. Thomas. They are little more than half the distance of the British Santa Lucia

and the French Martinique. The formidable island
and military stronghold of Jamaica, *within* the sea,
is nearer the Isthmus than Guantanamo is, by one
hundred and fifty miles, and than Cienfuegos by
yet more.

Taking into consideration situation only, Jamaica
is admirably placed for the control of the Caribbean.
It is equidistant from Colon, from the Yucatan
Passage, and from the Mona Passage. It shares
with Guantanamo and Santiago control of the Windward Passage, and of that along the south coast of
Cuba; while, with but a slight stretching out of its
arm, it reaches the routes from the Gulf of Mexico
to the Isthmus. Above all, as towards Cuba, it so
blocks the road to the Isthmus that any attempt
directed upon the Isthmus from Cuba must first
have to account with the military and naval forces
of Jamaica.

There are, however, certain deductions to be
made from the strength of Jamaica that do not
apply as forcibly to Cuba. Leaving to one side the
great and widely scattered colonial system of Great
Britain, which always throws that empire on the
defensive and invites division of the fleet, owing to
the large number of points open to attack, and confining our attention strictly to the field before us, it
will be observed that in a scheme of British operations Jamaica is essentially, as has been said before,
an advanced post; singularly well situated, it is true,
but still with long and difficult communications. Its
distance from Antigua, a possible intermediate base
of supplies, is over nine hundred miles; from Santa

Lucia, the chief British naval station in the Lesser Antilles, over one thousand miles, not less than three days' economical steaming. Great Britain, if at war with a state possessing Cuba, is shut out from the Windward Passage by Guantanamo, and from the Gulf of Mexico by Havana. The Mona Passage, also, though not necessarily closed, will be too dangerous to be relied upon. For these reasons, in order to maintain communications with Jamaica, an intermediate position and depot, like Santa Lucia, will be urgently needed. Supplies coming from Bermuda, Halifax, or England would probably have to be collected first there, or at Antigua, and thence make a more secure, but still exposed, voyage to Kingston. The north coasts of Cuba and Haiti must be looked upon as practically under the control of the Cuban fleet, in consequence of the command which it exercises over the Windward Passage, by virtue of position.

The possessor of Cuba, on the contrary, by his situation has open communication with the Gulf of Mexico, which amounts to saying that he has all the resources of the United States at his disposal, through the Mississippi Valley. Cruisers from Jamaica attempting to intercept that trade would be at a great disadvantage, especially as to coal, compared with their enemy resting upon Havana. Cruisers from Havana, reaching their cruising ground with little or no consumption, can therefore remain longer, and consequently are equivalent to a greater number of ships. On the other hand, cruisers from Santiago could move almost with im-

punity by the north side of Haiti as far as the Mona
Passage, and beyond that without any other risk
than that of meeting and fighting vessels of equal
size. If they stretch their efforts toward the Anegada
Passage, they would feel the same disadvantage,
relatively to cruisers from Santa Lucia, that Jamaica
cruisers in the Gulf would undergo as compared with
those from Havana; but by inclining their course
more to the northward, to or about the point Q (see
map, page 101), they would there be equidistant from
Guantanamo and Santa Lucia, and so on an equality
with the latter, while at the same time in a position
gravely to endanger supplies from any point in
North America. If it be replied that Bermuda can
take care of these cruisers at Q, the answer is plain:
on the supposition of equal forces, it can do so only
by diminishing the force at Santa Lucia. In short,
when compared with Jamaica, in repect of strategic
relations to Bermuda, Halifax, and Santa Lucia,
Cuba enjoys the immense advantage of a central position, and of interior lines of communication, with
consequent concentration of force and effort.

It is not easy to see how, in the face of these
difficulties, Great Britain, in the supposed case of
equal force in this theater of war, could avoid dividing her fleet sufficiently to put Jamaica at a disadvantage as to Cuba. In truth, Cuba here enjoys
not only the other advantages of situation already
pointed out, but also that of being central as regards the enemy's positions; and what is, perhaps,
even more important, she possesses secure interior

land lines of supply and coal between the points of her base, while covering the sea lines in her rear, in the Gulf of Mexico. For Guantanamo and Santiago have communication by rail with Havana, while the island itself covers the lines from Havana to the Gulf coast of the United States; whereas Jamaica depends wholly upon the sea, by lines of communication not nearly as well sheltered.

Contrasted with Cuba, Jamaica is seen to be, as has been more than once said, a strong advanced post, thrust well forward into the face of an enemy to which it is much inferior in size and resources, and therefore dependent for existence upon its power of holding out, despite uncertain and possibly suspended communication. Its case resembles that of Minorca, Malta, Gibraltar, the endurance of which, when cut off from the sea, has always been measurable. The question here before us, however, is not that of mere holding out on the defensive, which would be paralysis. If Cuba can reduce Jamaica to a passive defensive, Jamaica disappears as a factor in the control of the Caribbean and Isthmus — no obstacle then stands in the way of Cuba using her nearness to Panama. If Cuba can bring about a scarcity of coal at Kingston she achieves a strategic advantage; if a coal famine, the enemy's battle fleet must retire, probably to the Lesser Antilles.

The case of Jamaica, contrasted with Cuba, covers that of all strategic points on the borders of the Caribbean Sea, east, west, north, or south. Almost on the border itself, although within it, Jamaica has in nearness, in situation, in size, and in resources, a decisive advantage over any of the ports of Haiti or of the smaller islands. If Jamaica is inferior to Cuba, then is each of the other points on the circumference, and, it may be added, all of them together. . . .

[It is shown that, while Santa Lucia is essential to Jamaica, the two are too far apart to work together in concert. As for the Lesser Antilles, they may be said to control the approaches from Europe, while Cuba controls those from North America; but the Antilles are twice as far from the Isthmus as Cuba is, and much weaker in resources. — EDITOR.]

As to resources, those of all the West India islands for war will depend mainly upon the policy and preparation of the governments. Except Cuba, they are deficient in natural resources adequately developed. Outside of direct governmental action it can only be said that the much greater population of Cuba will draw more supplies and furnish more material for troops and garrisons. At present, as already noted, the resources of the United States are in effect also the resources of Cuba.

As between the three possible bases for attempted control of the Caribbean, no doubts can remain that Cuba is the most powerful, Jamaica next, and the Antilles least. Jamaica being where it is, Cuba cannot put forth her power against the Isthmus or against the lines of transit in the Caribbean, until she has materially reduced, if not neutralized, the offensive power of her smaller opponent. Upon the supposition of equal fleets, if the Cuban fleet move against the Isthmus, or into the Caribbean, it uncovers its communications; if it seeks to cover these, it divides its force. Jamaica exactly meets the case supposed in a previous chapter: " If, in moving upon the coveted objective you pass by a strategic point held by the enemy, capable of sheltering his ships — a point from which he may probably intercept your supplies of coal or ammunition, the circle of influence of that point will require your attention and reduce your force."

In that case it was laid down that, if you cannot observe the port without reducing your fleet below that of the enemy, you must not divide it; either the intermediate point must be taken, or, if you think you can accomplish your special aim with the supplies on board, you may cut loose from your base, giving up your communications. Undoubtedly, the same difficulty would be felt by the Jamaica fleet, if it moved away from home leaving the Cuban fleet in port in Santiago or Guantanamo; but, of the two, Jamaica has the inside track. It is not so with operations based upon the Lesser Antilles only, and directed against the Isthmus, or against any position in the western basin of the Caribbean, Cuba being hostile; the line of communication in that case is so long as to be a very serious comparative disadvantage.

Upon the whole, then, Jamaica, though less powerful than Cuba, seems to deserve the title of the " key to the Caribbean." Only when Cuba has mastered it can she predominantly control the positions of that sea. But if Jamaica in this sense be the

key, Cuba has the grip that can wrest it away.
Secure as to her own communications, in the rear,
towards the Gulf of Mexico, Cuba has it in her
power to impose upon her enemy a line so long and
insecure as to be finally untenable. First a scarcity
of coal, then a famine, lastly the retreat of the
Jamaica fleet to the most available coal station.
Such is the solution I believe possible to the military
problem of the Caribbean as dependent upon geographical conditions, — that is, upon positions; concerning which Napoleon has said that " War is a
business of positions." The instant the Cuban fleet
has gained a decided superiority over that of Jamaica, it can take a position covering at once the approaches to that island and the Windward Channel,
keeping all its own ships in hand while cutting off
the enemy's supplies and reinforcements. The con-
verse is not true of the Jamaica fleet, in case it gains
a momentary superiority, because the southern ports
of Cuba should be able to receive supplies by land,
from the Gulf of Mexico through Havana.

The general discussion of the strategic features
of the Gulf of Mexico and Caribbean ends here;
but the treatment of the subject will not be complete,
unless there be some further specific consideration
of the bearing which the conclusions reached have
upon the facilities of the United States for naval
action in the region studied.

[The political developments between 1887 and
1911 are here considered, including the growth of
the American Navy; the construction of the Panama
Canal; the acquisition by the United States of

strategic points along the line from Key West to Culebra Island, centering at Guantanamo and " most effectual for military and naval action in the Caribbean; " and, finally, our increased responsibilities arising from the growth of the German Navy and the consequent limitation of England's co-operation in support of the Monroe Doctrine. — EDITOR.]

. . . The Caribbean Sea and the Isthmus of Panama furnish the student of naval strategy with a very marked illustration of the necessity of such cohesion and mutual support between military positions assumed; as well as between those positions and the army in the field, — that is, the navy. It affords therefore a subject of the first importance for such a student to master, and that in fuller detail than is expedient for a series of lectures, the object of which should be to suggest lines of thought, rather than to attempt exhaustive treatment. For an American naval officer, the intimate relation of the Isthmus and its coming canal to the mutual support of the Atlantic and Pacific coasts renders the subject doubly interesting. This interest is yet farther increased by the consideration that the general international importance to commerce of such a point as the Canal can scarcely fail to make the conditions of its tenure and use a source of international difference and negotiation, which often are war under another form; that is, the solution depends upon military power, even though held in the background. There are questions other than commercial dependent upon the tenure of the Isthmus, of which I will not here speak explicitly. To appreciate them fully there must be constant reading and reflection upon the general topics of the day.

One thing is sure: in the Caribbean Sea is the strategic key to the two great oceans, the Atlantic and Pacific, our own chief maritime frontiers.

12. Principles of Naval Administration
Opposing Elements [1]

ADMINISTRATION being a term of very general application, it will be expected that that of the navy should present close analogies, and even points of identity, with other forms of administration; for instance, that in it, as elsewhere, efficiency of result will be better secured by individual responsibility than by collective responsibility. But, along with general resemblance, naval administration is very clearly and sharply differentiated by the presence of an element which is foreign to almost all other activities of life in countries like Great Britain and the United States. The military factor is to it not merely incidental, but fundamental; whatever other result may be achieved, naval administration has failed unless it provides to the nation an efficient fighting body, directed by well-trained men, animated by a strong military spirit. On the other hand, many of the operations connected with it differ from those common to civil life only in a certain particularity of method. This is true in principal measure of the financial management, of the medical establishment, and to a considerable though much smaller degree of the manufacturing processes connected with the production of naval material. The business routine of even the most military depart-

[1] "Naval Administration and Warfare" (1903), pp. 5–11.

ment of a naval administration is in itself more akin to civil than to military life: but it by no means follows that those departments would be better administered under men of civil habits of thought than by those of military training. The method exists for the result, and an efficient fighting body is not to be attained by weakening the appreciation of military necessities at the very fountain head of their supply in the administration. This necessary appreciation can be the result only of personal experience of good and bad through the formative period of life.

We find, therefore, at the very outset of our inquiry two fundamental yet opposing elements, neither of which can be eliminated. Nor can they be reconciled, in the sense of becoming sympathetic. In its proper manifestation the jealousy between the civil and military spirits is a healthy symptom. They can be made to work together harmoniously and efficiently; to complement, not to antagonize each other; provided means are taken to ensure to each its due relative precedence and weight in the determination of practical questions.

Historically, the institution and development of naval administration has been essentially a civil process, the object of which has been to provide and keep in readiness a national weapon for war. The end is war — fighting; the instrument is the navy; the means are the various activities which we group under the head of administration. Of these three, the end necessarily conditions the others. The proverb is familiar, " He who wills the end wills the means." Whatever is essential to the spirit and organization of the navy afloat, to its efficiency for war, must find itself adequately represented in the administration, in order that the exigencies of fighting may be kept well to the front in governmental and national consideration. Since armies and navies have existed as permanent national institutions, there has been a constant struggle on the part of the military element to keep the end — fighting, or readiness to fight — superior to mere administrative considerations. This is but natural, for all men tend to magnify their office. The military man having to do the fighting, considers that the chief necessity; the administrator equally naturally tends to think the smooth running of the machine the most admirable quality. Both are necessary; but the latter cannot obtain under the high pressure of war unless in peace the contingency of war has dictated its system. There is a quaint, well-worn story, which yet may be new to some readers, of an administrator who complained that his office was working admirably until war came and threw everything out of gear.

The opposition between civil and military, necessitating their due adjustment, may be said to be original, of the nature of things. It is born with naval administration. Corresponding roughly to these primary factors are the two principal activities in which administration is exerted — organization and execution. These also bear to each other the relation of means to end. Organization is not for itself, but is a means to an ultimate executive action; in the case of a navy, to war or to the prevention of war. It is, therefore, in its end — war — that organization must find the conditions dictating its character. Whatever the system adopted, it must aim above all at perfect efficiency in military action; and the nearer it approaches to this ideal the better it is. It would seem that this is too obvious for mention. It may be for mention; but not for reiteration. The long record of naval history on the side of administration shows a constant predominance of other considerations, and the abiding necessity for insisting, in season and out of season, that the one test of naval administration is not the satisfactory or economical working of the office, as such, but the readiness of the navy in all points for war. The one does not exclude the other; but there is between them the relation of greater and less.

Both organization and execution are properties alike of the active navy, the instrument for war, and of the naval administration, the means which has been constituted to create and maintain the instrument; but from their respective spheres, and in proportion to their relative nearness to the great final end of war, the one or the other characteristic is found predominant. The naval officer on board his ship, face to face with the difficulties of the profession, and in daily contact with the grim implements which remind him of the eventualities of his calling, naturally sees in organization mainly a means to an end. Some indeed fall short. The martinet is a man to whom the organization is more than a means; but he is the exception. Naval administration, on the other hand, in the common acceptation of the term, is mostly office work. It comes into contact with the navy proper chiefly through official correspondence, less by personal intercourse with the officers concerned; still less by immediate contact with the daily life of the profession, which it learns at second hand. It consequently tends to overvalue the orderly routine and observance of the system by which it receives information, transmits orders, checks expenditure, files returns, and, in general, keeps with the service the touch of paper; in short, the organization which has been created for facilitating its own labors. In due measure these are imperatively necessary; but it is undeniable that the practical tendency is to exaggerate their importance relatively to the executive end proposed. The writer was once visiting a French captain, who in the course of the interview took up wearily a mass of papers from a desk beside him. " I wonder," said he, " whether all this is as bad with you as with us. Look at our Navy Register; " and dividing the pages into two parts, severally about one-sixth and five-sixths of the whole, he continued, " This, the smaller, is the Navy; and that is the Administration." No wonder he had papers galore; administration needs papers, as a mill needs grist.

Even in the case of naval officers entering administrative offices, the influence of prolonged tenure is in the same direction. The habits of a previous lifetime doubtless act as a check, in proportion to the strength they have acquired in the individual. They serve as an invaluable leaven, not only to his own thought but to that of his associates. Nevertheless, the experience is general that permanence in an office essentially civil tends to deaden the intimate appreciation of naval exigencies; yet upon this alone can thrive that sympathy between the administrative and executive functions of the navy which is requisite to efficiency. The habit of the arm-chair easily prevails over that of the quarter-deck; it is more comfortable. For this reason, in the best-considered systems, a frequent exchange between the civil and military parts of their profession, between the administrative offices and the army or fleet, is thought expedient for officers who show aptitude for the former. It is better for them personally, better for the administration, and consequently better for the service at large. It prevails extensively in the United States Navy, where it is frequently the subject of ill-instructed outside criticism on the score of sea-officers being on " shore duty." Without asserting that the exact proportions of service are always accurately observed, it may be confidently affirmed that the interchange between the civil and military occupations tends to facilitate the smooth working of both, by promoting mutual understanding of conditions and difficulties.

The British System [1]

[From 1660 to 1832, British naval administration was divided between a civilian " Navy Board " and a military " Board of Admiralty." — EDITOR.]

[1] "Naval Administration and Warfare" (1903), pp. 26–31.

Divided control means divided responsibility; and that in turn means no responsibility, or at least one very hard to fix. The abuses that grew up, especially in the dockyards, the effect of which of course was transmitted to the navy that depended upon them, led to a loud outcry throughout the service towards the end of the eighteenth century; but horses are not swapped when crossing streams, and the exigencies of the great wars which ended in 1815 made it long impossible to attempt the revolutionary change needed. This was carried out in 1832 by the Government which came in with the Reform Bill of 1830. The spirit of the innovation was summarized in the expression, "Individual (undivided) Responsibility." The Navy Board disappeared altogether. The civil functions which in the process of centuries had accumulated in its hands, and had culminated by successive additions into a very numerous and loose aggregation of officials, were concentrated into five heads, having separate and independent responsibilities; in this resembling the chiefs of bureau in the United States Naval Administration. Each of the five was specifically under one of the members of the Admiralty Board, who thus represented that particular interest of the Navy in the Board regarded as a consultative body. Admiral Sir Vesey Hamilton writes: "This was a consolidation of functions and a subordination of the civil branches to the Admiralty as a whole . . . under the Board of Admiralty collectively and under the Lords individually." While the First Lord is a civilian, the majority of the other members of the

Admiralty are naval officers. Authority, therefore, is in civil hands, while military influence enters strongly.

While I highly appreciate the value of this latter factor, particularly as the sea lords do not consequently give up their profession, but remain actively connected with it, it appears to my observation of human nature that the system has some of the disadvantages of a council of war, tending to make responsibility elusive. I question, in short, the entire soundness of a scheme which by its nature, if not by specific provision, inclines to place executive action in the hands of a consultative body. It seems to sap individual responsibility; not perhaps in subordinates, but, what is much worse, in the head, in the commander-in-chief of the administration, upon whom depend the great determinative lines of provision and of policy. In conception, the Admiralty is primarily a Board, secondarily individual members. For individual responsibility at the head, too much depends upon the personality of the First Lord, too little upon his position. Since these lines were first written, five years ago, it may fairly be inferred, from the language of the English Press, that very decisive changes of policy have been adopted which are attributed popularly, and even professionally, to the dominating influence of one of the "Sea" Lords. During a brief period in 1827, as two centuries before, an arrangement more formally ideal obtained. The Duke of Clarence, afterwards William IV, being appointed Lord High Admiral, the Admiralty Board lapsed as a board and became his council. The modification here made in deference to royal blood might well serve as a model for naval administration; a head with advisers feels responsibility more than a head with associates. It should go without saying that in any case the head must be good.

In the United States Naval Administration the head is one man, with no division of responsibility. His own superior, the President, may control his action, as may Congress by law; but this, as far as it goes, is simply a transfer of responsibility in its entirety. It is not a division. The Secretary of the Navy has no associates, but he has subordinates. In them he has capable advisers, so far as he chooses to use them; but he can transfer to them no responsibility, except that of doing as he tells them. The responsibility of decision is his alone. The law constitutes them subordinate executive officers, just as it constitutes a lieutenant in the navy; but it does not constitute them advisers, and there is in their position nothing which compels the Secretary to hear their advice, still less to accept it. Each is independent of the others, and there is nothing in law to compel conference between them. The Secretary may assemble them, or any number of them, as a board for consultation, in his presence or otherwise; but there is nothing in the system which obliges him to do so. Unity of action between several naval technical experts, each of whom is represented in the planning and maintenance of every naval vessel, and some in every element of naval military efficiency, depends entirely upon the co-ordinating force of the Secretary, who is a civilian, possibly with only more or less outside knowledge of the subject. The system provides no strictly professional unifying force, such as the Board of Admiralty, which has a numerical preponderance of combatant sea-officers, each of whom has in individual control one or more of the technical administrative departments, and may be supposed therefore to be fully informed of its arguments in any technical matter under discussion. The constitution of the Admiralty Board also ensures that all technical details and their effect upon naval efficiency shall be scrutinized from the point of view of the men who shall do the work of war. The American plan fixes the very strictest individual responsibility in the Secretary, and in his principal subordinates, the chiefs of bureau. His duties are universal and supreme, theirs sharply defined and mutually independent. This result appears to me superior to the British, but it has the defects of its qualities; not too much independence in responsibility, but, so far as the system goes, too little co-ordination. As I said of the responsibility of the First Lord, unity of action depends too much on the personality of the Secretary.

The United States System [1]

The United States system of naval administration has progressed successively, and without breach of legislative continuity, from the simple rudimentary organ, the one man, in whom all functions as well

---

[1] "Naval Administration and Warfare" (1903), pp. 46-48.

as all responsibility were centered, through the phase of a complex organ with aggregate functions and responsibilities, defined, but still undifferentiated, into an organization elaborate in form, if not final in development. The process has been from first to last consistent in principle. The sole control and single responsibility of the Secretary — the representative of the President — have been preserved throughout, and all other responsibility is, and has been, not only subordinate to him but derivative from him, as a branch derives its being from the root. Moreover, consistency has also been maintained in restricting the administration thus evolved to the civil function which it essentially is. From the first departure, in the institution of the Board of Commissioners, to the present time, it has not had military authority properly so called. It has had necessary authority in matters pertaining to a military establishment, but it has had no direction of activities in themselves essentially military; that has remained with the Secretary, and is by him transferred only to officers properly military in function. Finally, the principle of particular responsibility has been strictly followed. Within the limits of the duty assigned, the corporate responsibility of the Board in its day was, and the individual responsibility of each bureau chief now is, as certain and defined as that of the Secretary.

The defect of the system is that no means is provided for co-ordinating the action of the bureaus,[1]

[1] These bureaus are seven in number: Yards and Docks, Navigation, Ordnance, Construction and Repairs, Steam Engineering, Sup-

except the single authority of the Secretary. This,
in his beginning days of inexperience, together with
his preoccupations with the numerous collateral en-
gagements attendant upon all positions of public
responsibility, will most usually be inadequate to the
task. To indicate a defect is not to prescribe a
remedy; and the purpose of this article is to show
things as they are, not to advocate particular
changes. One of the ablest administrative sea-
officers, both afloat and ashore, that I have known in
my professional career, stated before a Congressional committee that he had " always believed it
would be wise to have a board of five officers for the
purpose of harmonizing difficulties between bureaus,
settling upon a ship-building policy, and other matters that embarrass the head of the Department on
account of a lack of professional knowledge." I do
not undertake to pass an opinion upon this particular
suggestion, but confine myself to remarking that the
fault in the system certainly exists, and that any
remedy requires the careful observance of two
points : 1, that the adviser, one or a board, be wholly
clear of administrative activity; and, 2, that he or
they be advisers only, pure and simple, with no
power to affect the individual responsibility of
decision. This must be preserved under whatever
method, as the Secretary's privilege as well as his
obligation.

plies and Accounts, and Medicine and Surgery. The Chief of Naval
Operations, whose office was created in 1915, stands second to the Secretary and acts as his expert professional adviser, with the specific task
of co-ordinating the work of the navy, preparing plans, and directing
operations in war. He is, *ex officio*, a member of the General Board of
the Navy, created in 1900, which serves as an expert advisory body. —
EDITOR.

13. The Military Rule of Obedience [1]

IT may be asserted, as perhaps the most tenable general definition of the principle upon which the rule of obedience rests, that the spirit of obedience, as distinguished from its letter, consists in faithfully forwarding the general object to which the officer's particular command is contributing. This finds expression in the well-known directive maxim, " March to the sound of the guns." In doubtful cases, however, — and by doubtful I mean cases where action other than that prescribed in the orders seems expedient, — liberty of judgment is conditioned by the officer's acquaintance with the plans of his superior. If his knowledge is imperfect, or altogether lacking, the doing that which at the moment seems wise to himself may be to defeat a much more important object, or to dissolve the bonds of a combined movement to which his co-operation is essential. If, under such circumstances of ignorance, resting only upon his own sagacity or surmises, he errs either in his reading of his commander's general purpose, or in his decision as to his own action, and through such error disobeys, he cannot complain if he receive censure or punishment. He has violated a recognized rule without adequate reason. The rectitude of his intentions may clear him of moral blame, though not necessarily even so; for the duty of obedience is not merely military, but moral. It is not an arbitrary rule, but one essential and fundamental;

[1] "Retrospect and Prospect," pp. 258–259, 270–272.

the expression of a principle without which military organization would go to pieces, and military success be impossible. Consequently, even where the individual purpose may be demonstrably honest, not willful, blame adheres and punishment may follow, according to the measure of the delinquency, though that be due to nothing worse than personal incompetency. . . .

No man wrestled with the question more vigorously than Nelson; none found greater exasperation than he did in the too often successful opposition of the letter to the demands of his impetuous spirit for co-operation, addressed to men over whom he had not immediate control; none was more generous in his attitude to subordinates who overrode or overpassed his own orders, provided he saw in their acts the intelligent and honest will to forward his purposes. Obedience he certainly required; but he recognized that, given a capable and zealous man, better work would usually be had by permitting a certain elasticity of initiative, provided it was accompanied by accurate knowledge of his general wishes. These he was always most careful to impart; in nothing was he more precise or particular. If he allowed large liberty in the letter, he expected close observance of, nay, rather, participation in, the spirit of his ideas. He was not tolerant of incapacity, nor would he for a moment bear willful disregard of his plans. When considerations of high policy entertained by himself were crossed by Sidney Smith, his language became peremptory. "*As this is in strict opposition to my opinion, which is never to suffer any one individual Frenchman to quit Egypt, I strictly charge and command you* never to give any French ship or man leave to quit Egypt." The italics are his own; and he adds again, as though distrustful still: "You are to put my orders in force, not on any pretense to permit a single Frenchman to leave Egypt." The severity of the tone sufficiently proves his disposition to enforce the strictest rule, where necessary to control individuals; but a more liberal reliance upon principle, in preference to rule, was his habit. None, it may be added, illustrated more copiously than he, when a junior, the obedience of the spirit and the disobedience of the letter. His practice was in this consistent in all stages of his career. Unfortunately, the example may tempt smaller men to follow where their heads are not steady enough to keep their feet.

Of course, thinking and feeling thus, he gave frequent expression to his views, and these, coming from a man of his military genius, are often very illuminative. There is one such that is singularly applicable to our present purpose, of searching for the underlying principle which governs the duty and observance of obedience, and determines its absolute necessity to all military action. "I find few think as I do, but to obey orders is all perfection. What would my superiors direct, did they know what is passing under my nose? To serve my King and to destroy the French I consider as the great order of all, from which little ones spring, and if one of these little ones militate against it, I go back to obey the great order."

14. Preparedness for Naval War [1]

PREPARATION for war, rightly understood, falls under two heads, — preparation and preparedness. The one is a question mainly of material, and is constant in its action. The second involves an idea of completeness. When, at a particular moment, preparations are completed, one is prepared — not otherwise. There may have been made a great deal of very necessary preparation for war without being prepared. Every constituent of preparation may be behindhand, or some elements may be perfectly ready, while others are not. In neither case can a state be said to be prepared.

In the matter of preparation for war, one clear idea should be absorbed first by every one who, recognizing that war is still a possibility, desires to see his country ready. This idea is that, however defensive in origin or in political character a war may be, the assumption of a simple defensive in war is ruin. War, once declared, must be waged offensively, aggressively. The enemy must not be fended off, but smitten down. You may then spare him every exaction, relinquish every gain; but till down he must be struck incessantly and remorselessly.

Preparation, like most other things, is a question both of kind and of degree, of quality and of quantity. As regards degree, the general lines upon

[1] "The Interest of America in Sea Power" (1896), pp. 192–200.

which it is determined have been indicated broadly in the preceding part of this article. The measure of degree is the estimated force which the strongest probable enemy can bring against you, allowance being made for clear drawbacks upon his total force, imposed by his own embarrassments and responsibilities in other parts of the world. The calculation is partly military, partly political, the latter, however, being the dominant factor in the premises.

In kind, preparation is twofold, — defensive and offensive. The former exists chiefly for the sake of the latter, in order that offense, the determining factor in war, may put forth its full power, unhampered by concern for the protection of the national interests or for its own resources. In naval war, coast defense is the defensive factor, the navy the offensive. Coast defense, when adequate, assures the naval commander-in-chief that his base of operations — the dock-yards and coal depots — is secure. It also relieves him and his government, by the protection afforded to the chief commercial centers, from the necessity of considering them, and so leaves the offensive arm perfectly free.

Coast defense implies coast attack. To what attacks are coast liable? Two, principally, — blockade and bombardment. The latter, being the more difficult, includes the former, as the greater does the lesser. A fleet that can bombard can still more easily blockade. Against bombardment the necessary precaution is gun-fire, of such power and range that a fleet cannot lie within bombarding distance. This condition is obtained, where surroundings permit, by advancing the line of guns so far from the city involved that bombarding distance can be reached only by coming under their fire. But it has been demonstrated, and is accepted, that, owing to their rapidity of movement, — like a flock of birds on the wing, — a fleet of ships can, without disabling loss, pass by guns before which they could not lie. Hence arises the necessity of arresting or delaying their progress by blocking channels, which in modern practice is done by lines of torpedoes. The mere moral effect of the latter is a deterrent to a dash past, — by which, if successful, a fleet reaches the rear of the defenses, and appears immediately before the city, which then lies at its mercy.

Coast defense, then, implies gun-power and torpedo lines placed as described. Be it said in passing that only places of decisive importance, commercially or militarily, need such defenses. Modern fleets cannot afford to waste ammunition in bombarding unimportant towns, — at least when so far from their own base as they would be on our coast. It is not so much a question of money as of frittering their fighting strength. It would not pay.

Even coast defense, however, although essentially passive, should have an element of offensive force, local in character, distinct from the offensive navy, of which nevertheless it forms a part. To take the offensive against a floating force it must itself be afloat — naval. This offensive element of coast defense is to be found in the torpedo-boat, in its various developments. It must be kept distinct in idea from the sea-going fleet, although it is, **of** course, possible that the two may act in concert. The war very well may take such a turn that the sea-going navy will find its best preparation for initiating an offensive movement to be by concentrating in a principal seaport. Failing such a contingency, however, and in and for coast defense in its narrower sense, there should be a local flotilla of small torpedo-vessels, which by their activity should make life a burden to an outside enemy. A distinguished British admiral, now dead, has said that he believed half the captains of a blockading fleet would break down — " go crazy " were the words repeated to me — under the strain of modern conditions. The expression, of course, was intended simply to convey a sense of the immensity of suspense to be endured. In such a flotilla, owing to the smallness of its components, and to the simplicity of their organization and functions, is to be found the best sphere for naval volunteers; the duties could be learned with comparative ease, and the whole system is susceptible of rapid development. Be it remembered, however, that it is essentially defensive, only incidentally offensive, in character.

Such are the main elements of coast defense — guns, lines of torpedoes, torpedo-boats. Of these none can be extemporized, with the possible exception of the last, and that would be only a makeshift. To go into details would exceed the limits of an article, — require a brief treatise. Suffice it to say, without the first two, coast cities are open to bombardment; without the last, they can be blockaded freely, unless relieved by the sea-going navy. Bombardment and blockade are recognized modes of warfare, subject only to reasonable notification, — a concession rather to humanity and equity than to strict law.[1] Bombardment and blockade directed against great national centers, in the close and complicated network of national and commercial interests as they exist in modern times, strike not only the point affected, but every corner of the land.

The offensive in naval war, as has been said, is the function of the sea-going navy — of the battleships, and of the cruisers of various sizes and purposes, including sea-going torpedo-vessels capable of accompanying a fleet, without impeding its movements by their loss of speed or unseaworthiness. Seaworthiness, and reasonable speed under all weather conditions, are qualities necessary to every constituent of a fleet; but, over and above these, the backbone and real power of any navy are the vessels which, by due proportion of defensive and offensive powers, are capable of taking and giving hard knocks. All others are but subservient to these, and exist only for them.

What is that strength to be? Ships answering to this description are the *kind* which make naval strength; what is to be its *degree?* What their number? The answer — a broad formula — is that it must be great enough to take the sea, and to fight, with reasonable chances of success, the largest force likely to be brought against it, as shown by calcula-

---

[1] Bombardment of *undefended* ports, towns, etc., is forbidden by Convention IX of the Hague conference of 1907, with the broad concession, however, that depots, store houses, and all constructions that serve military purposes may be destroyed. — EDITOR.

tions which have been indicated previously. Being, as we claim, and as our past history justifies us in claiming, a nation indisposed to aggression, unwilling to extend our possessions or our interests by war, the measure of strength we set ourselves depends, necessarily, not upon our projects of aggrandizement, but upon the disposition of others to thwart what we consider our reasonable policy, which they may not so consider. When they resist, what force can they bring against us? That force must be naval; we have no exposed point upon which land operations, decisive in character, can be directed. This is the kind of the hostile force to be apprehended. What may its size be? There is the measure of our needed strength. The calculation may be intricate, the conclusion only approximate and probable, but it is the nearest reply we can reach. So many ships of such and such sizes, so many guns, so much ammunition — in short, so much naval material.

In the material provisions that have been summarized under the two chief heads of defense and offense — in coast defense under its three principal requirements, guns, lines of stationary torpedoes, and torpedo-boats, and in a navy able to keep the sea in the presence of a probable enemy — consist what may be called most accurately preparations for war. In so far as the United States is short in them, she is at the mercy of an enemy whose naval strength is greater than that of her own available navy. If her navy cannot keep the enemy off the coast, blockade at least is possible. If, in addition, there are no harbor torpedo-boats, blockade is easy. If, further, guns and torpedo lines are deficient, bombardment comes within the range of possibility, and may reach even the point of entire feasibility. There will be no time for preparation after war begins.

[The remainder of the essay considers the vital problem of supplying the navy with trained men, both in active service and in reserve. It is pointed out that, of the two systems, compulsory enlistments for short service and voluntary enlistments for long service, the second system, which is the one employed by the United States, produces fewer though better trained reserves; and it therefore necessitates a larger standing force. — EDITOR.]

PART II

SEA POWER IN HISTORY

PART II: SEA POWER IN HISTORY

15. A NATION EXHAUSTED BY ISOLATION [1]

France under Louis XIV

THE peace signed at Ryswick in 1697 was most disadvantageous to France; she lost all that had been gained since the Peace of Nimeguen, nineteen years before, with the single important exception of Strasburg. All that Louis XIV had gained by trick or force during the years of peace was given up. Immense restitutions were made to Germany and to Spain. In so far as the latter were made in the Netherlands, they were to the immediate advantage of the United Provinces, and indeed of all Europe as well as of Spain. To the two sea nations the terms of the treaty gave commercial benefits, which tended to the increase of their own sea power and to the consequent injury of that of France.

France had made a gigantic struggle; to stand alone as she did then, and as she has since done more than once, against all Europe is a great feat. Yet it may be said that as the United Provinces taught the lesson that a nation, however active and enterprising, cannot rest upon external resources alone, if intrinsically weak in numbers and territory, so

<hr>

[1] "The Influence of Sea Power upon History" (1660–1783), pp. 197–200. Admiral Mahan's major historical works treat consecutively the history of naval warfare from 1660 to 1815; and his essays and shorter studies cover subsequent wars. The selections in Part II are arranged in chronological order. — EDITOR.

France in its measure shows that a nation cannot
subsist indefinitely off itself, however powerful in
numbers and strong in internal resources.

It is said that a friend once found Colbert looking
dreamily from his windows, and on questioning him
as to the subject of his meditations, received this
reply: " In contemplating the fertile fields before
my eyes, I recall those which I have seen elsewhere;
what a rich country is France!" This conviction
supported him amid the many discouragements of
his official life, when struggling to meet the financial
difficulties arising from the extravagance and wars
of the king; and it has been justified by the whole
course of the nation's history since his days. France
is rich in natural resources as well as in the industry
and thrift of her people. But neither individual
nations nor men can thrive when severed from
natural intercourse with their kind; whatever the
native vigor of constitution, it requires healthful
surroundings, and freedom to draw to itself from
near and from far all that is conducive to its growth
and strength and general welfare. Not only must
the internal organism work satisfactorily, the processes of decay and renewal, of movement and circulation, go on easily, but, from sources external to
themselves, both mind and body must receive healthful and varied nourishment. With all her natural
gifts France wasted away because of the want of
that lively intercourse between the different parts of
her own body and constant exchange with other
people, which is known as commerce, internal or external. To say that war was the cause of these de-

fects is to state at least a partial truth; but it does not exhaust the matter. War, with its many acknowledged sufferings, is above all harmful when it cuts a nation off from others and throws it back upon itself. There may indeed be periods when such rude shocks have a bracing effect, but they are exceptional, and of short duration, and they do not invalidate the general statement. Such isolation was the lot of France during the later wars of Louis XIV, and it well-nigh destroyed her; whereas to save her from the possibility of such stagnation was the great aim of Colbert's life.

War alone could not entail it, if only war could be postponed until the processes of circulation within and without the kingdom were established and in vigorous operation. They did not exist when he took office; they had to be both created and firmly rooted in order to withstand the blast of war. Time was not given to accomplish this great work, nor did Louis XIV support the schemes of his minister by turning the budding energies of his docile and devoted subjects into paths favorable to it. So when the great strain came upon the powers of the nation, instead of drawing strength from every quarter and through many channels, and laying the whole outside world under contribution by the energy of its merchants and seamen, as England has done in like straits, it was thrown back upon itself, cut off from the world by the navies of England and Holland, and the girdle of enemies which surrounded it upon the continent. The only escape from this process of gradual starvation was by an effectual

control of the sea; the creation of a strong sea power
which should ensure free play for the wealth of the
land and the industry of the people. For this, too,
France had great natural advantages in her three
seaboards, on the Channel, the Atlantic, and the
Mediterranean; and politically she had had the fair
opportunity of joining to her own maritime power
that of the Dutch in friendly alliance, hostile or at
least wary toward England. In the pride of his
strength, conscious of absolute control in his kingdom, Louis cast away this strong reinforcement to
his power, and proceeded to rouse Europe against
him by repeated aggressions. In the period which
we have just considered, France justified his confidence by a magnificent, and upon the whole successful, maintenance of his attitude against all Europe;
she did not advance, but neither did she greatly
recede. But this display of power was exhausting;
it ate away the life of the nation, because it drew
wholly upon itself and not upon the outside world,
with which it could have been kept in contact by the
sea. In the war that next followed, the same energy
is seen, but not the same vitality; and France was
everywhere beaten back and brought to the verge
of ruin. The lesson of both is the same; nations,
like men, however strong, decay when cut off from
the external activities and resources which at once
draw out and support their internal powers. A
nation, as we have already shown, cannot live indefinitely off itself, and the easiest way by which it
can communicate with other peoples and renew its
own strength is the sea.

16. The Growth of British Sea Power [1]

England after the Peace of Utrecht, 1715

WHILE England's policy thus steadily aimed at widening and strengthening the bases of her sway upon the ocean, the other governments of Europe seemed blind to the dangers to be feared from her sea growth. The miseries resulting from the overweening power of Spain in days long gone by seemed to be forgotten; forgotten also the more recent lesson of the bloody and costly wars provoked by the ambition and exaggerated power of Louis XIV. Under the eyes of the statesmen of Europe there was steadily and visibly being built up a third overwhelming power, destined to be used as selfishly, as aggressively, though not as cruelly, and much more successfully than any that had preceded it. This was the power of the sea, whose workings, because more silent than the clash of arms, are less often noted, though lying clearly enough on the surface. It can scarcely be denied that England's uncontrolled dominion of the seas, during almost the whole period chosen for our subject, was by long odds the chief among the military factors that determined the final issue. [2] So far, however, was

[1] "The Influence of Sea Power upon History," pp. 63–67.
[2] An interesting proof of the weight attributed to the naval power of Great Britain by a great military authority will be found in the opening chapter of Jomini's "History of the Wars of the French Revolution." He lays down, as a fundamental principle of European policy, that an

this influence from being foreseen after Utrecht, that France for twelve years, moved by personal exigencies of her rulers, sided with England against Spain; and when Fleuri came into power in 1726, though this policy was reversed, the navy of France received no attention, and the only blow at England was the establishment of a Bourbon prince, a natural enemy to her, upon the throne of the two Sicilies in 1736. When war broke out with Spain in 1739, the navy of England was in numbers more than equal to the combined navies of Spain and France; and during the quarter of a century of nearly uninterrupted war that followed, this numerical disproportion increased. In these wars England, at first instinctively, afterward with conscious purpose under a government that recognized her opportunity and the possibilities of her great sea power, rapidly built up that mighty colonial empire whose foundations were already securely laid in the characteristics of her colonists and the strength of her fleets. In strictly European affairs her wealth, the outcome of her sea power, made her play a conspicuous part during the same period. The system of subsidies, which began half a century before in the wars of Marlborough and received its most extensive development half a century later in the Napoleonic wars, maintained the efforts of her allies, which would have been crippled, if not paralyzed, without them. Who can deny that the

unlimited expansion of naval force should not be permitted to any nation which cannot be approached by land, — a description which can apply only to Great Britain.

government which with one hand strengthened its fainting allies on the continent with the life-blood of money, and with the other drove its own enemies off the sea and out of their chief possessions, Canada, Martinique, Guadeloupe, Havana, Manila, gave to its country the foremost rôle in European politics; and who can fail to see that the power which dwelt in that government, with a land narrow in extent and poor in resources, sprang directly from the sea? The policy in which the English government carried on the war is shown by a speech of Pitt, the master-spirit during its course, though he lost office before bringing it to an end. Condemning the Peace of 1763, made by his political opponent, he said: " France is chiefly, if not exclusively, formidable to us as a maritime and commercial power. What we gain in this respect is valuable to us, above all, through the injury to her which results from it. You have left to France the possibility of reviving her navy." Yet England's gains were enormous; her rule in India was assured, and all North America east of the Mississippi in her hands. By this time the onward path of her government was clearly marked out, had assumed the force of a tradition, and was consistently followed. The war of the American Revolution was, it is true, a great mistake, looked at from the point of view of sea power; but the government was led into it insensibly by a series of natural blunders. Putting aside political and constitutional considerations, and looking at the question as purely military or naval, the case was this: The American colonies were large

and growing communities at a great distance from
England. So long as they remained attached to the
mother-country, as they then were enthusiastically,
they formed a solid base for her sea power in that
part of the world; but their extent and population
were too great, when coupled with the distance from
England, to afford any hope of holding them by
force, *if* any powerful nations were willing to help
them. This "if," however, involved a notorious
probability; the humiliation of France and Spain
was so bitter and so recent that they were sure to
seek revenge, and it was well known that France in
particular had been carefully and rapidly building
up her navy. Had the colonies been thirteen islands,
the sea power of England would quickly have settled the question; but instead of such a physical
barrier they were separated only by local jealousies
which a common danger sufficiently overcame. To
enter deliberately on such a contest, to try to hold
by force so extensive a territory, with a large hostile
population, so far from home, was to renew the
Seven Years' War with France and Spain, and with
the Americans, against, instead of for, England.
The Seven Years' War had been so heavy a burden
that a wise government would have known that the
added weight could not be borne, and have seen it
was necessary to conciliate the colonists. The government of the day was not wise, and a large element of England's sea power was sacrificed; but
by mistake, not willfully; through arrogance, not
through weakness.

This steady keeping to a general line of policy

was doubtless made specially easy for successive English governments by the clear indications of the country's conditions. Singleness of purpose was to some extent imposed. The firm maintenance of her sea power, the haughty determination to make it felt, the wise state of preparation in which its military element was kept, were yet more due to that feature of her political institutions which practically gave the government, during the period in question, into the hands of a class, — a landed aristocracy. Such a class, whatever its defects otherwise, readily takes up and carries on a sound political tradition, is naturally proud of its country's glory, and comparatively insensible to the sufferings of the community by which that glory is maintained. It readily lays on the pecuniary burden necessary for preparation and for endurance of war. Being as a body rich, it feels those burdens less. Not being commercial, the sources of its own wealth are not so immediately endangered, and it does not share that political timidity which characterizes those whose property is exposed and business threatened, — the proverbial timidity of capital. Yet in England this class was not insensible to anything that touched her trade for good or ill. Both houses of Parliament vied in careful watchfulness over its extension and protection, and to the frequency of their inquiries a naval historian attributes the increased efficiency of the executive power in its management of the navy. Such a class also naturally imbibes and keeps up a spirit of military honor, which is of the first importance in ages when military institutions have

not yet provided the sufficient substitute in what is
called *esprit-de-corps*. But although full of class
feeling and class prejudice, which made themselves
felt in the navy as well as elsewhere, their practical
sense left open the way of promotion to its highest
honors to the more humbly born; and every age
saw admirals who had sprung from the lowest of
the people. In this the temper of the English upper
class differed markedly from that of the French.
As late as 1789, at the outbreak of the Revolution,
the French Navy List still bore the name of an
official whose duty was to verify the proofs of noble
birth on the part of those intending to enter the
naval school.

Since 1815, and especially in our own day, the
government of England has passed very much more
into the hands of the people at large. Whether her
sea power will suffer therefrom remains to be seen.
Its broad basis still remains in a great trade, large
mechanical industries, and an extensive colonial
system. Whether a democratic government will
have the foresight, the keen sensitiveness to national
position and credit, the willingness to ensure its
prosperity by adequate outpouring of money in
times of peace, all of which are necessary for military preparation, is yet an open question. Popular
governments are not generally favorable to military
expenditure, however necessary, and there are signs
that England tends to drop behind.

17. Results of the Seven Years' War [1]

NEVERTHELESS, the gains of England were very great, not only in territorial increase, nor yet in maritime preponderance, but in the prestige and position achieved in the eyes of the nations, now fully opened to her great resources and mighty power. To these results, won by the sea, the issue of the continental war offered a singular and suggestive contrast. France had already withdrawn, along with England, from all share in that strife, and peace between the other parties to it was signed five days after the Peace of Paris. The terms of the peace was simply the *status quo ante bellum.* By the estimate of the King of Prussia, one hundred and eighty thousand of his soldiers had fallen or died in this war, out of a kingdom of five million souls, while the losses of Russia, Austria, and France aggregated four hundred and sixty thousand men. The result was simply that things remained as they were.[2] To attribute this only to a difference between the possibilities of land and sea war is of course absurd. The genius of Frederick, backed by the money of England, had proved an equal

[1] "The Influence of Sea Power upon History," pp. 323–329. By the Treaty of Paris, 1763, England secured Canada, all French possessions east of the Mississippi, and Florida; she also retained Gibraltar and Minorca, and gained ascendancy in India. — EDITOR.

[2] See Annual Register, 1762, p. 63.

match for the mismanaged and not always hearty
efforts of a coalition numerically overwhelming.

What does seem a fair conclusion is, that States
having a good seaboard, or even ready access to the
ocean by one or two outlets, will find it to their advantage to seek prosperity and extension by the way
of the sea and of commerce, rather than in attempts
to unsettle and modify existing political arrangements
in countries where a more or less long possession
of power has conferred acknowledged rights, and
created national allegiance or political ties. Since
the Treaty of Paris in 1763, the waste places of the
world have been rapidly filled; witness our own
continent, Australia, and even South America. A
nominal and more or less clearly defined political
possession now generally exists in the most forsaken
regions, though to this statement there are some
marked exceptions; but in many places this political
possession is little more than nominal, and in others
of a character so feeble that it cannot rely upon
itself alone for support or protection. The familiar
and notorious example of the Turkish Empire, kept
erect only by the forces pressing upon it from opposing sides, by the mutual jealousies of powers that
have no sympathy with it, is an instance of such
weak political tenure; and though the question is
wholly European, all know enough of it to be aware
that the interest and control of the sea powers is
among the chief, if not the first, of the elements that
now fix the situation; and that they, if intelligently
used, will direct the future inevitable changes.
Upon the western continents the political condition

of the Central American and tropical South American States is so unstable as to cause constant anxiety about the maintenance of internal order, and seriously to interfere with commerce and with the peaceful development of their resources. So long as — to use a familiar expression — they hurt no one but themselves, this may go on; but for a long time the citizens of more stable governments have been seeking to exploit their resources, and have borne the losses arising from their distracted condition. North America and Australia still offer large openings to immigration and enterprise; but they are filling up rapidly, and as the opportunities there diminish, the demand must arise for a more settled government in those disordered States, for security to life and for reasonable stability of institutions enabling merchants and others to count upon the future. There is certainly no present hope that such a demand can be fulfilled from the existing native materials; if the same be true when the demand arises, no theoretical positions, like the Monroe Doctrine, will prevent interested nations from attempting to remedy the evil by some measure, which, whatever it may be called, will be a political interference. Such interferences must produce collisions, which may be at times settled by arbitration, but can scarcely fail at other times to cause war. Even for a peaceful solution, that nation will have the strongest arguments which has the strongest organized force.

It need scarcely be said that the successful piercing of the Central American Isthmus at any point may

precipitate the moment that is sure to come sooner
or later. The profound modification of commercial
routes expected from this enterprise, the political
importance to the United States of such a channel
of communication between her Atlantic and Pacific
seaboards, are not, however, the whole nor even
the principal part of the question. As far as can be
seen, the time will come when stable governments
for the American tropical States must be assured by
the now existing powerful and stable States of
America or Europe. The geographical position of
those States, the climatic conditions, make it plain
at once that sea power will there, even more than in
the case of Turkey, determine what foreign State
shall predominate, — if not by actual possession, by
its influence over the native governments. The
geographical position of the United States and her
intrinsic power give her an undeniable advantage;
but that advantage will not avail if there is a great
inferiority of organized brute-force, which still remains the last argument of republics as of kings.

Herein lies to us the great and still living interest
of the Seven Years' War. In it we have seen and
followed England, with an army small as compared
with other States, as is still her case to-day, first
successfully defending her own shores, then carrying
her arms in every direction, spreading her rule and
influence over remote regions, and not only binding
them to her obedience, but making them tributary
to her wealth, her strength, and her reputation. As
she loosens the grasp and neutralizes the influence of
France and Spain in regions beyond the sea, there

is perhaps seen the prophecy of some other great
nation in days yet to come, that will incline the
balance of power in some future sea war, whose
scope will be recognized afterward, if not by contemporaries, to have been the political future and
the economical development of regions before lost
to civilization; but that nation will not be the United
States if the moment find her indifferent, as now, to
the empire of the seas.

The direction then given to England's efforts, by
the instinct of the nation and the fiery genius of
Pitt, continued after the war, and has profoundly
influenced her subsequent policy. Mistress now of
North America, lording it in India, through the
company whose territorial conquests had been rati-
fied by native princes, over twenty millions of inhabitants, — a population larger than that of Great
Britain and having a revenue respectable alongside
of that of the home government, — England, with
yet other rich possessions scattered far and wide over
the globe, had ever before her eyes, as a salutary
lesson, the severe chastisement which the weakness of
Spain had allowed her to inflict upon that huge disjointed empire. The words of the English naval historian of that war, speaking about Spain, apply with
slight modifications to England in our own day.

" Spain is precisely that power against which
England can always contend with the fairest prospect of advantage and honor. That extensive
monarchy is exhausted at heart, her resources lie at
a great distance, and whatever power commands the
sea, may command the wealth and commerce of

Spain. The dominions from which she draws her resources, lying at an immense distance from the capital and from one another, make it more necessary for her than for any other State to temporize, until she can inspire with activity all parts of her enormous but disjointed empire." [1]

It would be untrue to say that England is exhausted at heart; but her dependence upon the outside world is such as to give a certain suggestiveness to the phrase.

This analogy of positions was not overlooked by England. From that time forward up to our own day, the possessions won for her by her sea power have combined with that sea power itself to control her policy. The road to India — in the days of Clive a distant and perilous voyage on which she had not a stopping-place of her own — was reinforced as opportunity offered by the acquisition of St. Helena, of the Cape of Good Hope, of the Mauritius. When steam made the Red Sea and Mediterranean route practicable, she acquired Aden, and yet later has established herself at Socotra. Malta had already fallen into her hands during the wars of the French Revolution; and her commanding position, as the corner-stone upon which the coalitions against Napoleon rested, enabled her to claim it at the Peace of 1815. Being but a short thousand miles from Gibraltar, the circles of military command exercised by these two places intersect. The present day has seen the stretch from Malta to the Isthmus of Suez, formerly without a

1 Campbell, "Lives of the Admirals."

station, guarded by the cession to her of Cyprus.
Egypt, despite the jealousy of France, has passed
under English control. The importance of that
position to India, understood by Napoleon and
Nelson, led the latter at once to send an officer overland to Bombay with the news of the battle of the
Nile and the downfall of Bonaparte's hopes. Even
now, the jealousy with which England views the advance of Russia in Central Asia is the result of those
days in which her sea power and resources triumphed over the weakness of D'Aché and the genius
of Suffren, and wrenched the peninsula of India
from the ambition of the French.

" For the first time since the Middle Ages," says
M. Martin, speaking of the Seven Years' War,
" England had conquered France single-handed
almost without allies, France having powerful
auxiliaries. She had conquered solely by the superiority of her government."

Yes! but by the superiority of her government
using the tremendous weapon of her sea power.
This made her rich and in turn protected the trade
by which she had her wealth. With her money she
upheld her few auxiliaries, mainly Prussia and
Hanover, in their desperate strife. Her power was
everywhere that her ships could reach, and there
was none to dispute the sea to her. Where she
would she went, and with her went her guns and her
troops. By this mobility her forces were multiplied,
those of her enemies distracted. Ruler of the
seas, she everywhere obstructed its highways. The
enemies' fleets could not join; no great fleet could

get out, or if it did, it was only to meet at once, with uninured officers and crews, those who were veterans in gales and warfare. Save in the case of Minorca, she carefully held her own sea-bases and eagerly seized those of the enemy. What a lion in the path was Gibraltar to the French squadrons of Toulon and Brest! What hope for French succor to Canada, when the English fleet had Louisburg under its lee?

The one nation that gained in this war was that which used the sea in peace to earn its wealth, and ruled it in war by the extent of its navy, by the number of its subjects who lived on the sea or by the sea, and by its numerous bases of operations scattered over the globe. Yet it must be observed that these bases themselves would have lost their value if their communications remained obstructed. Therefore the French lost Louisburg, Martinique, Pondicherry; so England herself lost Minorca. The service between the bases and the mobile force, between the ports and the fleets, is mutual.[1] In this respect the navy is essentially a light corps; it keeps open the communications between its own ports, it obstructs those of the enemy; but it sweeps the sea for the service of the land, it controls the desert that man may live and thrive on the habitable globe.

---

[1] These remarks, always true, are doubly so now since the introduction of steam. The renewal of coal is a want more frequent, more urgent, more peremptory, than any known to the sailing-ship. It is vain to look for energetic naval operations distant from coal stations. It is equally vain to acquire distant coaling stations without maintaining a powerful navy; they will but fall into the hands of the enemy. But the vainest of all delusions is the expectation of bringing down an enemy by commerce-destroying alone, with no coaling stations outside the national boundaries.

18. Eighteenth Century Formalism in Naval Tactics [1]

TOURVILLE,[2] though a brilliant seaman, thus not only typified an era of transition, with which he was contemporary, but fore-shadowed the period of merely formal naval warfare, precise, methodical, and unenterprising, emasculated of military virility, although not of mere animal courage. He left to his successors the legacy of a great name, but also unfortunately that of a defective professional tradition. The splendid days of the French Navy under Louis XIV passed away with him, — he died in 1701 ; but during the long period of naval lethargy on the part of the state, which followed, the French naval officers, as a class, never wholly lost sight of professional ideals. They proved themselves, on the rare occasions that offered, before 1715 and during the wars of Hawke and Rodney, not only gallant seamen after the pattern of Tourville, but also exceedingly capable tacticians, upon a system good as far as it went, but defective on Tourville's express lines, in aiming rather at exact dispositions and defensive security than at the thorough-going initiative and persistence which confounds and destroys the enemy. "War," to use Napoleon's

[1] "Types of Naval Officers," pp. 14–17.
[2] A celebrated French admiral, in command at the battles of Beachy Head (1690) and La Hogue (1692). — EDITOR.

phrase, "was to be waged without running risks." The sword was drawn, but the scabbard was kept ever open for its retreat.

The English, in the period of reaction which succeeded the Dutch wars, produced their own caricature of systematized tactics. Even under its influence, up to 1715, it is only just to say they did not construe naval skill to mean anxious care to keep one's own ships intact. Rooke, off Malaga, in 1704, illustrated professional fearlessness of consequences as conspicuously as he had shown personal daring in the boat attack at La Hogue; but his plans of battle exemplified the particularly British form of inefficient naval action. There was no great difference in aggregate force between the French fleet and that of the combined Anglo-Dutch under his orders. The former, drawing up in the accustomed line of battle, ship following ship in a single column, awaited attack. Rooke, having the advantage of the wind, and therefore the power of engaging at will, formed his command in a similar and parallel line a few miles off, and thus all stood down together, the ships maintaining their line parallel to that of the enemy, and coming into action at practically the same moment, van to van, center to center, rear to rear. This ignored wholly the essential maxim of all intelligent warfare, which is so to engage as markedly to outnumber the enemy at a point of main collision. If he be broken there, before the remainder of his force come up, the chances all are that a decisive superiority will be established by this alone, not to mention the moral effect of partial defeat and disorder. Instead of this, the impact at Malaga was so distributed as to produce a substantial equality from one end to the other of the opposing fronts. The French, indeed, by strengthening their center relatively to the van and rear, to some extent modified this condition in the particular instance; but the fact does not seem to have induced any alteration in Rooke's dispositions. Barring mere accident, nothing conclusive can issue from such arrangements. The result accordingly was a drawn battle, although Rooke says that the fight, which was maintained on both sides " with great fury for three hours, . . . was the sharpest day's service that I ever saw; " and he had seen much, — Beachy Head, La Hogue, Vigo Bay, not to mention his own great achievement in the capture of Gibraltar.

This method of attack remained the ideal — if such a word is not a misnomer in such a case — of the British Navy, not merely as a matter of irreflective professional acceptance, but laid down in the official " Fighting Instructions." [1] It cannot be said that these err on the side of lucidity; but their meaning to contemporaries in this particular respect is ascertained, not only by fair inference from their contents, but by the practical commentary of numerous actions under commonplace commanders-in-chief. It further received authoritative formulation in the specific finding of the Court-Martial

---

[1] The most famous of these were issued in 1665 by the Duke of York, afterward James II, who was then Lord High Admiral. They were revised but not greatly altered in 1740 and again in 1756. — EDITOR.

upon Admiral Byng, which was signed by thirteen experienced officers. " Admiral Byng should have caused his ships to tack together, and should immediately have borne down upon the enemy; his van steering for the enemy's van, his rear for its rear, each ship making for the one opposite to her in the enemy's line, under such sail as would have enabled the worst sailer to preserve her station in the line of battle." [1] Each phrase of this opinion is a reflection of an article in the Instructions. The line of battle was the naval fetish of the day; and, be it remarked, it was the more dangerous because in itself an admirable and necessary instrument, constructed on principles essentially accurate. A standard wholly false may have its error demonstrated with comparative ease; but no servitude is more hopeless than that of unintelligent submission to an idea formally correct, yet incomplete. It has all the vicious misleading of a half-truth unqualified by appreciation of modifying conditions; and so seamen who disdained theories, and hugged the belief in themselves as " practical," became *doctrinaires* in the worst sense.

[1] Byng's offense, for which he was sentenced to be shot, occurred in an action with a French squadron off Minorca in 1756. — EDITOR.

19. THE NEW TACTICS [1]

Rodney and De Guichen, April 17, 1780

DESPITE his brilliant personal courage and professional skill, which in the matter of tactics was far in advance of his contemporaries in England, Rodney, as a commander-in-chief, belongs rather to the wary, cautious school of the French tacticians than to the impetuous, unbounded eagerness of Nelson. As in Tourville we have seen the desperate fighting of the seventeenth century, unwilling to leave its enemy, merging into the formal, artificial — we may almost say trifling — parade tactics of the eighteenth, so in Rodney we shall see the transition from those ceremonious duels to an action which, while skillful in conception, aimed at serious results. For it would be unjust to Rodney to press the comparison to the French admirals of his day. With a skill that De Guichen recognized as soon as they crossed swords, Rodney meant mischief, not idle flourishes. Whatever incidental favors fortune might bestow by the way, the objective from which his eye never wandered was the French fleet, — the organized military force of the enemy on the sea. And on the day when Fortune forsook the opponent who had neglected her offers, when the conqueror of Cornwallis failed to strike while he had Rodney at

[1] "The Influence of Sea Power upon History," pp. 377-380.

a disadvantage, the latter won a victory [1] which
redeemed England from the depths of anxiety, and
restored to her by one blow all those islands which
the cautious tactics of the allies had for a moment
gained, save only Tobago.

De Guichen and Rodney met for the first time on
the 17th of April, 1780, three weeks after the arrival of the latter. The French fleet was beating
to windward in the channel between Martinique
and Dominica, when the enemy was made in the
southeast. A day was spent in maneuvering for the
weather-gage, which Rodney got. The two fleets
being now well to leeward of the islands (see Plate),
both on the starboard tack heading to the northward and the French on the lee bow of the English,
Rodney, who was carrying a press of sail, signalled
to his fleet that he meant to attack the enemy's rear
and center with his whole force; and when he had
reached the position he thought suitable, ordered
them to keep away eight points (90°) together
(A, A, A). De Guichen, seeing the danger of the
rear, wore his fleet all together and stood down to
succor it. Rodney, finding himself foiled, hauled
up again on the same tack as the enemy, both fleets
now heading to the southward and eastward.[2]

---

[1] De Grasse, whose victory over Graves off the Chesapeake forced
the surrender of Cornwallis, was afterward defeated by Rodney in the
famous battle of the Saints' Passage, April 12, 1782. Three days earlier,
De Grasse had neglected an opportunity to attack in superior force.

While the battle of the Saints' Passage is more celebrated, the action
here described better illustrates Rodney's merits as a tactician. In his
later years Rodney wrote that he "thought little of his victory of the
12th of April," and looked upon this earlier action as "one by which,
but for the disobedience of his captains, he might have gained im-
mortal renown." — Mahan, "Types of Naval Officers," p. 203. — EDITOR.

[2] The black ships, in position A, represent the English ships bearing

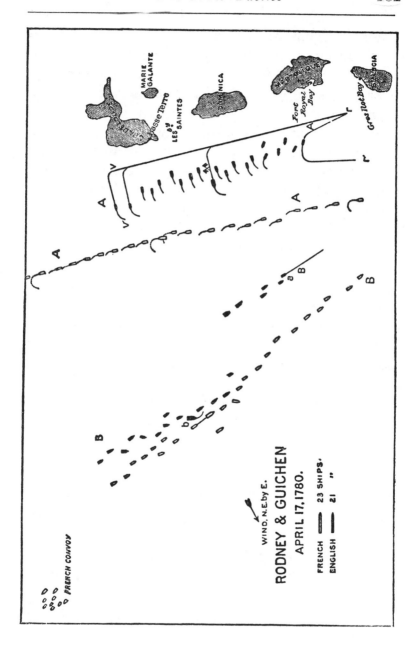

MARIE
GALANTE

BASSE TERRE

D'
LES SAINTES

DOMINICA

MARTINIQUE

Fort
Royal
Bay

St LUCIA

Gros Ilot Bay

A

B

B

B

FRENCH CONVOY

WIND. N.E by E.

RODNEY & GUICHEN
APRIL 17, 1780.

FRENCH ⚍ 23 SHIPS.
ENGLISH ── 21 "

Later, he again made signal for battle, followed an hour after, just at noon, by the order (quoting his own despatch), " for every ship to bear down and steer for her opposite in the enemy's line." This, which sounds like the old story of ship to ship, Rodney explains to have meant her opposite at the moment, not her opposite in numerical order. His own words are: " In a slanting position, that my leading ships might attack the van ships of the enemy's center division, and the whole British fleet be opposed to only two thirds of the enemy " (B, B). The difficulty and misunderstanding which followed seem to have sprung mainly from the defective character of the signal book. Instead of doing as the admiral wished, the leading ships (a) carried sail so as to reach their supposed station abreast their numerical opposite in the order. Rodney stated afterward that when he bore down the second time, the French fleet was in a very extended line of battle; and that, had his orders been obeyed, the center and rear must have been disabled before the van could have joined.

There seems every reason to believe that Rodney's intentions throughout were to double on the French, as asserted. The failure sprang from the signal book and tactical inefficiency of the fleet; for which he, having lately joined, was not answerable. But the ugliness of his fence was so apparent to De Guichen, that he exclaimed, when the English

down upon the French center and rear. The line v r is the line of battle from van to rear before bearing down. The positions v', r' are those of the van and rear ships after hauling up on the port tack, when the French wore. — Editor.

fleet kept away the first time, that six or seven of his ships were gone; and sent word to Rodney that if his signals had been obeyed he would have had him for his prisoner.[1] A more convincing proof that he recognized the dangerousness of his enemy is to be found in the fact that he took care not to have the lee-gage in their subsequent encounters. Rodney's careful plans being upset, he showed that with them he carried all the stubborn courage of the most downright fighter; taking his own ship close to the enemy and ceasing only when the latter hauled off, her foremast and mainyard gone, and her hull so damaged that she could hardly be kept afloat.

[1] In a severe reprimand addressed to Captain Carkett, commanding the leading ship of the English line, by Rodney, he says: "Your leading in the manner you did, induced others to follow so bad an example; and thereby, forgetting that the signal for the line was at only two cables' length distance from each other, the van division was led by you to *more than two leagues distance* from the center division, which was thereby exposed to the greatest strength of the enemy, and not properly supported" (Life, Vol. I, p. 351). By all rules of tactical common-sense it would seem that the other ships should have taken their distance from their next astern, that is, should have closed toward the center. In conversation with Sir Gilbert Blane, who was not in this action, Rodney stated that the French line extended four leagues in length, "as if De Guichen thought we meant to run away from him" (*Naval Chronicle*, Vol. XXV, p. 402).

20. SEA POWER IN THE AMERICAN REVOLUTION [1]

Graves and De Grasse off the Chesapeake

[**P**RELIMINARY to the events narrated, the general naval situation was as follows: The main British and French fleets, under Rodney and De Grasse, respectively, were in the West Indies, while a small British division was under Graves at New York, and a French squadron under De Barras was based on Newport, R. I. The squadrons on the American coast had met in a desultory action off the Virginia capes on March 16, 1781, after which the French commander had returned to Newport and left the British in control. — EDITOR.]

The way of the sea being thus open and held in force, two thousand more English troops sailing from New York reached Virginia on the 26th of March, and the subsequent arrival of Cornwallis in May raised the number to seven thousand. The operations of the contending forces during the spring and summer months, in which Lafayette commanded the Americans, do not concern our subject. Early in August, Cornwallis, acting under orders from Clinton, withdrew his troops into the peninsula between the York and James rivers, and occupied Yorktown.

Washington and Rochambeau had met on the 21st of May, and decided that the situation de-

---

[1] "The Influence of Sea Power upon History," pp. 387–391, 397.

manded that the effort of the French West Indian fleet, when it came, should be directed against either New York or the Chesapeake. This was the tenor of the despatch found by De Grasse at Cap Français,[1] and meantime the allied generals drew their troops toward New York, where they would be on hand for the furtherance of one object, and nearer the second if they had to make for it.

In either case the result, in the opinion both of Washington and of the French government, depended upon superior sea power; but Rochambeau had privately notified the admiral that his own preference was for the Chesapeake as the scene of the intended operations, and moreover the French government had declined to furnish the means for a formal siege of New York.[2] The enterprise therefore assumed the form of an extensive military combination, dependent upon ease and rapidity of movement, and upon blinding the eyes of the enemy to the real objective,—purposes to which the peculiar qualities of a navy admirably lent themselves. The shorter distance to be traversed, the greater depth of water and easier pilotage of the Chesapeake, were further reasons which would commend the scheme to the judgment of a seaman; and De Grasse readily accepted it, without making difficulties or demanding modifications which would have involved discussion and delay.

Having made his decision, the French admiral acted with great good judgment, promptitude, and

---

[1] Now Cape Haitien, Haiti. — EDITOR.
[2] Bancroft, "History of the United States."

vigor. The same frigate that brought despatches from Washington was sent back, so that by August 15 the allied generals knew of the intended coming of the fleet. Thirty-five hundred soldiers were spared by the governor of Cap Français, upon the condition of a Spanish squadron anchoring at the place, which De Grasse procured. He also raised from the governor of Havana the money urgently needed by the Americans; and finally, instead of weakening his force by sending convoys to France, as the court had wished, he took every available ship to the Chesapeake. To conceal his coming as long as possible, he passed through the Bahama Channel, as a less frequented route, and on the 30th of August anchored in Lynnhaven Bay, just within the capes of the Chesapeake, with twenty-eight ships-of-the-line. Three days before, August 27, the French squadron at Newport, eight ships-of-the-line with four frigates and eighteen transports under M. de Barras, sailed for the rendezvous; making, however, a wide circuit out to sea to avoid the English. This course was the more necessary as the French siege-artillery was with it. The troops under Washington and Rochambeau [1] had crossed the Hudson on the 24th of August, moving toward the head of Chesapeake Bay. Thus the different armed forces, both land and sea, were converging toward their objective, Cornwallis.

The English were unfortunate in all directions.

---

[1] With the reinforcement brought by De Grasse, Lafayette's army numbered about 8,000; the troops brought by Washington and Rochambeau consisted of 2,000 Americans and 4,000 French. — EDITOR.

Rodney, learning of De Grasse's departure, sent fourteen ships-of-the-line under Admiral Hood to North America, and himself sailed for England in August, on account of ill health. Hood, going by the direct route, reached the Chesapeake three days before De Grasse, looked into the bay, and finding it empty went on to New York. There he

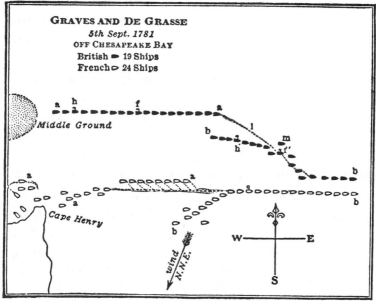

met five ships-of-the-line under Admiral Graves, who, being senior officer, took command of the whole force and sailed on the 31st of August for the Chesapeake, hoping to intercept De Barras before he could join De Grasse. It was not till two days later that Sir Henry Clinton was persuaded that the allied armies had gone against Cornwallis, and had too far the start to be overtaken.

Admiral Graves was painfully surprised, on making the Chesapeake, to find anchored there a fleet which from its numbers could only be an enemy's. Nevertheless, he stood in to meet it, and as De Grasse got under way, allowing his ships to be counted, the sense of numerical inferiority — nineteen to twenty-four — did not deter the English admiral from attacking. The clumsiness of his method, however, betrayed his gallantry; many of his ships were roughly handled, without any advantage being gained.[1] De Grasse, expecting De Barras, remained outside five days, keeping the English fleet in play without coming to action; then returning to port he found De Barras safely at anchor. Graves went back to New York, and with him disappeared the last hope of succor that was to gladden Cornwallis's eyes. The siege was steadily endured, but the control of the sea made only one issue possible, and the English forces were surrendered October 19, 1781. With this disaster the hope of subduing the colonies died in England. The conflict

[1] The action itself is more fully described in Mahan's "Major Operations of the Navies in the War of American Independence," from which the diagram on page 167 is taken. In the diagram, a a indicates the positions of the two fleets when De Grasse came out of the bay; b b, the positions when the order to engage was given; f, Graves's flagship, and h, Hood. Having approached the enemy with his twelve leading ships, Graves gave the order to bear down and engage, though he still kept the signal for "line ahead" flying. Whether through inability or misinterpretation of orders, the rear under Hood failed to get in range.

Hood afterward criticised his superior severely on the grounds, (1) that the fleet was not brought into proper position to engage, and (2) that, upon engaging, the "line ahead" signal should have been hauled down. He interpreted this signal as meaning that no ship could close beyond a line through the flagship and parallel to the enemy line.

Graves next day issued a memorandum to the effect that the line ahead was a means to an end, not an end in itself, and "that the signal for battle should not be rendered ineffective by strict adherence to the former." The confusion was such as frequently arose in this period of transition from one system of tactics to another. — EDITOR.

flickered through a year longer, but no serious operations were undertaken.

. . . The defeat of Graves and subsequent surrender of Cornwallis did not end the naval operations in the western hemisphere. On the contrary, one of the most interesting tactical feats and the most brilliant victory of the whole war were yet to grace the English flag in the West Indies; but with the events at Yorktown the patriotic interest for Americans closes. Before quitting that struggle for independence, it must again be affirmed that its successful ending, at least at so early a date, was due to the control of the sea, — to sea power in the hands of the French, and its improper distribution by the English authorities. This assertion may be safely rested on the authority of the one man who, above all others, thoroughly knew the resources of the country, the temper of the people, the difficulties of the struggle, and whose name is still the highest warrant for sound, quiet, unfluttered good sense and patriotism.

The keynote to all Washington's utterances is set in the " Memorandum for concerting a plan of operations with the French army," dated July 15, 1780, and sent by the hands of Lafayette:

" The Marquis de Lafayette will be pleased to communicate the following general ideas to Count de Rochambeau and the Chevalier de Ternay, as the sentiments of the underwritten:

" I. *In any operation, and under all circumstances, a decisive naval superiority is to be considered as a fundamental principle, and the basis upon which every hope of success must ultimately depend."*

This, however, though the most formal and decisive expression of Washington's views, is but one among many others equally distinct.

21. The French Navy Demoralized by the Revolution [1]

. . . The seamen and the navy of France were swept away by the same current of thought and feeling which was carrying before it the whole nation; and the government, tossed to and fro by every wave of popular emotion, was at once too weak and too ignorant of the needs of the service to repress principles and to amend defects which were fatal to its healthy life.

It is particularly instructive to dwell upon this phase of the revolutionary convulsions of France, because the result in this comparatively small, but still most important, part of the body politic was so different from that which was found elsewhere. Whatever the mistakes, the violence, the excesses of every kind, into which this popular rising was betrayed, they were symptomatic of strength, not of weakness, — deplorable accompaniments of a movement which, with all its drawbacks, was marked by overwhelming force.

It was the inability to realize the might in this outburst of popular feeling, long pent up, that caused the mistaken forecasts of many statesmen of the day; who judged of the power and reach of the movement by indications — such as the finances, the condition of the army, the quality of the known

[1] "Types of Naval Officers," pp. 35–37, 41.

leaders — ordinarily fairly accurate tests of a country's endurance, but which utterly misled those who looked to them only and did not take into account the mighty impulse of a whole nation stirred to its depths.   Why, then, was the result so different in the navy?   Why was it so weak, not merely nor chiefly in quantity, but in quality? and that, too, in days so nearly succeeding the prosperous naval era of Louis XVI.   Why should the same throe which brought forth the magnificent armies of Napoleon have caused the utter weakness of the sister service, not only amid the disorders of the Republic, but also under the powerful organization of the Empire?

The immediate reason was that, to a service of a very special character, involving special exigencies, calling for special aptitudes, and consequently demanding special knowledge of its requirements in order to deal wisely with it, were applied the theories of men wholly ignorant of those requirements, — men who did not even believe that they existed.   Entirely without experimental knowledge, or any other kind of knowledge, of the conditions of sea life, they were unable to realize the obstacles to those processes by which they would build up their navy, and according to which they proposed to handle it.   This was true not only of the wild experiments of the early days of the Republic; the reproach may fairly be addressed to the great emperor himself, that he had scarcely any appreciation of the factors conditioning efficiency at sea; nor did he seemingly ever reach any such sense of them as would enable him to understand why the French navy failed. " Disdaining," says Jean Bon Saint-André, the Revolutionary commissioner whose influence on naval organization was unbounded, " *disdaining*, through calculation and reflection, *skillful evolutions*, perhaps our seamen will think it more fitting and useful to try those boarding actions in which the Frenchman was always conqueror, and thus astonish Europe by new prodigies of valor." [1] " Courage and audacity," says Captain Chevalier, " had become in his eyes the only qualities necessary to our officers." " The English," said Napoleon, " will become very small when France shall have two or three admirals willing to die." [2] So commented, with pathetic yet submissive irony, the ill-fated admiral, Villeneuve, upon whom fell the weight of the emperor's discontent with his navy: " Since his Majesty thinks that nothing but audacity and resolve are needed to succeed in the naval officer's calling, I shall leave nothing to be desired." [3]

. . . In truth men's understandings, as well as their *morale* and beliefs, were in a chaotic state. In the navy, as in society, the *morale* suffered first. Insubordination and mutiny, insult and murder, preceded the blundering measures which in the end destroyed the fine *personnel* that the monarchy bequeathed to the French republic. This insubordination broke out very soon after the affairs of the Bastille and the forcing of the palace at Versailles; that is, very soon after the powerlessness of the

[1] Chevalier, "Mar. Fran. sous la République," p. 49.
[2] Nap. to Decrès, Aug. 29, 1805.
[3] Troude, "Batailles Nav.," Vol. III, p. 370.

executive was felt. Singularly, yet appropriately the first victim was the most distinguished flag officer of the French navy.[1]

During the latter half of 1789 disturbances occurred in all the seaport towns; in Havre, in Cherbourg, in Brest, in Rochefort, in Toulon. Everywhere the town authorities meddled with the concerns of the navy yards and of the fleet, discontented seamen and soldiers, idle or punished, rushed to the town halls with complaints against their officers. The latter, receiving no support from Paris, yielded continually, and things naturally went from bad to worse.

---

[1] Commodore de Rions, a member of the nobility, who was imprisoned at Toulon and afterward fled from the country. — EDITOR.

22. Howe's Victory of June 1, 1794[1]

[PRIOR to the engagement, the French fleet had met and was convoying to port 180 vessels from America with food-stuffs of which France was then in dire need. The British fleet encountered the French 400 miles west of Ushant on May 28, and in the four days of maneuvering and pursuit which followed, Howe displayed marked energy and tactical skill. Though the French fleet was defeated in the ensuing battle, it covered the escape of the convoy. — EDITOR.]

The French admiral on the evening of the 29th saw that he now must fight, and at a disadvantage; consequently, he could not hope to protect the convoy. As to save this was his prime object, the next best thing was to entice the British out of its path. With this view he stood away to the northwest; while a dense fog coming on both favored his design and prevented further encounter during the two ensuing days, throughout which Howe continued to pursue. In the evening of May 31 the weather cleared, and at daybreak the next morning the enemies were in position, ready for battle, two long

[1] "Types of Naval Officers," pp. 308–317. The "Glorious First of June" is one of the most important naval actions in the wars of the French Revolution, and illustrates the work of an officer who stood in his own day conspicuously at the head of his profession. The selection is interesting also as showing that, when it suited his purpose, Admiral Mahan could write with notable ease and pictorial vigor. — EDITOR.

columns of ships, heading west, the British twenty-
five, the French again twenty-six through the junction of the four vessels mentioned. Howe now had
cause to regret his absent six, and to ponder Nelson's
wise saying, " Only numbers can annihilate."

This time for maneuvering was past. Able tactician as he personally was, and admirable as had
been the direction of his efforts in the two days'
fighting, Howe had been forced in them to realize
two things, namely, that his captains were, singly,
superior in seamanship, and their crews in gunnery,
to the French; and again, that in the ability to work
together as a fleet the British were so deficient as
to promise very imperfect results, if he attempted
any but the simplest formation. To such, therefore,
he resorted; falling back upon the old, unskillful,
sledge-hammer fashion of the British navy. Arranging his ships in one long line, three miles from
the enemy, he made them all go down together,
each to attack a specified opponent, coming into
action as nearly as might be at the same instant.
Thus the French, from the individual inferiority of
the units of their fleet, would be at all points over-
powered. The issue justified the forecast; but the
manner of performance was curiously and happily
marked by Howe's own peculiar phlegm. There
was a long summer day ahead for fighting, and no
need for hurry. The order was first accurately
formed, and canvas reduced to proper proportions.
Then the crews went to breakfast. After breakfast,
the ships all headed for the hostile line, under short
sail, the admiral keeping them in hand during the

approach as an infantry officer dresses his company.
Hence the shock from end to end was so nearly
simultaneous as to induce success unequalled in any
engagement conducted on the same primitive plan.

Picturesque as well as sublime, animating as well
as solemn, on that bright Sunday morning, was this
prelude to the stern game of war about to be played:
the quiet summer sea stirred only by a breeze sufficient to cap with white the little waves that ruffled
its surface; the dark hulls gently rippling the water
aside in their slow advance, a ridge of foam curling
on either side of the furrow ploughed by them in
their onward way; their massive sides broken by
two, or at times three, rows of ports, whence, the
tompions drawn, yawned the sullen lines of guns,
behind which, unseen, but easily realized by the instructed eye, clustered the groups of ready seamen
who served each piece. Aloft swung leisurely to
and fro the tall spars, which ordinarily, in so light
a wind, would be clad in canvas from deck to truck,
but whose naked trimness now proclaimed the
deadly purpose of that still approach. Upon the
high poops, where floated the standard of either
nation, gathered round each chief the little knot of
officers through whom commands were issued and
reports received, the nerves along which thrilled the
impulses of the great organism, from its head, the
admiral, through every member to the dark lowest
decks, nearly awash, where, as farthest from the
captain's own oversight, the senior lieutenants controlled the action of the ships' heaviest batteries.

On board the *Queen Charlotte,* Lord Howe,

whose burden of sixty-eight years had for four days
found no rest save what he could snatch in an arm-
chair, now, at the prospect of battle, " displayed
an animation," writes an eye-witness, " of which,
at his age, and after such fatigue of body and mind,
I had not thought him capable. He seemed to con-
template the result as one of unbounded satisfaction." By his side stood his fleet-captain, Curtis,
of whose service among the floating batteries, and
during the siege of Gibraltar, the governor of the
fortress had said, " He is the man to whom the king
is chiefly indebted for its security; " and Codrington, then a lieutenant, who afterwards commanded
the allied fleets at Navarino. Five ships to the left,
Collingwood, in the *Barfleur*, was making to the
admiral whose flag she bore the remark that stirred
Thackeray: " Our wives are now about going to
church, but we will ring about these Frenchmen's
ears a peal which will drown their bells." The
French officers, both admirals and captains, were
mainly unknown men, alike then and thereafter.
The fierce flames of the Revolution had swept away
the men of the old school, mostly aristocrats, and
time had not yet brought forward the very few
who during the Napoleonic period showed marked
capacity. The commander-in-chief, Villaret-Joyeuse,
had three years before been a lieutenant. He had
a high record for gallantry, but was without antecedents as a general officer. With him, on the poop
of the *Montagne,* which took her name from Robes-
pierre's political supporters, stood that anomalous
companion of the generals and admirals of the day,

the Revolutionary commissioner, Jean Bon Saint-André, about to learn by experience the practical working of the system he had advocated, to disregard all tests of ability save patriotism and courage, depreciating practice and skill as unnecessary to the valor of the true Frenchman.

As the British line drew near the French, Howe said to Curtis, " Prepare the signal for close action." " There is no such signal," replied Curtis. " No," said the admiral, " but there is one for closer action, and I only want that to be made in case of captains not doing their duty." Then closing a little signal book he always carried, he continued to those around him, " Now, gentlemen, no more book, no more signals. I look to you to do the duty of the *Queen Charlotte* in engaging the flag-ship. I don't want the ships to be bilge to bilge, but if you can lock the yardarms, so much the better; the battle will be the quicker decided." His purpose was to go through the French line, and fight the *Montagne* on the far side. Some doubted their succeeding, but Howe overbore them. " That 's right, my lord! " cried Bowen, the sailing-master, who looked to the ship's steering. " The *Charlotte* will make room for herself." She pushed close under the French ship's stern, grazing her ensign, and raking her from stern to stem with a withering fire, beneath which fell three hundred men. A length or two beyond lay the French *Jacobin*. Howe ordered the *Charlotte* to luff, and place herself between the two. " If we do," said Bowen, " we shall be on board one of them." " What is that to you, sir? "

asked Howe quickly. " Oh! " muttered the master, not inaudibly. " D—n my eyes if I care, if you don't. I 'll go near enough to singe some of our whiskers." And then, seeing by the *Jacobin's* rudder that she was going off, he brought the *Charlotte* sharp round, her jib boom grazing the second Frenchman as her side had grazed the flag of the first.

From this moment the battle raged furiously from end to end of the field for nearly an hour, — a wild scene of smoke and confusion, under cover of which many a fierce ship duel was fought, while here and there men wandered, lost, in a maze of bewilderment that neutralized their better judgment. An English naval captain tells a service tradition of one who was so busy watching the compass, to keep his position in the ranks, that he lost sight of his antagonist, and never again found him. Many a quaint incident passed, recorded or unrecorded, under that sulphurous canopy. A British ship, wholly dismasted, lay between two enemies, her captain desperately wounded. A murmur of surrender was somewhere heard; but as the first lieutenant checked it with firm authority, a cock flew upon the stump of a mast and crowed lustily. The exultant note found quick response in hearts not given to despair, and a burst of merriment, accompanied with three cheers, replied to the bird's triumphant scream. On board the *Brunswick*, in her struggle with the *Vengeur*, one of the longest and fiercest fights the sea has ever seen, the cocked hat was shot off the effigy of the Duke of Brunswick, which she bore as a figure-head. A deputation from the crew gravely requested the captain to allow the use of his spare chapeau, which was securely nailed on, and protected his grace's wig during the rest of the action. After this battle with the ships of the new republic, the partisans of monarchy noted with satisfaction that, among the many royal figures that surmounted the stems of the British fleet, not one lost his crown. Of a harum-scarum Irish captain are told two droll stories. After being hotly engaged for some time with a French ship, the fire of the latter slackened, and then ceased. He called to know if she had surrendered. The reply was, " No." " Then," shouted he, " d—n you, why don't you fire?" Having disposed of his special antagonist without losing his own spars, the same man kept along in search of new adventures, until he came to a British ship totally dismasted and otherwise badly damaged. She was commanded by a captain of rigidly devout piety. " Well, Jemmy," hailed the Irishman, " you are pretty well mauled; but never mind, Jemmy, whom the Lord loveth he chasteneth."

The French have transmitted to us less of anecdote, nor is it easy to connect the thought of humor with those grimly earnest republicans and the days of the Terror. There is, indeed, something unintentionally funny in the remark of the commander of one of the captured ships to his captors. They had, it was true, dismasted half the French fleet, and had taken over a fourth; yet he assured them it could not be considered a victory, " but merely a butchery, in which the British had shown neither science nor tactics." The one story, noble and enduring, that will ever be associated with the French on the 1st of June is in full keeping with the temper of the times and the enthusiasm of the nation. The seventy-four-gun ship *Vengeur,* after a three hours' fight, yardarm to yardarm, with the British *Brunswick,* was left in a sinking state by her antagonist, who was herself in no condition to help. In the confusion, the *Vengeur's* peril was for some time not observed; and when it was, the British ships that came to her aid had time only to remove part of her survivors. In their report of the event the latter said: " Scarcely had the boats pulled clear of the sides, when the most frightful spectacle was offered to our gaze. Those of our comrades who remained on board the *Vengeur du Peuple,* with hands raised to heaven, implored, with lamentable cries, the help for which they could no longer hope. Soon disappeared the ship and the unhappy victims it contained. In the midst of the horror with which this scene inspired us all, we could not avoid a feeling of admiration mingled with our grief. As we drew away, we heard some of our comrades still offering prayers for the welfare of their country. The last cries of these unfortunates were, ' Vive la République! ' They died uttering them." Over a hundred Frenchmen thus went down.

Seven French ships were captured, including the sunk *Vengeur.* Five more were wholly dismasted, but escaped, — a good fortune mainly to be attributed to Howe's utter physical prostration, due to his advanced years and the continuous strain of the past five days. He now went to bed, completely worn out. "We all got round him," wrote an officer, Lieutenant Codrington, who was present; "indeed, I saved him from a tumble, he was so weak that from a roll of the ship he was nearly falling into the waist. 'Why, you hold me up as if I were a child,' he said good-humoredly." Had he been younger, there can be little doubt that the fruits of victory would have been gathered with an ardor which his assistant, Curtis, failed to show.

23. Nelson's Strategy at Copenhagen [1]

[In 1800 Russia, Sweden, and Denmark, under the manipulation of Napoleon, formed a "League of Armed Neutrality" to resist British restrictions on their trade with France. To reinforce diplomatic pressure, Great Britain sent against the league a fleet of twenty ships, of which Nelson was second in command under Sir Hyde Parker. Throughout the campaign, writes Mahan, Nelson "lifted and carried on his shoulders the dead weight of his superior." — Editor.]

The fleet sailed from Yarmouth on the 12th of March, 1801; and on the 19th, although there had been some scattering in a heavy gale, nearly all were collected off the Skaw, the northern point of Jutland at the entrance of the Kattegat. The wind being northwest was fair for going to Copenhagen, and Nelson, if in command, would have advanced at once with the ambassador on board. "While the negotiation is going on," he said, "the Dane should see our flag waving every moment he lifted his head." As it was, the envoy went forward with a frigate alone and the fleet waited. On the 12th it was off Elsineur, where the envoy rejoined, Denmark having rejected the British terms.

[1] "The Influence of Sea Power upon the French Revolution and Empire," Vol. II, pp. 42–47. The campaign is treated more fully in "The Life of Nelson," Vol. II, p. 70 *ff*. — Editor.

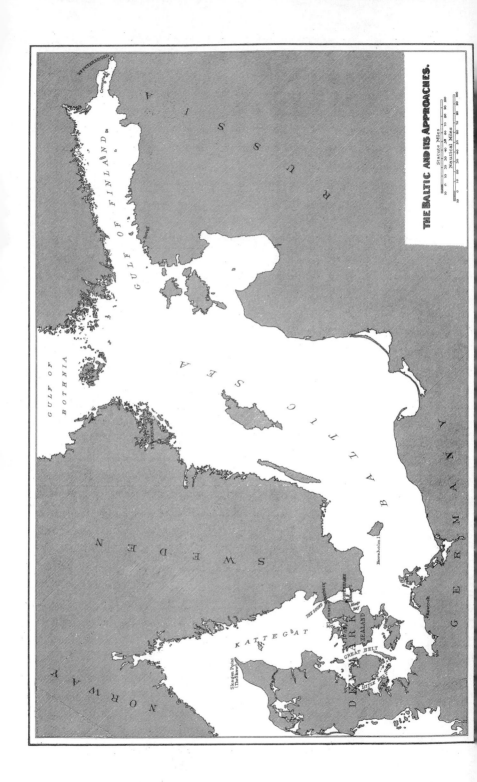

THE BALTIC AND ITS APPROACHES.

Statute Miles

Nautical Miles

This amounted to an acceptance of hostilities, and it only remained to the commander-in-chief to act at once; for the wind was favorable, an advantage which at any moment might be lost. On this day Nelson addressed Parker a letter, summing up in a luminous manner the features of the situation and the different methods of action. " Not a moment should be lost in attacking," he said; " we shall never be so good a match for them as at this moment." He next hinted, what he had probably already said, that the fleet ought to have been off Copenhagen, and not at Elsineur, when the negotiation failed. " Then you might instantly attack and there would be scarcely a doubt but the Danish fleet would be destroyed, and the capital made so hot that Denmark would listen to reason and its true interest." Since, however, the mistake of losing so much time had been made, he seeks to stir his superior to lose no more. " Almost the safety, certainly the honor, of England is more entrusted to you than ever yet fell to the lot of any British officer; . . . never did our country depend so much on the success of any fleet as of this."

Having thus shown the necessity for celerity, Nelson next discussed the plan of operations. Copenhagen is on the east side of the island of Zealand, fronting the coast of Sweden, from which it is separated by the passage called the Sound. On the west the island is divided from the other parts of Denmark by the Great Belt. The navigation of the latter being much the more difficult, the preparations of the Danes had been made on the side of the Sound, and chiefly about Copenhagen itself. For half a mile from the shore in front of the city, flats extend, and in the Sound itself, at a distance of little over a mile, is a long shoal called the Middle Ground. Between these two bodies of shallow water is a channel, called the King's, through which a fleet of heavy ships could sail, and from whose northern end a deep pocket stretches toward Copenhagen, forming the harbor proper. The natural point of attack therefore appears to be at the north; and there the Danes had erected powerful works, rising on piles out of the shoal water off the harbor's mouth and known as the Three-Crown Batteries. Nelson, however, pointed out that not only was this head of the line exceedingly strong, but that the wind that was fair to attack would be foul to return; therefore a disabled ship would have no escape but by passing through the King's Channel. Doing so she would have to run the gantlet of a line of armed hulks, which the Danes had established as floating batteries along the inner edge of the channel — covering the front of Copenhagen — and would also be separated from her fleet. Nor was this difficulty, which may be called tactical, the only objection to a plan that he disparaged as "taking the bull by the horns." He remarked that so long as the British fleet remained in the Sound, without entering the Baltic, the way was left open for both the Swedes and the Russians, if released by the ice, to make a junction with the Danes. Consequently, he advised that a sufficiently strong force of the lighter ships-of-the-line should pass outside the Middle Ground, despite the difficulties of navigation, which were not insuperable, and come up in rear of the city. There they would interpose between the Danes and their allies, and be in position to assail the weaker part of the hostile order. He offered himself to lead this detachment.

This whole letter of March 24, 1801,[1] possesses peculiar interest; for it shows with a rare particularity, elicited by the need he felt of arousing and convincing his superior, Nelson's clear discernment of the decisive features of a military situation. The fame of this great admiral has depended less upon his conduct of campaigns than upon the renowned victories he won in the actual collision of fleet with fleet; and even then has been mutilated by the obstinacy with which, despite the perfectly evident facts, men have persisted in seeing in them nothing but dash, — heart, not head. Throughout his correspondence, it is true, there are frequent traces of the activity of his mental faculties and of the general accuracy of his military conclusions; but ordinarily it is from his actions that his reasonings and principles must be deduced. In the present case we have the views he held and the course he evidently would have pursued clearly formulated by himself; and it cannot but be a subject of regret that the naval world should have lost so fine an illustration as he would there have given of the principles and conduct of naval warfare. He concluded his letter with a suggestion worthy of Napoleon himself, and which, if

[1] Nelson's Letters and Dispatches, Vol. IV, p. 295.

adopted, would have brought down the Baltic Confederacy with a crash that would have resounded throughout Europe. " Supposing us through the Belt with the wind first westerly, would it not be possible to go with the fleet, or detach ten ships of three and two decks, with one bomb and two fireships, to Revel, to destroy the Russian squadron at that place? I do not see the great risk of such a detachment, and with the remainder to attempt the business at Copenhagen. The measure may be thought bold, but I am of opinion the boldest are the safest; and our country demands a most vigorous exertion of her force, directed with judgment."

Committed as the Danes were to a stationary defense, this recommendation to strike at the soul of the confederacy evinced the clearest perception of the key to the situation, which Nelson himself summed up in the following words: " I look upon the Northern League to be like a tree, of which Paul was the trunk and Sweden and Denmark the branches. If I can get at the trunk and hew it down, the branches fall of course; but I may lop the branches and yet not be able to fell the tree, and my power must be weaker when its greatest strength is required " [1] — that is, the Russians should have been attacked before the fleet was weakened, as it inevitably must be, by the battle with the Danes. " If we could have cut up the Russian fleet," he said again, " that was my object." Whatever Denmark's wishes about fighting, she was by her continental possessions tied to the policy of Russia and

[1] Nelson's Dispatches, Vol. IV., p. 355.

Prussia, either of whom could overwhelm her by land. She dared not disregard them. The course of both depended upon the czar; for the temporizing policy of Prussia would at once embrace his withdrawal from the league as an excuse for doing the same. At Revel were twelve Russian ships-of-the-line, fully half their Baltic fleet, whose destruction would have paralyzed the remainder and the naval power of the empire. To persuade Parker to such a step was, however, hopeless. " Our fleet would never have acted against Russia and Sweden," wrote Nelson afterwards, " although Copenhagen would have been burned; for Sir Hyde Parker was determined not to leave Denmark hostile in his rear;" [1] a reason whose technical accuracy under all the circumstances was nothing short of pedantic, and illustrates the immense distance between a good and accomplished officer, which Parker was, and a genius whose comprehension of rules serves only to guide, not to fetter, his judgment.

Although unable to rise equal to the great opportunity indicated by Nelson, Sir Hyde Parker adopted his suggestion as to the method and direction of the principal attack upon the defenses of Copenhagen. For this, Nelson asked ten ships-of-the-line and a number of smaller vessels, with which he undertook to destroy the floating batteries covering the front of the city. These being reduced, the bomb vessels could be placed so as to play with effect upon the dockyard, arsenals, and the town, in case further resistance was made.

[1] Nelson's Dispatches, April 9, 1801, Vol. IV, pp. 339, 341.

[The fleet entered the Sound and anchored off Copenhagen on March 26. On April 2 Nelson attacked from the southward as he had suggested, and after a hard-fought battle forced a fourteen weeks' armistice which practically secured the British aims, since it gave opportunity to proceed against Sweden and Russia. Nelson was given chief command on May 5, and two days later sailed for Revel, but the death of the Czar Paul had already brought a favorable change in Russia's policy and made further action unnecessary. — EDITOR.]

24. ENGLAND'S FIRST LINE OF DEFENSE [1]

[AFTER the Copenhagen campaign, for a brief period in 1801, Nelson commanded the naval defense forces in the Channel. When, after two years of peace, hostilities were renewed in 1803, he sailed in the *Victory* to take command in the Mediterranean. During the following years of the war, "The British squadrons, hugging the French coasts and blocking the French arsenals, were the first line of defense, covering British interests from the Baltic to Egypt, the British colonies in the four quarters of the globe, and the British merchantmen which whitened every sea." [2] — EDITOR.]

Meanwhile that period of waiting from May, 1803, to August, 1805, when the tangled net of naval and military movements began to unravel, was a striking and wonderful pause in the world's history. On the heights above Boulogne, and along the narrow strip of beach from Étaples to Vimereux, were encamped one hundred and thirty thousand of the most brilliant soldiery of all time, the soldiers who had fought in Germany, Italy, and Egypt, soldiers who were yet to win, from Austria, Ulm and Austerlitz, and from Prussia, Auerstadt and Jena, to hold their own, though barely, at Eylau

---

[1] "The Influence of Sea Power upon the French Revolution and Empire," Vol. II, pp. 117–120.
[2] *Ibid.*, p. 106.

against the army of Russia, and to overthrow it also, a few months later, on the bloody field of Friedland.   Growing daily more vigorous in the bracing sea air and the hardy life laid out for them, they could on fine days, as they practised the varied maneuvers which were to perfect the vast host in embarking and disembarking with order and rapidity, see the white cliffs fringing the only country that to the last defied their arms.   Far away, Cornwallis off Brest, Collingwood off Rochefort, Pellew off Ferrol, were battling the wild gales of the Bay of Biscay, in that tremendous and sustained vigilance which reached its utmost tension in the years preceding Trafalgar, concerning which Collingwood wrote that admirals need to be made of iron, but which was forced upon them by the unquestionable and imminent danger of the country.   Farther distant still, severed apparently from all connection with the busy scene at Boulogne, Nelson before Toulon was wearing away the last two years of his glorious but suffering life, fighting the fierce northwesters of the Gulf of Lyon and questioning, questioning continually with feverish anxiety, whether Napoleon's object was Egypt again or Great Britain really.   They were dull, weary, eventless months, those months of watching and waiting of the big ships before the French arsenals.   Purposeless they surely seemed to many, but they saved England.   The world has never seen a more impressive demonstration of the influence of sea power upon its history.   Those far distant, storm-beaten ships, upon which the Grand Army never looked, stood between it and the dominion of the world. Holding the interior positions they did, before — and therefore between — the chief dockyards and detachments of the French navy, the latter could unite only by a concurrence of successful evasions, of which the failure of any one nullified the result. Linked together as the various British fleets were by chains of smaller vessels, chance alone could secure Bonaparte's great combination, which depended upon the covert concentration of several detachments upon a point practically within the enemy's lines.   Thus, while bodily present before Brest, Rochefort, and Toulon, strategically the British squadrons lay in the Straits of Dover barring the way against the Army of Invasion.

The Straits themselves, of course, were not without their own special protection.   Both they and their approaches, in the broadest sense of the term, from the Texel to the Channel Islands, were patrolled by numerous frigates and smaller vessels, from one hundred to a hundred and fifty in all. These not only watched diligently all that happened in the hostile harbors and sought to impede the movements of the flat-boats, but also kept touch with and maintained communication between the detachments of ships-of-the-line.   Of the latter, five off the Texel watched the Dutch navy, while others were anchored off points of the English coast with reference to probable movements of the enemy. Lord St. Vincent, whose ideas on naval strategy were clear and sound, though he did not use the technical terms of the art, discerned and provided against the very purpose entertained by Bonaparte, of a concentration before Boulogne by ships drawn from the Atlantic and Mediterranean. The best security, the most advantageous strategic positions, were doubtless those before the enemy's ports; and never in the history of blockades has there been excelled, if ever equalled, the close locking of Brest by Admiral Cornwallis, both winter and summer, between the outbreak of war and the battle of Trafalgar. It excited not only the admiration but the wonder of contemporaries.[1] In case, however, the French at Brest got out, so the prime minister of the day informed the speaker of the House, Cornwallis's rendezvous was off the Lizard (due north of Brest), so as to go for *Ireland, or follow the French up Channel,* if they took either direction. *Should the French run for the Downs,* the five sail-of-the-line at Spithead would also follow them; and Lord Keith (in the Downs) would in addition to his six, and six block ships, have also the North Sea fleet at his command.[2] Thus provision was made, in case of danger, for the outlying detachments to fall back on the strategic center, gradually accumulating strength, till they formed a body of from twenty-five to thirty heavy and disciplined ships-of-the-line, sufficient to meet all probable contingencies.

Hence, neither the Admiralty nor British naval officers in general shared the fears of the country

[1] See "Naval Chronicle," Vol. X, pp. 508, 510; Vol. XI, p. 81; Nelson's Dispatches, Vol. V, p. 438.
[2] Pellew's "Life of Lord Sidmouth," Vol. II, p. 237.

concerning the peril from the flotilla. " Our first
defense," wrote Nelson in 1801, " is close to the
enemy's ports; and the Admiralty have taken such
precautions, by having such a respectable force
under my orders, that I venture to express a well-
grounded hope that the enemy would be annihilated
before they get ten miles from their own shores." [1]

[1] Nelson's Dispatches, Vol. IV, p. 452.

25. THE BATTLE OF TRAFALGAR[1]

[W]HILE Napoleon's plans for control of the Channel underwent many changes, the movements actually carried out were as follows: On March 27, Villeneuve with eighteen ships left Toulon and sailed for the West Indies, arriving at Martinique May 12, where he was to be joined by the Brest fleet. Baffled at first by head winds and uncertainty as to the enemy's destination, Nelson reached Barbados twenty-three days later.

Learning of his arrival, Villeneuve at once sailed for Europe, on June 9, again followed, four days later by Nelson. The brig *Curieux,* despatched by Nelson to England on the 12th, sighted the enemy fleet and reported its approach to the Admiralty, thus enabling Calder to meet Villeneuve in an indecisive action on July 22 off Ferrol, Spain. Nelson steered for Gibraltar, and thence, having learned that Villeneuve was to the northward, for the Channel, where on August 15 he left his ships with the Channel fleet under Cornwallis.

The French now had twenty-one ships at Brest and twenty-nine under Villeneuve at Ferrol, while Cornwallis stood between with thirty-four or thirty-five. An effective French combination was still possible, especially as Cornwallis made the cardinal

1 "The Influence of Sea Power upon the French Revolution and Empire," Vol. II, pp. 184-197, 199-202, 356-357.

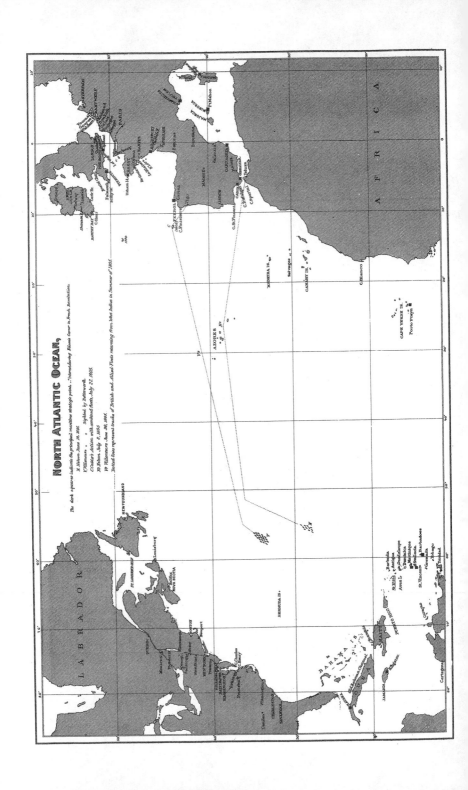

NORTH ATLANTIC OCEAN,

The dark squares indicate the principal maritime strategic points. ...Interrupting Nelson Career in French Revolution.

N. Nelson June 19, 1805.

V. Villeneuve " " Sighted by Bellerouth.

C.Calder's Action with combined fleets, July 22. 1805.

N. Nelson, July 9, 1805.

VV. Villeneuve June 30, 1805.

.... Dotted lines represent tracks of British and Allied Fleets returning from West Indies in Summer of 1805.

error of dividing his fleet. Accordingly, Villeneuve, under an imperative summons from Napoleon, left Ferrol on August 13; but, with his ships demoralized by their long cruise, with head winds, and disturbed by false reports from a Danish merchantman regarding the British strength, the French admiral two days later turned for Cadiz. Here he was watched by Collingwood; and on September 28 Nelson, after three weeks in England, took command of the blockading fleet. " Thus ended, and forever," writes Mahan, " Napoleon's profoundly conceived and laboriously planned scheme for the invasion of England. If it be sought to fix a definite moment which marked the final failure of so vast a plan, that one may well be chosen when Villeneuve made signal to bear up for Cadiz." [1] On August 25 the Boulogne army broke camp and marched against the Austrian forces advancing toward the Rhine. — EDITOR.]

The importance attached by the emperor to his project was not exaggerated. He might, or he might not, succeed; but, if he failed against Great Britain, he failed everywhere. This he, with the intuition of genius, felt; and to this the record of his after history now bears witness. To the strife of arms with the great Sea Power succeeded the strife of endurance. Amid all the pomp and circumstance of the war which for ten years to come desolated the Continent, amid all the tramping to and fro over Europe of the French armies and their

[1] "The Influence of Sea Power upon the French Revolution and Empire, Vol. II, p. 181.

auxiliary legions, there went on unceasingly that
noiseless pressure upon the vitals of France, that
compulsion, whose silence, when once noted, becomes to the observer the most striking and awful
mark of the working of Sea Power. Under it the
resources of the Continent wasted more and more
with each succeeding year; and Napoleon, amid all
the splendor of his imperial position, was ever
needy. To this, and to the immense expenditures
required to enforce the Continental System, are to
be attributed most of those arbitrary acts which
made him the hated of the peoples, for whose en-
franchisement he did so much. Lack of revenue
and lack of credit, such was the price paid by
Napoleon for the Continental System, through
which alone, after Trafalgar, he hoped to crush the
Power of the Sea. It may be doubted whether, amid
all his glory, he ever felt secure after the failure
of the invasion of England. To borrow his own
vigorous words, in the address to the nation issued
before he joined the army, " To live without commerce, without shipping, without colonies, subjected
to the unjust will of our enemies, is to live as
Frenchmen should not." Yet so had France to live
throughout his reign, by the will of the one enemy
never conquered.

On the 14th of September, before quitting Paris,
Napoleon sent Villeneuve orders to take the first
favorable opportunity to leave Cadiz, to enter the
Mediterranean, join the ships at Cartagena, and
with this combined force move upon southern Italy.
There, at any suitable point, he was to land the

troops embarked in the fleet to reinforce General St. Cyr, who already had instructions to be ready to attack Naples at a moment's notice.[1] The next day these orders were reiterated to Decrès, enforcing the importance to the general campaign of so powerful a diversion as the presence of this great fleet in the Mediterranean; but, as " Villeneuve's excessive pusillanimity will prevent him from undertaking this, you will send to replace him Admiral Rosily, who will bear letters directing Villeneuve to return to France and give an account of his conduct." [2] The emperor had already formulated his complaints against the admiral under seven distinct heads.[3] On the 15th of September, the same day the orders to relieve Villeneuve were issued, Nelson, having spent at home only twenty-five days, left England for the last time. On the 28th, when he joined the fleet off Cadiz, he found under his command twenty-nine ships-of-the-line, which successive arrivals raised to thirty-three by the day of the battle; but, water running short, it became necessary to send the ships, by divisions of six, to fill up at Gibraltar. To this cause was due that only twenty-seven British vessels were present in the action, — an unfortunate circumstance; for, as Nelson said, what the country wanted was not merely a splendid victory, but annihilation; " numbers only can annihilate." [4] The force under his command was thus disposed: the main body about fifty miles west-south-west of Cadiz, seven lookout frigates close in with the port,

---

[1] Napoleon to St. Cyr, Sept. 2, 1805.
[2] Napoleon to Decrès, Sept. 15. [3] *Ibid.*, Sept. 4.
[4] Nelson's Dispatches, Vol. VII, p. 80.

and between these extremes, two small detachments of ships-of-the-line, — the one twenty miles from the harbor, the other about thirty-five. " By this chain," he wrote, " I hope to have constant communication with the frigates."

" *The Nelson Touch* " [1]

At 6 P.M. of Saturday, September 28, the *Victory* reached the fleet, then numbering twenty-nine of the line; the main body being fifteen to twenty miles west of Cadiz, with six ships close in with the port. The next day was Nelson's birthday — forty-seven years old. The junior admirals and the captains visited the commander-in-chief, as customary, but with demonstrations of gladness and confidence that few leaders have elicited in equal measure from their followers. " The reception I met with on joining the fleet caused the sweetest sensation of my life. The officers who came on board to welcome my return, forgot my rank as commander-in-chief in the enthusiasm with which they greeted me. As soon as these emotions were past, I laid before them the plan I had previously arranged for attacking the enemy; and it was not only my pleasure to find it generally approved, but clearly perceived and understood." To Lady Hamilton he gave an account of this scene which differs little from the above, except in its greater vividness. " I believe my arrival was most welcome,

[1] The following account of Nelson's arrival and his plan of battle is taken from the fuller narrative in "The Life of Nelson," Vol. II, pp. 339–351. — EDITOR.

not only to the commander of the fleet, but also to every individual in it; and, when I came to explain to them the ' *Nelson touch*,' it was like an electric shock. Some shed tears, all approved — ' It was new — it was singular — it was simple ! ' and, from admirals downwards, it was repeated — ' It must succeed, if ever they will allow us to get at them ! You are, my Lord, surrounded by friends whom you inspire with confidence.' Some may be Judas's; but the majority are certainly much pleased with my commanding them." No more joyful birthday levee was ever held than that of this little naval court. Besides the adoration for Nelson personally, which they shared with their countrymen in general, there mingled with the delight of the captains the senti- ment of professional appreciation and confidence, and a certain relief, noticed by Codrington, from the dry, unsympathetic rule of Collingwood, a man just, conscientious, highly trained, and efficient, but self- centered, rigid, uncommunicative; one who fostered, if he did not impose, restrictions upon the inter- course between the ships, against which he had in- veighed bitterly when himself one of St. Vincent's captains. Nelson, on the contrary, at once invited cordial social relations with the commanding officers. Half of the thirty-odd were summoned to dine on board the flagship the first day, and half the second. Not till the third did he permit himself the luxury of a quiet dinner chat with his old chum, the second in command, whose sterling merits, under a crusty exterior, he knew and appreciated. Codrington mentions also an incident, trivial in itself, but illustrative of that outward graciousness of manner, which, in a man of Nelson's temperament and position, is rarely the result of careful cultivation, but bespeaks rather the inner graciousness of the heart that he abundantly possessed. They had never met before, and the admiral, greeting him with his usual easy courtesy, handed him a letter from his wife, saying that being entrusted with it by a lady, he made a point of delivering it himself, instead of sending it by another.

The "Nelson Touch," or Plan of Attack, expounded to his captains at the first meeting, was afterwards formulated in an Order, copies of which were issued to the fleet on the 9th of October. In this "Memorandum," which was doubtless sufficient for those who had listened to the vivid oral explanation of its framer, the writer finds the simplicity, but not the absolute clearness, that they recognized. It embodies, however, the essential ideas, though not the precise method of execution, actually followed at Trafalgar, under conditions considerably different from those which Nelson probably anticipated; and it is not the least of its merits as a military conception that it could thus, with few signals and without confusion, adapt itself at a moment's notice to diverse circumstances. This great order not only reflects the ripened experience of its author, but contains also the proof of constant mental activity and development in his thought; for it differs materially in detail from the one issued a few months before to the fleet, when in pursuit of Villeneuve to the West Indies.

MEMORANDUM

(Secret)

Victory, off CADIZ, 9th October, 1805.

Thinking it almost impossible to bring a Fleet of forty Sail of the Line into a Line of Battle in variable winds, thick weather, and other circumstances which must occur, without such a loss of time that the opportunity would probably be lost of bringing the Enemy to Battle in such a manner as to make the business decisive, I have therefore made up my mind to keep the Fleet in that position of sailing (with the exception of the First and Second in Command) that the Order of Sailing is to be the Order of Battle, placing the Fleet in two Lines of sixteen Ships each, with an Advanced Squadron of eight of the fastest sailing Two-decked Ships, which will always make, if wanted, a Line of twenty-four Sail, on whichever Line the Commander-in-Chief may direct.

The Second in Command will, after my intentions are made known to him, have the entire direction of his Line to make the attack upon the Enemy, and to follow up the blow until they are captured or destroyed.

If the Enemy's Fleet should be seen to windward in Line of Battle, and that the two Lines and the Advanced Squadron can fetch them, they will probably be so extended that their Van could not succor their Rear.

I should therefore probably make the Second in Command's signal to lead through, about their twelfth Ship from their Rear, (or wherever he could fetch, if not able to get so far advanced) ; my Line would lead through about their Center, and the Advanced Squadron to cut two or three or four Ships a-head of their Center, so as to ensure getting at their Commander-in-Chief, on whom every effort must be made to capture.

The whole impression of the British Fleet must be to overpower from two or three Ships a-head of their Commander-in-Chief, supposed to be in the Center, to the Rear of their Fleet. I will suppose twenty Sail of the Enemy's Line to be untouched, it must be some time before they could perform a maneuver to bring their force compact to attack any part of the British Fleet engaged, or to succor their own Ships, which indeed would be impossible without mixing with the Ships engaged.

Something must be left to chance; nothing is sure in a Sea Fight beyond all others. Shot will carry away the masts and yards of friends as well as foes; but I look with confidence to a Victory before the Van of the Enemy could succor their Rear, and then that the British Fleet would most of them be ready to receive their twenty Sail of the Line, or to pursue them, should they endeavor to make off.

If the Van of the Enemy tacks, the Captured Ships must run to leeward of the British Fleet; if the Enemy wears, the British must place themselves between the Enemy and the Captured, and disabled British Ships; and should the Enemy close, I have no fears as to the result.

The Second in Command will in all possible things direct the movements of his Line, by keeping them as compact as the nature of the circumstances will admit. Captains are to look to their particular Line as their rallying point. But, in case Signals can neither be seen or perfectly understood, no Captain can do very wrong if he places his Ship alongside that of an Enemy.

Of the intended attack from to windward, the Enemy in Line of Battle ready to receive an attack,

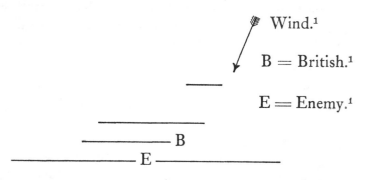

Wind.[1]

B = British.[1]

E = Enemy.[1]

The divisions of the British Fleet will be brought nearly within gun shot of the Enemy's Center. The signal will most probably then be made for the Lee Line to bear up together, to set all their sails, even steering sails, in order to get as quickly as possible to the Enemy's Line, and to cut through, beginning from the 12 Ship from the Enemy's Rear. Some Ships may not get through their exact place, but they will always be at hand to assist their friends; and if any are thrown round the Rear of the Enemy, they will effectually complete the business of twelve Sail of the Enemy.

Should the Enemy wear together, or bear up and

---

[1] Inserted by author.

sail large, still the twelve Ships composing, in the first position, the Enemy's Rear, are to be the object of attack of the Lee Line, unless otherwise directed from the Commander-in-Chief, which is scarcely to be expected, as the entire management of the Lee Line, after the intentions of the Commander-in-Chief is signified, is intended to be left to the judgment of the Admiral commanding that Line.

The remainder of the Enemy's Fleet, 34 Sail, are to be left to the management of the Commander-in-Chief who will endeavor to take care that the movements of the Second in Command are as little interrupted as is possible.

NELSON AND BRONTÉ.

After a statement of general considerations, and a frank attribution of full powers to the second in command for carrying out his part, Nelson lays down the manner of attack from to leeward. This condition not obtaining at Trafalgar, the plan cannot be contrasted with the performance of that day. Upon this follows a luminous enunciation of the general idea, namely, Collingwood's engaging the twelve rear ships, which underlies the method prescribed for each attack — from to leeward and to windward. Of the latter Nelson fortunately gives an outline diagram, which illustrates the picture before his own mind, facilitating our comprehension of his probable expectations, and allowing a comparison between them and the event as it actually occurred. It is not to the discredit, but greatly to the credit, of his conception, that it was susceptible of large modification in practice while retaining its characteristic idea.

Looking at his diagram, and following his words, it will be seen that the British lines are not formed perpendicularly to that of the enemy (as they were at Trafalgar), but parallel to it. Starting from this disposition, near the enemy and abreast his center, the lee line of sixteen ships was to bear up *together*, and advance in line, not in column (as happened at Trafalgar); their object being the twelve rear ships of the enemy. This first move stands by itself; the action of the weather line, and of the reserve squadron still farther to windward, are held in suspense under the eye of the commander-in-chief, to take the direction which the latter shall prescribe as the struggle develops. The mere menace of such a force, just out of gunshot to windward, would be sufficient to prevent any extensive maneuver of the unengaged enemies. Nelson doubtless had in mind the dispositions, more than a century old, of Tourville and De Ruyter, by which a few ships, spaced to windward of an enemy's van, could check its tacking, because of the raking fire to which they would subject it. Unquestionably, he would not have kept long in idle expectancy twenty-four ships, the number he had in mind; but clearly also he proposed to hold them until he saw how things went with Collingwood. Thus much time would allow, granting the position he assumed and a reasonable breeze. His twenty-four to windward held an absolute check over the supposed thirty-four unengaged, of the enemy.

The attack as planned, therefore, differed from that executed (1) in that the lee line was not to advance in column, but in line, thereby dispersing the enemy's fire, and avoiding the terrific concentration which crushed the leaders at Trafalgar; and (2) in that the weather squadrons were not to attack simultaneously with the lee, but after it had engaged, in order to permit the remedying of any mishap that might arise in delivering the crucial blow. In both these matters of detail the plan was better than the modification; but the latter was forced upon Nelson by conditions beyond his control.[1]

The Battle

Napoleon's commands to enter the Mediterranean reached Villeneuve on September 27. The following day, when Nelson was joining his fleet, the admiral acknowledged their receipt, and submissively reported his intention to obey as soon as the wind served. Before he could do so, accurate intelligence was received of the strength of Nelson's force, which the emperor had not known. Villeneuve assembled a council of war to consider the situation, and the general opinion was adverse to sailing; but the commander-in-chief, alleging the orders of Napoleon, announced his determination to follow them. To this all submitted. An event, then unforeseen by Villeneuve, precipitated his action.

Admiral Rosily's approach was known in Cadiz

---

[1] Here the narrative is resumed from "The Influence of Sea Power upon the French Revolution and Empire." — EDITOR.

some time before he could arrive. It at first made little impression upon Villeneuve, who was not expecting to be superseded. On the 11th of October, however, along with the news that his successor had reached Madrid, there came to him a rumor of the truth. His honor took alarm. If not allowed to remain afloat, how remove the undeserved imputation of cowardice which he knew had by some been attached to his name. He at once wrote to Decrès that he would have been well content if permitted to continue with the fleet in a subordinate capacity; and closed with the words, " I will sail to-morrow, if circumstances favor."

The wind next day was fair, and the combined fleets began to weigh. On the 19th eight ships got clear of the harbor, and by ten A.M. Nelson, far at sea, knew by signal that the long-expected movement had begun. He at once made sail toward the Straits of Gibraltar to bar the entrance of the Mediterranean to the allies. On the 20th, all the latter, thirty-three ships-of-the-line accompanied by five frigates and two brigs, were at sea, steering with a south-west wind to the northward and westward to gain the offing needed before heading direct for the Straits. That morning Nelson, for whom the wind had been fair, was lying to off Cape Spartel to intercept the enemy; and learning from his frigates that they were north of him, he stood in that direction to meet them.

During the day the wind shifted to west, still fair for the British and allowing the allies, by going about, to head south. It was still very weak, so that the progress of the fleets was slow. During the night both maneuvered; the allies to gain, the British to retain, the position they wished. At daybreak of the 21st they were in presence, the French and Spaniards steering south in five columns; of which the two to windward, containing together twelve ships, constituted a detached squadron of observation under Admiral Gravina. The remaining twenty-one formed the main body, commanded by Villeneuve. Cape Trafalgar, from which the battle took its name, was on the south-eastern horizon, ten or twelve miles from the allies; and the British fleet was at the same distance from them to the westward.

Soon after daylight Villeneuve signalled to form line of battle on the starboard tack, on which they were then sailing, heading south. In performing this evolution Gravina with his twelve ships took post in the van of the allied fleet, his own flag-ship heading the column. It is disputed between the French and Spaniards whether this step was taken by Villeneuve's order, or of Gravina's own motion. In either case, these twelve, by abandoning their central and windward position, sacrificed to a great extent their power to reinforce any threatened part of the order, and also unduly extended a line already too long. In the end, instead of being a reserve well in hand, they became the helpless victims of the British concentration.

At eight A.M. Villeneuve saw that battle could not be shunned. Wishing to have Cadiz under his lee in case of disaster, he ordered the combined fleet to wear together. The signal was clumsily executed; but by ten all had gone round and were heading north in inverse order, Gravina's squadron in the rear. At eleven Villeneuve directed this squadron to keep well to windward, so as to be in position to succor the center, upon which the enemy seemed about to make his chief attack; a judicious order, but rendered fruitless by the purpose of the British to concentrate on the rear itself. When this signal was made, Cadiz was twenty miles distant in the north-north-east, and the course of the allies was carrying them toward it.

Owing to the lightness of the wind Nelson would lose no time in maneuvering. He formed his fleet rapidly in two divisions, each in single column, the simplest and most flexible order of attack, and the one whose regularity is most easily preserved. The simple column, however, unflanked, sacrifices during the critical period of closing the support given by the rear ships to the leader, and draws upon the latter the concentrated fire of the enemy's line. Its use by Nelson on this occasion has been much criticized. It is therefore to be remarked that, although his orders, issued several days previous to the battle, are somewhat ambiguous on this point, their natural meaning seems to indicate the intention, if attacking from to windward, to draw up with his fleet in two columns parallel to the enemy and abreast his rear. Then the column nearest the enemy, the lee, keeping away together, would advance in line against the twelve rear ships; while the weather column, moving forward, would hold in check the remainder of the hostile fleet. In either event, whether attacking in column or in line, the essential feature of his plan was to overpower twelve of the enemy by sixteen British, while the remainder of his force covered this operation. The destruction of the rear was entrusted to the second in command; he himself with a smaller body took charge of the more un-certain duties of the containing force. " The second in command," wrote he in his memorable order, " will, after my instructions are made known to him, have the entire direction of his line."

The justification of Nelson's dispositions for battle at Trafalgar rests therefore primarily upon the sluggish breeze, which would so have delayed formations as to risk the loss of the opportunity. It must also be observed that, although a column of ships does not possess the sustained momentum of a column of men, whose depth and mass combine to drive it through the relatively thin resistance of a line, and so cut the latter in twain, the results nevertheless are closely analogous. The leaders in either case are sacrificed, — success is won over their prostrate forms; but the continued impact upon one part of the enemy's order is essentially a concentration, the issue of which, if long enough maintained, cannot be doubtful. Penetration, sever-ance, and the enveloping of one of the parted frag-ments, must be the result. So, exactly, it was at Trafalgar. It must also be noted that the rear ships of either column, until they reached the hostile line, swept with their broadsides the sea over which enemy's ships from either flank might try to come to the support of the attacked center. No such attempt was in fact made from either extremity of the combined fleet.

The two British columns were nearly a mile apart and advanced on parallel courses, — heading nearly east, but a little to the northward to allow for the gradual advance in that direction of the hostile fleet. The northern or left-hand column, commonly called the " weather line " because the wind came rather from that side, contained twelve ships, and was led by Nelson himself in the *Victory*, a ship of one hundred guns. The *Royal Sovereign,* of the same size and carrying Collingwood's flag, headed the right column, of fifteen ships.

To the British advance the allies opposed the traditional order of battle, a long single line, close-hauled, — in this case heading north, with the wind from west-north-west. The distance from one flank to the other was nearly five miles. Owing partly to the lightness of the breeze, partly to the great number of ships, and partly to the inefficiency of many of the units of the fleet, the line was very imperfectly formed. Ships were not in their places, intervals were of irregular width, here vessels were not closed up, there two overlapped, one masking the other's fire. The general result was that, instead of a line, the allied order showed a curve of gradual sweep, convex toward the east. To the British approach from the west, therefore, it presented a disposition resembling a re-entrant angle; and Collingwood, noting with observant eye the advantage of this arrangement for a cross-fire, com-

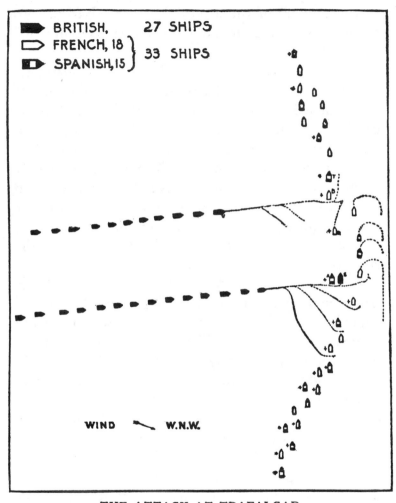

THE ATTACK AT TRAFALGAR
OCTOBER 21, 1805
5 minutes past noon

The French and Spanish ships marked + were taken or destroyed in the action.

REFERENCES

A. Santa Ana, Alava's Flagship
B. Bucentaure, Villeneuve's Flagship
P. Principe De Asturias, Gravina's Flagship
R. Redoutable

S. Royal Sovereign, Collingwood's Flagship
T. Santisima Trinidad
V. Victory, Nelson's Flagship

Recent investigation has shown that Collingwood's division was much more nearly parallel to the enemy than is indicated in this diagram, and thus in a formation more closely resembling Nelson's original plan. — *Editor.*

mented favorably upon it in his report of the battle. It was, however, the result of chance, not of intention, — due, not to the talent of the chief, but to the want of skill in his subordinates.

The commander-in-chief of the allies, Villeneuve, was in the *Bucentaure,* an eighty-gun ship, the twelfth in order from the van of the line. Immediately ahead of him was the huge Spanish four-decker, the *Santisima Trinidad,* a Goliath among ships, which had now come forth to her last battle. Sixth behind the *Bucentaure,* and therefore eighteenth in the order, came a Spanish three-decker, the *Santa Ana,* flying the flag of Vice-Admiral Alava. These two admirals marked the right and left of the allied center, and upon them, therefore, the British leaders respectively directed their course, — Nelson upon the *Bucentaure*, Collingwood upon the *Santa Ana.*

The *Royal Sovereign* had recently been refitted, and with clean new copper easily outsailed her more worn followers. Thus it happened that, as Collingwood came within range, his ship, outstripping the others by three quarters of a mile, entered alone, and for twenty minutes endured, unsupported, the fire of all the hostile ships that could reach her. A proud deed, surely, but surely also not a deed to be commended as a pattern. The first shot of the battle was fired at her by the *Fougueux,* the next astern of the *Santa Ana.* This was just at noon, and with the opening guns the ships of both fleets hoisted their ensigns; the Spaniards also hanging large wooden crosses from their spanker booms.

The *Royal Sovereign* advanced in silence until, ten minutes later, she passed close under the stern of the *Santa Ana*. Then she fired a double-shotted broadside which struck down four hundred of the enemy's crew, and, luffing rapidly, took her position close alongside, the muzzles of the hostile guns nearly touching. Here the *Royal Sovereign* underwent the fire not only of her chief antagonist, but of four other ships; three of which belonged to the division of five that ought closely to have knit the *Santa Ana* to the *Bucentaure,* and so fixed an impassable barrier to the enemy seeking to pierce the center. The fact shows strikingly the looseness of the allied order, these three being all in rear and to leeward of their proper stations.

For fifteen minutes the *Royal Sovereign* was the only British ship in close action. Then her next astern entered the battle, followed successively by the rest of the column. In rear of the *Santa Ana* were fifteen ships. Among these, Collingwood's vessels penetrated in various directions; chiefly, however, at first near the spot where his flag had led the way, enveloping and destroying in detail the enemy's center and leading rear ships, and then passing on to subdue the rest. Much doubtless was determined by chance in such confusion and obscurity; but the original tactical plan ensured an overwhelming concentration upon a limited portion of the enemy's order. This being subdued with the less loss, because so outnumbered, the intelligence and skill of the various British captains readily compassed the destruction of the dwindling remnant.

Of the sixteen ships, including the *Santa Ana,* which composed the allied rear, twelve were taken or destroyed.

Not till one o'clock, or nearly half an hour after the vessels next following Collingwood came into action, did the *Victory* reach the *Bucentaure.* The latter was raked with the same dire results that befell the *Santa Ana;* but a ship close to leeward blocked the way, and Nelson was not able to grapple with the enemy's commander-in-chief. The *Victory,* prevented from going through the line, fell on board the *Redoutable,* a French seventy-four, between which and herself a furious action followed, — the two lying in close contact. At half-past one Nelson fell mortally wounded, the battle still raging fiercely.

The ship immediately following Nelson's came also into collision with the *Redoutable,* which thus found herself in combat with two antagonists. The next three of the British weather column each in succession raked the *Bucentaure,* complying thus with Nelson's order that every effort must be made to capture the enemy's commander-in-chief. Passing on, these three concentrated their efforts, first upon the *Bucentaure,* and next upon the *Santisima Trinidad.* Thus it happened that upon the allied commander-in-chief, upon his next ahead, and upon the ship which, though not his natural supporter astern, had sought and filled that honorable post, — upon the key, in short, of the allied order, — were combined under the most advantageous conditions the fires of five hostile vessels, three of them first-rates. Consequently, not only were the three added to the prizes, but also a great breach was made between the van and rear of the combined fleets. This breach became yet wider by the singular conduct of Villeneuve's proper next astern. Soon after the *Victory* came into action, that ship bore up out of the line, wore round, and stood toward the rear, followed by three others. This movement is attributed to a wish to succor the rear. If so, it was at best an indiscreet and ill-timed act, which finds little palliation in the fact that not one of these ships was taken.

Thus, two hours after the battle began, the allied fleet was cut in two, the rear enveloped and in process of being destroyed in detail, the *Bucentaure, Santisima Trinidad,* and *Redoutable* practically reduced, though not yet surrendered. Ahead of the *Santisima Trinidad* were ten ships, which as yet had not been engaged. The inaction of the van, though partly accounted for by the slackness of the wind, has given just cause for censure. To it, at ten minutes before two, Villeneuve made signal to get into action and to wear together. This was accomplished with difficulty, owing to the heavy swell and want of wind. At three, however, all the ships were about, but by an extraordinary fatality they did not keep together. Five with Admiral Dumanoir stood along to windward of the battle, three passed to leeward of it, and two, keeping away, left the field entirely. Of the whole number, three were intercepted, raising the loss of the allies to eighteen ships-of-the-line taken, one of which caught fire and was burned. The approach of Admiral Dumanoir, if made an hour earlier, might have conduced to save Villeneuve; it was now too late. Exchanging a few distant broadsides with enemy's ships, he stood off to the south-west with four vessels; one of those at first with him having been cut off.

At quarter before five Admiral Gravina, whose ship had been the rear of the order during the battle and had lost heavily, retreated toward Cadiz, making signal to the vessels which had not struck to form around his flag. Five other Spanish ships and five French followed him. As he was withdrawing, the last two to resist of the allied fleet struck their colors.

During the night of the 21st these eleven ships anchored at the mouth of Cadiz harbor, which they could not then enter, on account of a land wind from south-east. At the same time the British and their prizes were being carried shoreward by the heavy swell which had prevailed during the battle; the light air blowing from the sea not enabling them to haul off. The situation was one of imminent peril. At midnight the wind freshened much, but fortunately hauled to the southward, whence it blew a gale all the 22d. The ships got their heads to the westward and drew off shore, with thirteen of the prizes; the other four having had to anchor off Cape Trafalgar. That morning the *Bucentaure,* Villeneuve's late flag-ship, was wrecked on some rocks off the entrance to Cadiz; and toward evening the *Redoutable,* that had so nobly supported her, was found to be sinking astern of the British ship that had her in tow. During the night of the 22d she went down with a hundred and fifty of her people still on board. On the 24th the same fate befell the great *Santisima Trinidad,* which had been the French admiral's next ahead. Thus his own ship and his two supports vanished from the seas.

For several days the wind continued violent from north-west and south-west. On the 23d five of the ships that had escaped with Gravina put out, to cut off some of the prizes that were near the coast. They succeeded in taking two; but as these were battered to pieces, while three of the five rescuers were carried on the beach and wrecked with great loss of life, little advantage resulted from this well-meant and gallant sortie. Two other prizes were given up to their own crews by the British prize-masters, because the latter were not able with their scanty force to save them. These got into Cadiz. Of the remaining British prizes, all but four either went ashore or were destroyed by the orders of Collingwood, who despaired of saving them. No British ship was lost.

Of thirty-three combined French and Spanish ships which sailed out of Cadiz on the 20th of October, eleven, five French and six Spanish, mostly now disabled hulks, lay there at anchor on the last day of the month. The four that escaped to sea under Dumanoir fell in with a British squadron of the same size near Cape Ortegal, on the 4th of November, and were all taken. This raised the allied loss to twenty-two, — two more than the twenty for which Nelson, in his dying hour, declared that he had bargained.

No attempt to move from Cadiz was again made by the shattered relics of the fight. On the 25th of October Rosily arrived and took up his now blasted command. Nearly three years later, when the Spanish monarchy, so long the submissive tool of the Directory and of Napoleon, had been overthrown by the latter, and the Spanish people had risen against the usurper, the five French ships were still in the port. Surprised between the British blockade and the now hostile batteries of the coast, Rosily, after an engagement of two days with the latter, surrendered his squadron, with the four thousand seamen then on board. This event occurred on the 14th of June, 1808. It was the last echo of Trafalgar.

Such, in its leading outlines and direct consequences, was the famous battle of Trafalgar. Its lasting significance and far-reaching results have been well stated by a recent historian, more keenly alive than most of his fellows to the paramount, though silent, influence of Sea Power upon the course of events: " Trafalgar was not only the greatest naval victory, it was the greatest and most momentous victory won either by land or by sea during the whole of the Revolutionary War. No victory, and no series of victories, of Napoleon produced the same effect upon Europe. . . . A generation passed after Trafalgar before France again seriously threatened England at sea. The prospect of crushing the British navy, so long as England had the means to equip a navy, vanished. Napoleon henceforth set his hopes on exhausting

England's resources, by compelling every state on the Continent to exclude her commerce. Trafalgar forced him to impose his yoke upon *all* Europe, or to abandon the hope of conquering Great Britain. . . . Nelson's last triumph left England in such a position that no means remained to injure her but those which *must result in the ultimate deliverance of the Continent.*" [1]

These words may be accepted with very slight modification. Napoleon's scheme for the invasion of Great Britain, thwarted once and again by the strategic difficulties attendant upon its execution, was finally frustrated when Villeneuve gave up the attempt to reach Brest and headed for Cadiz. On the part of the allies Trafalgar was, in itself, a useless holocaust, precipitated in the end by the despair of the unfortunate admiral, upon whose irresolution Napoleon not unjustly visited the anger caused by the wreck of his plans. Villeneuve was perfectly clear-sighted and right in his appreciation of the deficiencies of his command, — of the many chances against success. Where he wretchedly failed was in not recognizing the simple duty of obedience, — the obligation to persist at all hazards in the part of a great scheme assigned to him, even though it led to the destruction of his whole force. Had he, upon leaving Ferrol, been visited by a little of the desperation which brought him to Trafalgar, the invasion of England might possibly — not probably — have been effected.

An event so striking as the battle of Trafalgar

[1] Fyffe's "History of Modern Europe," Vol. I, p. 281.

becomes, however, to mankind the symbol of all the circumstances — more important, perhaps, but less obvious — which culminate in it. In this sense it may be said that Trafalgar was the cause — as it certainly marked the period — of Napoleon's resolution to crush Great Britain by excluding her commerce from the Continent. Here, therefore, the story of the influence of Sea Power upon this great conflict ceases to follow the strictly naval events, and becomes concerned simply with commerce-destroying, ordinarily a secondary operation of maritime war, but exalted in the later years of Napoleon's reign to be the principal, if not the sole, means of action.

Commerce Warfare after Trafalgar

The warfare against commerce during the French Revolution, alike under the Republic and under Napoleon, was marked by the same passionate vehemence, the same extreme and far-reaching conceptions, the same obstinate resolve utterly to overthrow and extirpate every opposing force, that characterized the political and military enterprises of the period. In the effort to bring under the yoke of their own policy the commerce of the whole world, the two chief contestants, France and Great Britain, swayed back and forth in deadly grapple over the vast arena, trampling under foot the rights and interests of the weaker parties; who, whether as neutrals, or as subjects of friendly or allied powers, looked helplessly on, and found that in this great struggle for self-preservation, neither outcries, nor threats, nor despairing submission, availed to lessen the pressure that was gradually crushing out both hope and life. The question between Napoleon and the British people became simply one of endurance, as was tersely and powerfully shown by the emperor himself. Both were expending their capital, and drawing freely drafts upon the future, the one in money, the other in men, to sustain their present strength. Like two infuriated dogs, they had locked jaws over commerce, as the decisive element in the contest. Neither would let go his grip until failing vitality should loose it, or until some bystander should deal one a wound through which the powers of life should drain away. All now know that in the latter way the end came. The commercial policy of the great monarch, who, from the confines of Europe, had watched the tussle with all the eagerness of self-interest, angered Napoleon. To enforce his will, he made new and offensive annexations of territory. The czar replied by a commercial edict, sharp and decisive, and war was determined. " It is all a scene in the Opera," wrote Napoleon,[1] " and the English are the scene shifters." Words failed the men of that day to represent the grandeur and apparent solidity of the Empire in 1811, when Napoleon's heir was born. In December, 1812, it was shattered from turret to foundation stone; wrecked in the attempt " to conquer the sea by the land." The scene was shifted indeed.

[1] To the King of Wurtemburg, April 2, 1811; "Corr.," Vol. XXII, p. 19.

Great Britain remained victorious on the field, but she had touched the verge of ruin. Confronted with the fixed resolution of her enemy to break down her commerce by an absolute exclusion from the continent of Europe, and as far as possible from the rest of the world, she met the challenge by a measure equally extreme, forbidding all neutral vessels to enter ports hostile to her, unless they had first touched at one of her own. Shut out herself from the Continent, she announced that while this exclusion lasted she would shut the Continent off from all external intercourse. " No trade except *through* England," was the formula under which her leaders expressed their purpose. The entrance of Russia into this strife, under the provocations of Napoleon, prevented the problem, which of these two policies would overthrow the other, from reaching a natural solution; and the final result of the measures which it is one object of this and the following chapter to narrate must remain for ever uncertain. It is, however, evident that a commercial and manufacturing country like Great Britain must, in a strife the essence of which was the restriction of trade, suffer more than one depending, as France did, mainly upon her internal resources. The question, as before stated, was whether she could endure the greater drain by her greater wealth. Upon the whole, the indications were, and to the end continued to be, that she could do so; that Napoleon, in entering upon this particular struggle, miscalculated his enemy's strength.

But besides this, here, as in every contest where

the opponents are closely matched, where power and discipline and leadership are nearly equal, there was a further question: which of the two would make the first and greatest mistakes, and how ready the other party was to profit by his errors. In so even a balance, the wisest prophet cannot foresee how the scale will turn. The result will depend not merely upon the skill of the swordsman in handling his weapons, but also upon the wariness of his fence and the quickness of his returns; much, too, upon his temper. Here also Napoleon was worsted. Scarcely was the battle over commerce joined, when the uprising of Spain was precipitated by overconfidence; Great Britain hastened at once to place herself by the side of the insurgents. Four years later, when the British people were groaning in a protracted financial crisis, — when, if ever, there was a hope that the expected convulsion and ruin were at hand, — Napoleon, instead of waiting for his already rigorous blockade to finish the work he attributed to it, strove to draw it yet closer, by demands which were unnecessary and to which the czar could not yield. Again Great Britain seized her opportunity, received her late enemy's fleet, and filled his treasury. Admit the difficulties of Napoleon; allow as we may for the intricacy of the problem before him; the fact remains that he wholly misunderstood the temper of the Spanish people, the dangers of the Spanish enterprise, the resolution of Alexander. On the other hand, looking upon the principal charge against the policy of the British government, that it alienated the United States, it is still true that there was no miscalculation as to the long-suffering of the latter under the guidance of Jefferson, with his passion for peace. The submission of the United States lasted until Napoleon was committed to his final blunder, thus justifying the risk taken by Great Britain and awarding to her the strategic triumph.

. . . As regards the rightfulness of the action of the two parties, viewed separately from their policy, opinions will probably always differ, according to the authority attributed by individuals to the *dicta* of International Law. It may be admitted at once that neither Napoleon's decrees nor the British orders can be justified at that bar, except by the simple plea of self-preservation, — the first law of states even more than of men; for no government is empowered to assent to that last sacrifice, which the individual may make for the noblest motives. The beneficent influence of the mass of conventions known as International Law is indisputable, nor should its authority be lightly undermined; but it cannot prevent the interests of belligerents and neutrals from clashing, nor speak with perfect clearness in all cases where they do. Of this the Rule of 1756 offered, in its day, a conspicuous instance. The belligerent claimed that the neutral, by covering with his flag a trade previously the monopoly of the enemy, not only inflicted a grave injury by snatching from him a lawful prey, but was guilty likewise of a breach of neutrality; the neutral contended that the enemy had a right to change his commercial regulations, in war as well as in peace. To the author, though an American, the belligerent argument seems the stronger; nor was the laudable desire of the neutral for gain a nobler motive than the solicitude, about their national resources, of men who rightly believed themselves engaged in a struggle for national existence. The measure meted to Austria and Prussia was an ominous indication of the fate Great Britain might expect, if her strength failed her. But, whatever the decision of our older and milder civilization on the merits of the particular question, there can be no doubt of the passionate earnestness of the two disputants in their day, nor of the conviction of right held by either. In such a dilemma, the last answer of International Law has to be that every state is the final judge as to whether it should or should not make war; to its own self alone is it responsible for the rightfulness of this action. If, however, the condition of injury entailed by the neutral's course is such as to justify war, it justifies all lesser means of control. The question of the rightfulness of these disappears, and that of policy alone remains.

It is the business of the neutral, by his prepared condition, to make impolitic that which he claims is also wrong. The neutral which fails to do so, which leaves its ports defenseless and its navy stunted until the emergency comes, will then find, as the United States found in the early years of this century, an admirable opportunity to write State Papers.

26. General Strategy of the War of 1812 [1]

THE general considerations that have been advanced are sufficient to indicate what should have been the general plan of the war on the part of the United States. Every war must be aggressive, or, to use the technical term, offensive, in military character; for unless you injure the enemy, if you confine yourself, as some of the grumblers of that day would have it, to simple defense against his efforts, obviously he has no inducement to yield your contention. Incidentally, however, vital interests must be defended, otherwise the power of offense falls with them. Every war, therefore, has both a defensive and an offensive side, and in an effective plan of campaign each must receive due attention. Now, in 1812, so far as general natural conditions went, the United States was relatively weak on the sea frontier, and strong on the side of Canada. The seaboard might, indeed, in the preceding ten years, have been given a development of force, by the creation of an adequate navy, which would have prevented war, by the obvious danger to British interests involved in hostilities. But this had not been done; and Jefferson, by his gunboat policy, building some two hundred of those vessels, worth-

[1] "Sea Power in its Relations with the War of 1812," Vol. I, pp. 295–308; Vol. II, pp. 121–125.

less unless under cover of the land, proclaimed by act as by voice his adherence to a bare defensive. The sea frontier, therefore, became mainly a line of defense, the utility of which primarily was, or should have been, to maintain communication with the outside world; to support commerce, which in turn should sustain the financial potency that determines the issues of war.

. . . . . Such in general was the condition of the sea frontier, thrown inevitably upon the defensive. With the passing comment that, had it been defended as suggested [by a squadron of respectable battleships in concentrated strength. — EDITOR], Great Britain would never have forced the war, let us now consider conditions on the Canadian line, where circumstances eminently favored the offensive by the United States; for this war should not be regarded simply as a land war or a naval war, nor yet as a war of offense and again one of defense, but as being continuously and at all times both offensive and defensive, both land and sea, in reciprocal influence.

Disregarding as militarily unimportant the artificial boundary dividing Canada from New York, Vermont, and the eastern parts of the Union, the frontier separating the land positions of the two belligerents was the Great Lakes and the river St. Lawrence. This presented certain characteristic and unusual features. That it was a water line was a condition not uncommon; but it was exceptionally marked by those broad expanses which constitute inland seas of great size and depth, navigable by vessels of the largest sea-going dimensions. This water system, being continuous and in continual progress, is best conceived by applying to the whole, from Lake Superior to the ocean, the name of the great river, the St. Lawrence, which on the one hand unites it to the sea, and on the other divides the inner waters from the outer by a barrier of rapids, impassable to ships that otherwise could navigate freely both lakes and ocean.

The importance of the lakes to military operations must always be great, but it was much enhanced in 1812 by the undeveloped condition of land communications. With the roads in the state they then were, the movement of men, and still more of supplies, was vastly more rapid by water than by land. Except in winter, when iron-bound snow covered the ground, the routes of Upper Canada were well-nigh impassable; in spring and in autumn rains, wholly so to heavy vehicles. The mail from Montreal to York, — now Toronto, — three hundred miles, took a month in transit.[1] In October, 1814, when the war was virtually over, the British general at Niagara lamented to the commander-in-chief that, owing to the refusal of the navy to carry troops, an important detachment was left " to struggle through the dreadful roads from Kingston to York." [2] " Should reinforcements and provisions not arrive, the naval commander would," in his opinion, " have much to answer for." [3] The com-

[1] Kingsford's "History of Canada," Vol. VIII, p. 111.
[2] Drummond to Prevost, Oct. 20, 1814. Report on Canadian Archives, 1896, Upper Canada, p. 9.
[3] *Ibid.*, Oct. 15.

mander-in-chief himself wrote: " The command of
the lakes enables the enemy to perform in two days
what it takes the troops from Kingston sixteen to
twenty days of severe marching. Their men arrive
fresh; ours fatigued, and with exhausted equipment.
The distance from Kingston to the Niagara frontier
exceeds two hundred and fifty miles, and part of
the way is impracticable for supplies." [1] On the
United States side, road conditions were similar but
much less disadvantageous. The water route by
Ontario was greatly preferred as a means of transportation, and in parts and at certain seasons was
indispensable. Stores for Sackett's Harbor, for
instance, had in early summer to be brought to
Oswego, and thence coasted along to their destination, in security or in peril, according to the momentary predominance of one party or the other
on the lake. In like manner, it was more convenient to move between the Niagara frontier and
the east end of the lake by water; but in case of
necessity, men could march. An English traveler
in 1818 says: " I accomplished the journey from
Albany to Buffalo in October in six days with ease
and comfort, whereas in May it took ten of great
difficulty and distress." [2] In the farther West the
American armies, though much impeded, advanced
securely through Ohio and Indiana to the shores of
Lake Erie, and there maintained themselves in supplies sent over-country; whereas the British at the

[1] Prevost to Bathurst, Aug. 14, 1814. Report on Canadian Archives,
1896, Lower Canada, p. 36.
[2] "Travels," J. M. Duncan, Vol. II, p. 27.

western end of the lake, opposite Detroit, depended wholly upon the water, although no hostile force threatened the land line between them and Ontario. The battle of Lake Erie, so disastrous to their cause, was forced upon them purely by failure of food, owing to the appearance of Perry's squadron.

. . . The opinion of competent soldiers on the spot, such as Craig and Brock, in full possession of all the contemporary facts, may be accepted explicitly as confirming the inferences which in any event might have been drawn from the natural features of the situation. Upon Mackinac and Detroit depended the control and quiet of the Northwestern country, because they commanded vital points on its line of communication. Upon Kingston and Montreal, by their position and intrinsic advantages, rested the communication of all Canada, along and above the St. Lawrence, with the sea power of Great Britain, whence alone could be drawn the constant support without which ultimate defeat should have been inevitable. Naval power, sustained upon the Great Lakes, controlled the great line of communication between the East and West, and also conferred upon the party possessing it the strategic advantage of interior lines; that is, of shorter distances, both in length and time, to move from point to point of the lake shores, close to which lay the scenes of operations. It followed that Detroit and Michilimackinac, being at the beginning in the possession of the United States, should have been fortified, garrisoned, provisioned, in readiness for siege, and placed in close communication with home, as soon as war was seen to be imminent, which it was in December, 1811, at latest. Having in that quarter everything to lose, and comparatively little to gain, the country was thrown on the defensive. On the east the possession of Montreal or Kingston would cut off all Canada above from support by the sea, which would be equivalent to ensuring its fall. "I shall continue to exert myself to the utmost to overcome every difficulty," wrote Brock, who gave such emphatic proof of energetic and sagacious exertion in his subsequent course. "Should, however, the communication between Montreal and Kingston be cut off, the fate of the troops in this part of the province will be decided."[1] "The Montreal frontier," said the officer selected by the Duke of Wellington to report on the defenses of Canada, "is the most important, and at present [1826] confessedly most vulnerable and accessible part of Canada."[2] There, then, was the direction for offensive operations by the United States; preferably against Montreal, for, if successful, a much larger region would be isolated and reduced. Montreal gone, Kingston could receive no help from without; and, even if capable of temporary resistance, its surrender would be but a question of time. Coincidently with this military advance, naval development for the control of the lakes should have proceeded, as a discreet precaution; although, after the fall of Kingston and Montreal, there could have been little use of an

---

[1] "Life of Brock," p. 193.
[2] Smyth, "Précis of the Wars in Canada," p. 167.

inland navy, for the British local resources would then have been inadequate to maintain an opposing force.

Results of the Northern Campaign

[While control was more vital and the forces stronger on Lake Ontario than on either Erie or Champlain, no naval action of consequence occurred there in 1813 or in fact throughout the war. Yeo, the British commander, was enjoined by Admiralty orders to take no risks; and the American Commodore Chauncey, with no such justification, adopted a similar policy. Hence the important fleet actions of the war were in other waters — Perry's victory of September 10, 1813, on Lake Erie, and Macdonough's victory on Lake Champlain a year later. The first sentence in the paragraph following refers to a raid on Buffalo, December 30, 1813. — EDITOR.]

With this may be said to have terminated the northern campaign of 1813. The British had regained full control of the Niagara peninsula, and they continued to hold Fort Niagara, in the State of New York, till peace was concluded. The only substantial gain on the whole frontier, from the extreme east to the extreme west, was the destruction of the British fleet on Lake Erie, and the consequent transfer of power in the west to the United States. This was the left flank of the American position. Had the same result been accomplished on the right flank, — as it might have been, — at Montreal, or even at Kingston, the center and left must have fallen also. For the misdirection of effort to

Niagara, the local commanders, Dearborn and Chauncey, are primarily responsible; for Armstrong[1] yielded his own correct perceptions to the representations of the first as to the enemy's force, supported by the arguments of the naval officer favoring the diversion of effort from Kingston to Toronto. Whether Chauncey ever formally admitted to himself this fundamental mistake, which wrecked the summer's work upon Lake Ontario, does not appear; but that he had learned from experience is shown by a letter to the Secretary of the Navy,[2] when the squadrons had been laid up. In this he recognized the uselessness of the heavy sailing schooners when once a cruising force of ships for war had been created, thereby condemning much of his individual management of the campaign; and he added: " If it is determined to prosecute the war offensively, and secure our conquests in Upper Canada, Kingston ought unquestionably to be the first object of attack, and that so early in the spring as to prevent the enemy from using the whole of the naval force that he is preparing."

In the three chapters which here end, the Ontario operations have been narrated consecutively and at length, without interruption by other issues, — except the immediately related Lake Erie campaign, — because upon them turned, and upon them by the dispositions of the government this year were wrecked the fortunes of the war. The year 1813, from the opening of the spring to the closing in of

---

1 The United States Secretary of War. — EDITOR.
2 December 17, 1813. Captain's Letters, Navy Department.

winter, was for several reasons the period when conditions were most propitious to the American cause. In 1812 war was not begun until June, and then with little antecedent preparation; and it was waged half-heartedly, both governments desiring to nip hostilities. In 1814, on the other hand, when the season opened, Napoleon had fallen, and the United States no longer had an informal ally to divert the efforts of Great Britain. But in the intervening year, 1813, although the pressure upon the seaboard, the defensive frontier, was undoubtedly greater than before, and much vexation and harassment was inflicted, no serious injury was done beyond the suppression of commerce, inevitable in any event. In the north, on the lakes frontier, the offensive and the initiative continued in the hands of the United States. No substantial reinforcements reached Canada until long after the ice broke up, and then in insufficient numbers. British naval preparations had been on an inadequate scale, receiving no proper professional supervision. The American Government, on the contrary, had had the whole winter to prepare, and the services of a very competent naval organizer. It had also the same period to get ready its land forces; while incompetent Secretaries of War and of the Navy gave place in January to capable men in both situations.

With all this in its favor, and despite certain gratifying successes, the general outcome was a complete failure, the full measure of which could be realized only when the downfall of Napoleon revealed what disaster may result from neglect to seize opportunity while it exists. The tide then ebbed, and never again flowed. For this many causes may be alleged. The imbecile ideas concerning military and naval preparation which had prevailed since the opening of the century doubtless counted for much. The entrusting of chief command to broken-down men like Dearborn and Wilkinson was enough to ruin the best conceived schemes. But, despite these very serious drawbacks, the strategic misdirection of effort was the most fatal cause of failure.

There is a simple but very fruitful remark of a Swiss military writer, that every military line may be conceived as having three parts, the middle and the two ends, or flanks. As sound principle requires that military effort should not be distributed along the whole of an enemy's position, — unless in the unusual case of overwhelming superiority, — but that distinctly superior numbers should be concentrated upon a limited portion of it, this idea of a threefold division aids materially in considering any given situation. One third, or two thirds, of an enemy's line may be assailed, but very seldom the whole; and everything may depend upon the choice made for attack. Now the British frontier, which the United States was to assail, extended from Montreal on the east to Detroit on the west. Its three parts were: Montreal and the St. Lawrence on the east, or left flank; Ontario in the middle, centering at Kingston; and Erie on the right; the strength of the British position in the last-named section being at Detroit and Malden, because they commanded the straits upon which the Indian tribes depended for access to the east. Over against the British positions named lay those of the United States. Given in the same order, these were: Lake Champlain, and the shores of Ontario and of Erie, centering respectively in the naval stations at Sackett's Harbor and Presque Isle.

Accepting these definitions, which are too obvious to admit of dispute, what considerations should have dictated to the United States the direction of attack; the one, or two, parts out of the three, on which effort should be concentrated? The reply, as a matter of abstract, accepted, military principle, is certain. Unless very urgent reasons to the contrary exist, strike at one end rather than at the middle, because both ends can come up to help the middle against you quicker than one end can get to help the other; and, as between the two ends, strike at the one upon which the enemy most depends for reinforcements and supplies to maintain his strength. Sometimes this decision presents difficulties. Before Waterloo, Wellington had his own army as a center of interest; on his right flank the sea, whence came supplies and reinforcements from England; on his left the Prussian army, support by which was imminently necessary. On which flank would Napoleon throw the weight of his attack? Wellington reasoned, perhaps through national bias, intensified by years of official dependence upon sea support, that the blow would fall upon his right, and he strengthened it with a body of men sorely needed when the enemy came upon his left, in overwhelming numbers, seeking to separate him from the Prussians.

No such doubt was possible as to Canada in 1813. It depended wholly upon the sea, and it touched the sea at Montreal. The United States, with its combined naval and military strength, crude as the latter was, was at the beginning of 1813 quite able in material power to grapple two out of the three parts, — Montreal and Kingston. Had they been gained, Lake Erie would have fallen; as is demonstrated by the fact that the whole Erie region went down like a house of cards the moment Perry triumphed on the lake. His victory was decisive, simply because it destroyed the communications of Malden with the sea. The same result would have been achieved, with effect over a far wider region, by a similar success in the east.

27. LESSONS OF THE WAR WITH SPAIN [1]

The Possibilities of a " Fleet in Being "

[ADMIRAL Cervera left the Cape Verde Islands on April 29, 1898. After touching at Martinique on May 11, he coaled at Curaçao on the 15th, and entered Santiago on the 19th.

On news of Cervera's arrival at Martinique, Sampson's squadron from Porto Rico and Schley's Flying Squadron from Hampton Roads converged on Key West. Sampson had his full strength in the approaches to Havana by the 21st and Schley was off Cienfuegos, the chief southern port of Cuba, on the 22d.

"We cannot," writes Admiral Mahan, " expect ever again to have an enemy so entirely inapt as Spain showed herself to be; yet, even so, Cervera's division reached Santiago on the 19th of May, two days before our divisions appeared in the full force they could muster before Havana and Cienfuegos." [2] — EDITOR.]

As was before said, the disparity between the armored fleets of the two nations was nominally inconsiderable; and the Spaniards possessed one extremely valuable — and by us unrivalled — ad-

---

[1] "Lessons of the War with Spain" (1899), pp. 75–85.
[2] *Ibid.*, p. 157.

vantage in a nearly homogeneous group of five [1] armored cruisers, very fast, and very similar both in nautical qualities and in armament. It is difficult to estimate too highly the possibilities open to such a body of ships, regarded as a " fleet in being," to use an expression that many of our readers may have seen, but perhaps scarcely fully understood.

The phrase " fleet in being," having within recent years gained much currency in naval writing, demands — like the word " jingo " — preciseness of definition; and this, in general acceptance, it has not yet attained. It remains, therefore, somewhat vague, and so occasions misunderstandings between men whose opinions perhaps do not materially differ. The writer will not attempt to define, but a brief explanation of the term and its origin may not be amiss. It was first used, in 1690, by the British admiral Lord Torrington, when defending his course in declining to engage decisively, with an inferior force, a French fleet, then dominating in the Channel, and under cover of which it was expected that a descent upon the English coast would be made by a great French army. " Had I fought otherwise," he said, " our fleet had been totally lost, and the kingdom had lain open to invasion. As it was, most men were in fear that the French would invade; but I was always of another opinion, for I always said that whilst we had a fleet in being, they would not dare to make an attempt."

A " fleet in being," therefore, is one the existence

---

[1] In this number is included the *Emperador Carlos V*, which, however, did not accompany the other four under Cervera.

and maintenance of which, although inferior, on or near the scene of operations, is a perpetual menace to the various more or less exposed interests of the enemy, who cannot tell when a blow may fall, and who is therefore compelled to restrict his operations, otherwise possible, until that fleet can be destroyed or neutralized. It corresponds very closely to " a position on the flank and rear " of an enemy, where the presence of a smaller force, as every military student knows, harasses, and may even paralyze, offensive movements. When such a force is extremely mobile, as a fleet of armored cruisers may be, its power of mischief is very great; potentially, it is forever on the flank and rear, threatening the lines of communications. It is indeed as a threat to communications that the " fleet in being " is chiefly formidable.

The theory received concrete and convincing illustration during the recent hostilities, from the effect exerted — and justly exerted — upon our plans and movements by Cervera's squadron, until there had been assembled before Santiago a force at once so strong and so numerous as to make his escape very improbable. Even so, when a telegram was received from a capable officer that he had identified by night, off the north coast of Cuba, an armored cruiser, — which, if of that class, was most probably an enemy, — the sailing of Shafter's expedition was stopped until the report could be verified. So much for the positive, material influence — in the judgment of the writer, the reasonable influence — of a " fleet in being." As regards the moral effect, the effect upon the imagination, it is scarcely necessary more than to allude to the extraordinary play of the fancy, the kaleidoscopic effects elicited from our own people, and from some foreign critics, in propounding dangers for ourselves and ubiquity for Cervera. Against the infection of such tremors it is one of the tasks of those in responsibility to guard themselves and, if possible, their people. " Don't make pictures for yourself," was Napoleon's warning to his generals. " Every naval operation since I became head of the government has failed, because my admirals see double and have learned — where I don't know — that war can be made without running risks."

The probable value of a " fleet in being " has, in the opinion of the writer, been much overstated; for, even at the best, the game of evasion, which this is, if persisted in, can have but one issue. The superior force will in the end run the inferior to earth. In the meanwhile, however, vital time may have been lost. It is conceivable, for instance, that Cervera's squadron, if thoroughly effective, might, by swift and well-concealed movements, have detained our fleet in the West Indies until the hurricane of September, 1898, swept over the Caribbean. We had then no reserve to replace armored ships lost or damaged. But, for such persistence of action, there is needed in each unit of the " fleet in being " an efficiency rarely attainable, and liable to be lost by unforeseen accident at a critical moment. Where effect, nay, safety, depends upon mere celerity of movement, as in retreat, a crippled ship means a lost ship; or a lost fleet, if the body sticks to its disabled member. Such efficiency it is probable Cervera's division never possessed. The length of its passage across the Atlantic, however increased by the embarrassment of frequently re-coaling the torpedo destroyers, so far overpassed the extreme calculations of our naval authorities, that ready credence was given to an apparently authentic report that it had returned to Spain; the more so that such concentration was strategically correct, and it was incorrect to adventure an important detachment so far from home, without the reinforcement it might have received in Cadiz. This delay, in ships whose individual speed had originally been very high, has been commonly attributed in our service to the inefficiency of the engine-room force; and this opinion is confirmed by a Spanish officer writing in their " Revista de la Marina." " The Americans," he says, " keep their ships cruising constantly, in every sea, and therefore have a large and qualified engine-room force. We have but few machinists, and are almost destitute of firemen." This inequality, however, is fundamentally due to the essential differences of mechanical capacity and development in the two nations. An amusing story was told the writer some years ago by one of our consuls in Cuba. Making a rather rough passage between two ports, he saw an elderly Cuban or Spanish gentleman peering frequently into the engine-room, with evident uneasiness. When asked the cause of his concern, the reply was, " I don't feel comfortable unless the man in charge of the engines talks English to them."

When to the need of constant and sustained ability to move at high speed is added the necessity of frequent recoaling, allowing the hostile navy time to come up, it is evident that the active use of a " fleet in being," however perplexing to the enemy, must be both anxious and precarious to its own commander. The contest is one of strategic wits, and it is quite possible that the stronger, though slower, force, centrally placed, may, in these days of cables, be able to receive word and to corner its antagonist before the latter can fill his bunkers. Of this fact we should probably have received a very convincing illustration, had a satisfactory condition of our coast defenses permitted the Flying Squadron to be off Cienfuegos, or even off Havana, instead of in Hampton Roads. Cervera's entrance to Santiago was known to us within twenty-four hours. In twenty-four more it could have been communicated off Cienfeugos by a fast despatch boat, after which less than forty-eight would have placed our division before Santiago. The uncertainty felt by Commodore Schley, when he arrived off Cienfuegos, as to whether the Spanish division was inside or no, would not have existed had his squadron been previously blockading; and his consequent delay of over forty-eight hours — with the rare chance thus offered to Cervera — would not have occurred. To coal four great ships within that time was probably beyond the resources of Santiago; whereas the speed predicted for our own movements is rather below than above the dispositions contemplated to ensure it.

The great end of a war fleet, however, is not to chase, nor to fly, but to control the seas. Had Cervera escaped our pursuit at Santiago, it would have been only to be again paralyzed at Cienfuegos or at Havana. When speed, not force, is the reliance, destruction may be postponed, but can be escaped only by remaining in port. Let it not, therefore, be inferred, from the possible, though temporary, effect of a " fleet in being," that speed is the chief of all factors in the battleship. This plausible, superficial notion, too easily accepted in these days of hurry and of unreflecting dependence upon machinery as the all in all, threatens much harm to the future efficiency of the navy. Not speed, but power of offensive action, is the dominant factor in war. The decisive preponderant element of great land forces has ever been the infantry, which, it is needless to say, is also the slowest. The homely summary of the art of war, " To get there first with the most men," has with strange perverseness been so distorted in naval — and still more in popular — conception, that the second and more important consideration has been subordinated to the former and less essential. Force does not exist for mobility, but mobility for force. It is of no use to get there first unless, when the enemy in turn arrives, you have also the most men, — the greater force. This is especially true of the sea, because there inferiority of force — of gun power — cannot be compensated, as on land it at times may be, by judiciously using accidents of the ground. I do not propose to fall into an absurdity of my own by questioning the usefulness of higher speed, *provided* the increase is not purchased at the expense of strictly offensive power; but the time has come to say plainly that its value is being exaggerated; that it is in the battleship secondary to gun power; that a battle fleet can never attain, nor maintain, the highest rate of any ship in it, except of that one which at the moment is the slowest, for it is a commonplace of naval action that fleet speed is that of the slowest ship; that not exaggerated speed, but uniform speed — sustained speed — is the requisite of the battle fleet; that it is not machinery, as is often affirmed, but brains and guns, that win battles and control of the sea. The true speed of war is not headlong precipitancy, but the unremitting energy which wastes no time.

For the reasons that have been given, the safest, though not the most effective, disposition of an inferior " fleet in being " is to lock it up in an impregnable port or ports, imposing upon the enemy the intense and continuous strain of watchfulness against escape. This it was that Torrington, the author of the phrase, proposed for the time to do. Thus it was that Napoleon, to some extent before Trafalgar, but afterward with set and exclusive purpose, used the French Navy, which he was continually augmenting, and yet never, to the end of his reign, permitted again to undertake any serious expedition. The mere maintenance of several formidable detachments, in apparent readiness, from the Scheldt round to Toulon, presented to the British so many possibilities of mischief that they were compelled to keep constantly before each of the French ports a force superior to that within, entailing an expense and an anxiety by which the emperor hoped to exhaust their endurance. To some extent this was Cervera's position and function in Santiago, whence followed logically the advisability of a land attack upon the port, to force to a decisive issue a situation which was endurable only if incurable. " The destruction of Cervera's squadron," justly commented an Italian writer, before the result was known, " is the only really decisive fact that can result from the expedition to Santiago, because it will reduce to impotence the naval power of Spain. The determination of the conflict will depend throughout upon the destruction of the Spanish sea power, and not upon territorial descents, although the latter may aggravate the situation." The American admiral from before Santiago, when urging the expedition of a land force to make the bay untenable, telegraphed, " The destruction of this squadron will end the war; " and it did.

28. The Santiago Blockade [1]

OUR battle fleet before Santiago was more than powerful enough to crush the hostile squadron in a very short time if the latter attempted a stand-up fight. The fact was so evident that it was perfectly clear nothing of the kind would be hazarded; but, nevertheless, we could not afford to diminish the number of armored vessels on this spot, now become the determining center of the conflict. The possibility of the situation was twofold. Either the enemy might succeed in an effort at evasion, a chance which required us to maintain a distinctly superior force of battleships in order to allow the occasional absence of one or two for coaling or repairs, besides as many lighter cruisers as could be mustered for purposes of lookout, or, by merely remaining quietly at anchor, protected from attack by the lines of torpedoes, he might protract a situation which tended not only to wear out our ships, but also to keep them there into the hurricane season, — a risk which was not, perhaps, adequately realized by the people of the United States.

It is desirable at this point to present certain other elements of the naval situation which weightily affected naval action at the moment, and which, also, were probably overlooked by the nation at

1 "Lessons of the War with Spain" (1899), pp. 184–191.

large, for they give a concrete illustration of conditions, which ought to influence our national policy, as regards the navy, in the present and immediate future. We had to economize our ships because they were too few. There was no reserve. The Navy Department had throughout, and especially at this period, to keep in mind, not merely the exigencies at Santiago, but the fact that we had not a battleship in the home ports that could in six months be made ready to replace one lost or seriously disabled, as the *Massachusetts,* for instance, not long afterwards was, by running on an obstruction in New York Bay. Surprise approaching disdain was expressed, both before and after the destruction of Cervera's squadron, that the battle fleet was not sent into Santiago either to grapple the enemy's ships there, or to support the operations of the army, in the same way, for instance, that Farragut crossed the torpedo lines at Mobile. The reply — and, in the writer's judgment, the more than adequate reason — was that the country could not at that time, under the political conditions which then obtained, afford to risk the loss or disablement of a single battleship, unless the enterprise in which it was hazarded carried a reasonable probability of equal or greater loss to the enemy, leaving us, therefore, as strong as before relatively to the naval power which in the course of events might yet be arrayed against us. If we lost ten thousand men, the country could replace them; if we lost a battleship, it could not be replaced. The issue of the war, as a whole and in every locality to which it extended, depended upon naval force, and it was imperative to achieve, not success only, but success delayed no longer than necessary. A million of the best soldiers would have been powerless in face of hostile control of the sea. Dewey had not a battleship, but there can be no doubt that that capable admiral thought he ought to have one or more; and so he ought, if we had had them to spare. The two monitors would be something, doubtless, when they arrived; but, like all their class, they lacked mobility.

When Cámara started by way of Suez for the East, it was no more evident than it was before that we ought to have battleships there. That was perfectly plain from the beginning; but battleships no more than men can be in two places at once, and until Cámara's movement had passed beyond the chance of turning west, the Spanish fleet in the Peninsula had, as regarded the two fields of war, the West Indies and the Philippines, the recognized military advantage of an interior position. In accepting inferiority in the East, and concentrating our available force in the West Indies, thereby ensuring a superiority over any possible combination of Spanish vessels in the latter quarter, the Department acted rightly and in accordance with sound military precedent; but it must be remembered that the Spanish Navy was not the only possibility of the day. The writer was not in a position to know then, and does not know now, what weight the United States Government attached to the current rumors of possible political friction with other states whose people were notoriously sympathizers with our enemy. The public knows as much about that as he does; but it was clear that if a disposition to interfere did exist anywhere, it would not be lessened by a serious naval disaster to us, such as the loss of one of our few battleships would be. Just as in the maintenance of a technically "effective" blockade of the Cuban ports, so, also, in sustaining the entireness and vigor of the battle fleet, the attitude of foreign Powers as well as the strength of the immediate enemy had to be considered. For such reasons it was recommended that the orders on this point to Admiral Sampson should be peremptory; not that any doubt existed as to the discretion of that officer, who justly characterized the proposition to throw the ships upon the mine fields of Santiago as suicidal folly, but because it was felt that the burden of such a decision should be assumed by a superior authority, less liable to suffer in personal reputation from the idle imputations of over-caution, which at times were ignorantly made by some who ought to have known better, but did not. "The matter is left to your discretion," the telegram read, "except that the United States armored vessels must not be risked."

When Cervera's squadron was once cornered, an intelligent opponent would, under any state of naval preparedness, have seen the advisability of forcing him out of the port by an attack in the rear, which could be made only by an army. As Nelson said on one occasion, "What is wanted now is not more

ships, but troops." Under few conditions should
such a situation be prolonged. But the reasons
adduced in the last paragraph made it doubly in-
cumbent upon us to bring the matter speedily to an
issue, and the combined expedition from Tampa
was at once ordered. Having in view the number
of hostile troops in the country surrounding Santiago, as shown by the subsequent returns of
prisoners, and shrewdly suspected by ourselves
beforehand, it was undoubtedly desirable to employ
a larger force than was sent. The criticism made
upon the inadequate number of troops engaged in
this really daring movement is intrinsically sound,
and would be wholly accurate if directed, not against
the enterprise itself, but against the national short-
sightedness which gave us so trivial an army at the
outbreak of the war. The really hazardous nature
of the movement is shown by the fact that the
column of Escario, three thousand strong, from
Manzanillo, reached Santiago on July 3d; too
late, it is true, abundantly too late, to take part
in the defense of San Juan and El Caney, upon
holding which the city depended for food and
water; yet not so late but that it gives a shiver-
ing suggestion how much more arduous would have
been the task of our troops had Escario come
up in time. The incident but adds another to history's long list of instances where desperate energy
and economy of time have wrested safety out of the
jaws of imminent disaster. The occasion was one
that called upon us to take big risks; and success
merely justifies doubly an attempt which, from the

obvious balance of advantages and disadvantages, was antecedently justified by its necessity, and would not have been fair subject for blame, even had it failed.

The Navy Department did not, however, think that even a small chance of injury should be taken which could be avoided; and it may be remarked that, while the man is unfit for command who, on emergency, is unable to run a very great risk for the sake of decisive advantage, he, on the other hand, is only less culpable who takes even a small risk of serious harm against which reasonable precaution can provide. It has been well said that Nelson took more care of his topgallant masts, in ordinary cruising, than he did of his whole fleet when the enemy was to be checked or beaten; and this combination of qualities apparently opposed is found in all strong military characters to the perfection of which both are necessary.

29. "Fleet in Being" and "Fortress Fleet" [1]

The Port Arthur Squadron in the Russo-Japanese War

[At the outbreak of the Russo-Japanese War in February, 1904, Russia had three armored cruisers at Vladivostok, another at Chemulpo, Korea, and seven battleships, six cruisers, and a torpedo flotilla at Port Arthur. Three of the Port Arthur ships were badly damaged by torpedo attack on February 8, and the cruiser at Chemulpo was destroyed on the next day. Togo lost two of his six first-class battleships by running into a mine field off Port Arthur on May 15. In an attempt to escape to Vladivostok on August 10, the Port Arthur squadron lost a battleship and several cruisers; the remainder were sunk in the course of the Port Arthur siege. This lasted from May 27 to January 1, 1905. Even before February 8, 1904, the Japanese had begun transporting their troops to Korea; and after the fall of Port Arthur they were able to throw their full strength against General Kuropatkin in the decisive battle of Mukden, February 24, 1905. — EDITOR.]

I have been led, on an occasion not immediately connected with Naval Strategy, to observe that

1 "Naval Strategy," pp. 383–401.

errors and defeats are more obviously illustrative
of principles than successes are. It is from the
records of the beaten side that we are most surely
able to draw instruction. This is partly due to the
fact that the general or admiral who is worsted has
to justify himself to his people, perhaps also to his
Government. The naval practice of court-martial-
ing a defeated captain or admiral has been most
productive of the material which history, and the
art of war, both require for their treatment. Even
failing a court-martial, defeat cries aloud for explanation; whereas success, like charity, covers a
multitude of sins. To this day Marengo is the
victory of Napoleon, not of Desaix; and the
hazardous stretching of the French line which
caused the first defeat is by most forgotten in the
ultimate triumph. The man who has failed will of
his own motion bring out all that extenuates failure,
or relieves him from the imputation of it. The
victor is asked few questions; and if conscious of
mistakes he need not reveal them. More can be
found to criticize Kuropatkin and Rozhestvensky
than to recognize either their difficulties or their
merits. Probably few, even in this naval audience,
knew, or have noted, that on the day preceding that
on which two Japanese battleships, the *Hatsuse* and
Yashima, were sunk by Russian mines, not a Japanese scout was in sight, to notice the Russian vessel
engaged in the work which resulted so disastrously
to its foes. On that day, during that operation, no
Japanese vessel was visible to the lookouts at Port
Arthur.

For the reasons advanced, I turn at first, and more particularly, to the Russian naval action for illustration of principles, whether shown in right or wrong conduct; and here I first name *two* such principles, or formulation of maxims, as having been fundamental, and in my judgment fundamentally erroneous, in the Russian practice. These are mental conceptions, the first of which has been explicitly stated as controlling Russian plans, and influencing Russian military ideas; while the second may be deduced, inferentially, as exercising much effect. The first, under the title of " Fortress Fleet," is distinctly Russian; realized, that is, in Russian theory and practice, though not without representation in the military thought of other countries. The second is the well known " Fleet in Being; " a conception distinctly English in statement and in origin, although, like the first, it finds reflection in naval circles elsewhere. I shall not at this point define this conception " Fleet in Being." I shall attempt to do so later, by marking its extreme expression; but to do more will require more space than is expedient to give here, because full definition would demand the putting forward of various shades of significance, quite wide in their divergence, which are attributed to the expression — " Fleet in Being " — by those who range themselves as advocates of the theory embraced in the phrase.

It is, however, apt here to remark that, in extreme formulation, the two theories, or principles, summed up in the phrases, " Fortress Fleet " and

" Fleet in Being," are the antipodes of each other.
They represent naval, or military, thought polar-
ized, so to say. The one lays all stress on the fortress, making the fleet so far subsidiary as to have
no reason for existence save to help the fortress.
The other discards the fortress altogether, unless
possibly as a momentary refuge for the vessels of
the fleet while coaling, repairing, or refreshing.
The one throws national defense for the coast lines
upon fortifications only; the other relies upon the
fleet alone for actual defense. In each case, co-
operation between the two arms, fleet and coast-
works, is characterized by a supremacy of one or
the other, so marked as to be exclusive. Co-ordination of the two, which I conceive to be the proper
solution, can scarcely be said to exist. The relation
is that of subjection, rather than of co-ordination.
[Here a distinction is drawn between *compromise*,
which implies concessions and a middle course between divergent purposes, and the proper method
best expressed by the word *adjustment,* which sig-
nifies concentration on a single purpose and co-
ordination of all means to that end.]
   It is worthy of your consideration whether the
word " compromise " does not really convey to your
minds an impression that, when you come to design
a ship of war, you must be prepared to concede
something on every quality, in order that each of
the others may have its share. Granting, and I am
not prepared to deny, that in effect each several
quality must yield something, if only in order that
its own effectiveness be ensured, as in the case of

the central defense force just cited, is it of no consequence that you approach the problem in the
spirit of him who divided his force among several
passes, rather than of him who recognizes a central
conception to which all else is to minister? Take
the armored cruiser; a fad, I admit, with myself.
She is armored, and she is a cruiser; and what have
you got? A ship to "lie in the line?" as our
ancestors used to say. No, and Yes; that is to say,
she may on a pinch, and at a risk which exceeds her
powers. A cruiser? Yes, and No; for, in order
to give her armor and armament which do not fit
her for the line, you have given tonnage beyond
what is needed for the speed and coal endurance
proper to a cruiser. By giving this tonnage to
armor and armament you have taken it from other
uses; either from increasing her own speed and
endurance, or from providing an additional cruiser.
You have in her more cruiser than you ought to
have, and less armored vessel; or else less cruiser
and more armored ship. I do not call this a combination, though it is undoubtedly a compromise.
You have put two things together, but they remain
two, have not become one; and, considering the
tonnage, you have neither as much armored ship,
nor as much cruiser, as you ought to have. I do not
say you have a useless ship. I do say you have not
as useful a ship as, for the tonnage, you ought to
have. Whether this opinion of one man is right or
wrong, however, is a very small matter compared
with the desirability of officers generally considering
these subjects on proper lines of thought, and with

proper instruments of expression; that is, with correct principles and correct phraseology.

As an illustration of what I am here saying, the two expressions, " Fortress Fleet " and " Fleet in Being," themselves give proof in their ultimate effect upon Russian practice and principle. Fortress Fleet was a dominant conception in Russian military and naval thought. I quote with some reserve, because from a daily newspaper,[1] but as probably accurate, and certainly characteristic of Russian theory, the following: " Before his departure from Bizerta for the Suez Canal, Admiral Wirenius, in command of the Russian squadron, remarked that the Russian plan was to make Port Arthur and Vladivostok the two most important arsenals in the empire, each having a fleet of corresponding strength," — corresponding, that is, to the fortress, — " depending upon it as upon a base." The distribution would be a division in the face of the probable enemy, Japan, centrally situated, because the design has reference primarily to the fortress, not to naval efficiency. The conception is not wholly erroneous; if it were, the error would have been detected. It has an element of truth, and therein lies its greatest danger; the danger of half or quarter truths. A fleet *can* contribute to the welfare of coast fortresses; especially when the fortress is in a foreign possession of the nation. On the other hand, the Fleet in Being theory has also an element of truth, a very considerable element; and it

---

[1] The Kobe *Chronicle,* February 25, 1904; an English newspaper published in Japan.

has been before the naval public, explicitly, for so long a time that it is impossible it was not known in Russia. It was known and was appreciated. It had a strong following. The Russian Naval General Staff clamored for command of the sea; but in influence upon the government, the responsible director and formulator of national policy, it did not possess due weight. Not having been adequately grasped, — whether from neglect, or because the opposite factor of Fortress Fleet was already in possession of men's minds, — it was never able to secure expression in the national plans. There was compromise, possibly; both things, Fleet in Being and Fortress Fleet, were attempted; but there was not adjustment. The fortress throughout reduced the fleet, as fleet, to insignificance in the national conceptions. What resulted was that at Port Arthur the country got neither a fortress fleet, for, except the guns mounted from it, the fleet contributed nothing to the defense of the place; nor yet a Fleet in Being, for it was never used as such.

It is interesting to observe that this predominant conception of a fortress fleet reflects national temperament; that is, national characteristics, national bias. For, for what does Fortress Fleet stand? For the defensive idea. For what does Fleet in Being stand? For the offensive. In what kind of warfare has Russia most conspicuously distinguished herself? In defensive. She has had her Suvarof, doubtless; but in 1812, and in the Crimea, and now again, in 1904–1905, it is to the defensive that she has inclined. In virtue of her territorial bulk and vast population, she has, so to say, let the enemy hammer at her, sure of survival in virtue of mass. Militarily, Russia as a nation is not enterprising. She has an apathetic bias towards the defensive. She has not, as a matter of national, or governmental, decision, so grasped the idea of offense, nor, as a people, been so gripped by that idea, as to correct the natural propensity to defense, and to give to defense and offense their proper adjustment in national and military policy.

In these two well-known expressions, " Fortress Fleet " and " Fleet in Being," both current, and comparatively recent, we find ourselves therefore confronting the two old divisions of warfare, — defensive and offensive. We may expect these old friends to exhibit their well-known qualities and limitations in action; but, having recognized them under their new garb, we will also consider them under it, speaking not directly of offensive and defensive, but of Fortress Fleet and Fleet in Being, and endeavoring, first, to trace their influence in the Russian conduct. . . .

Why then was the fleet stationed in Port Arthur? Because, expecting the Japanese attack to fall upon Port Arthur, the purpose of the Russian authorities was not to use the fleet offensively against the enemy's navy, but defensively as a fortress fleet; defending the fortress by defensive action, awaiting attack, not making it. That is, the function of the fortress was conceived as defensive chiefly, and not as offensive. Later, I hope to show that the purpose, the *raison d'être,* of a coast fortress is in itself offensive; because it exists chiefly for the purpose of sheltering a fleet, and keeping it fit to act offensively. For the present, waiving the point, it will be sufficient to note that the conception of the fleet by the Russians, that it should act only in defense, led necessarily to imperfect action even in that respect. The Port Arthur division virtually never acted offensively, even locally. An observer on the spot says: " In the disposition of their destroyers, the authorities did not seem disposed to give them a free hand, or to allow them to take any chances." And again, " The torpedo boats were never sent out with the aim of attacking Japanese ships, or transports. If out, and attacked, they fought, but they did not go out for the purpose of attacking, although they would to cover an army flank." These two actions define the rôle indicated by the expression, " Fortress Fleet." The Japanese expressed surprise that no attempt by scouting was made to ascertain their naval base, which was also the landing place of their army; and, although the sinking of the two battleships on May 15 was seen from Port Arthur, no effort was made to improve such a moment of success, and of demoralization to the enemy, although there were twenty-one destroyers at Port Arthur; sixteen of which were under steam and outside. So, at the very last moment, the fleet held on to its defensive rôle; going out only when already damaged by enemy's shells, and then not to fight but to fly.

It is a curious commentary upon this course of action, that, as far as any accounts that have come under my eye show, the fleet contributed nothing to the defense of the fortress beyond landing guns, and, as the final death struggle approached, using their batteries in support of those of the fortress; but the most extreme theorist would scarcely advocate such an end as the object of maintaining a fleet. The same guns would be better emplaced on shore. As far as defense went, the Russian Port Arthur fleet might as well have been at Cronstadt throughout. Indeed, better; for then it would have accompanied Rozhestvensky in concentrated numbers, and the whole Russian navy there assembled, in force far superior, would have been a threat to the Japanese command of the sea much more effective, as a defense to Port Arthur, than was the presence of part of that fleet in the port itself.

The Russian fleet in the Far East, assembled as to the main body in Port Arthur, by its mere presence under the conditions announced that it was there to serve the fortress, to which it was subsidiary. Concentrated at Vladivostok, to one side of the theater of war, and flanking the enemy's line of communications to that which must be the chief scene of operations, it would have been a clear evident declaration that the fortress was subsidiary to the ships; that its chief value in the national military scheme was to shelter, and to afford repairs, in short, to maintain in efficiency, a body which meant to go out to fight, and with a definite object. The hapless Rozhestvensky gave voice to this fact in an expression which I have found attributed to him before the fatal battle at Tsushima: that; if twenty only of the numbers under his command reached Vladivostok, the Japanese communications would be seriously endangered. This is clear "Fleet in Being" theory, and quite undiluted; for it expresses the extreme view that the presence of a strong force, even though inferior, near the scene of operations, will produce a momentous effect upon the enemy's action. The extreme school has gone so far as to argue that it will stop an expedition; or should do so, if the enemy be wise. I have for years contended against this view as unsound; as shown to be so historically. Such a " fleet in being," inferior, should not be accepted by an enemy as a sufficient deterrent under ordinary circumstances. It has not been in the past, and the Japanese did not so accept it. The Russian " fleet in being," in Port Arthur, did not stop their transportation; although they recognized danger from it, and consistently took every step in their power to neutralize it. Their operations throughout were directed consistently to this end. The first partially successful torpedo attack; the attempts to block the harbor by sinking vessels; the distant bombardments; the mines laid outside; and the early institution and persistence in the siege operations, — all had but one end, the destruction of the fleet, in being, within; but, for all that, that fleet did not arrest the transport of the Japanese army.

These two simultaneous operations, the transport of troops despite the fleet in being, and the persevering effort at the same time to destroy it — or neutralize it — illustrate what I have called adjust-

ment between opposite considerations. The danger
from the fleet in being is recognized, but so also is
the danger in delaying the initiation of the land
campaign. The Fleet in Being School would condemn the transportation, so long as the Port Arthur
fleet existed. It actually did so condemn it. The
London *Times,* which is, or then was, under the
influence of this school, published six weeks before
the war began a summary of the situation, by naval
and military correspondents, in which appears this
statement: " With a hostile fleet behind the guns at
Port Arthur, the Japanese could hardly venture to
send troops into the Yellow Sea." And again, four
weeks later: " It is obvious that, until the Russian
ships are sunk, captured, or shut up in their ports
with their wings effectually clipped, there can be no
security for the sea communications of an expeditionary force." These are just as clear illustrations
of the exaggeration inherent in the Fleet in Being
theory, which assumes the deterrent influence of an
offensive threatened by inferior force, as the conduct of the Russian naval operations was of the
inefficiency latent in their theory of Fortress Fleet.

If security meant the security of peace, these
Fleet in Being statements could be accepted; but
military security is an entirely different thing; and
we know that, coincidently with the first torpedo
attack, before its result could be known, an expeditionary Japanese force was sent into the Yellow Sea
to Chemulpo, and that it rapidly received reinforcements to the estimated number of fifty or sixty
thousand. The enterprise in Manchuria, the land-

ing of troops west of the mouth of the Yalu, was delayed for some time — two months, more or less. What the reason of that delay, and what determined the moment of beginning, I do not know; but we do know, not only that it was made in face of four Russian battleships within Port Arthur, but that it continued in face of the increase of their number to six by the repair of those damaged in the first torpedo attack. As early as May 31, it was known in Tokyo that the damaged ships were nearly ready for the sortie, which they actually made on June 23.

It is doubtless open to say that, though the Japanese did thus venture, they ought not to have done so. Note therefore that the Japanese were perfectly alive to the risks run. From the first they were exceedingly careful of their battleships, knowing that on them depended the communications of their army. The fact was noted early in the war by observers on the spot. This shows that they recognized the full menace of all the conditions of the Russian fleet in Port Arthur, also of the one in the Baltic, and of the danger to their communications. Nevertheless, though realizing these various dangers from the hostile " fleets in being," they ventured.

About the middle of March, that is, six weeks after the war began, a report, partly believed by the Japanese authorities, came in that the Port Arthur ships had escaped in a snow storm, on March 11. It is reported that all transportation of troops stopped for some ten days. It may be remembered that in our war with Spain, a very similar report, from two different and competent witnesses, arrested the movement of Shafter's army from Key West until it could be verified. In the case of the Japanese, as in our own, the incident illustrates the possible dangers from a "fleet in being." In neither report was there an evident impossibility. Had either proved true the momentary danger to communications is evident; but the danger is one the chance of which has to be taken. As Napoleon said, "War cannot be made without running risks." The condition that an enemy's fleet watched in port may get out, and may do damage, is entirely different from the fact that it has gotten out. The possibility is not a sufficient reason for stopping transportation; the actual fact is sufficient for taking particular precautions, adjusting dispositions to the new conditions, as was done by ourselves and by the Japanese in the circumstances. The case is wholly different if the enemy has a fleet equal or superior; for then he is entirely master of his movement, does not depend upon evasion for keeping the sea, and communications in such case are in danger, not merely of temporary disarrangement but of permanent destruction. No special warning is needed to know this; the note of the "Fleet in Being" School is insistence on the paralyzing effect of an *inferior* fleet.

Divided Forces [1]

But among the most important lessons of this war — perhaps the most important, as also one

[1] "Naval Administration and Warfare," Retrospect upon the War between Russia and Japan (March, 1906) pp. 167–173.

easily understood and which exemplifies a principle of warfare of ageless application — is the inexpediency, the terrible danger, of dividing the battle fleet, even in times of peace, into fractions individually smaller than those of a possible enemy. The Russian divisions at Port Arthur, at Vladivostok, and in the European ports of Russia, if united, would in 1904 have outweighed decisively the navy of Japan, which moreover could receive no increase during hostilities. It would have been comparatively immaterial, as regards effect upon the local field of operations, whether the ships were assembled in the Baltic, in Vladivostok, or in Port Arthur. Present together, the fleet thus constituted could not have been disregarded by Japan without a risk transcending beyond comparison that caused by the Port Arthur division alone, which the Japanese deliberately put out of court. For, while they undertook, and successfully carried out, measures which during a period of four months disabled it as a body menacing their sea communications, they none the less before the torpedo attack of February 8 had begun the movement of their army to the continent. It is most improbable that they would have dared the same had the available Russian navy been united. It would have mattered nothing that it was frozen in in Vladivostok. The case of Japan would not have been better, but worse, for having utilized the winter to cross her troops to the mainland, if, when summer came, the enemy appeared in overwhelming naval force. If Togo, in face of Rozhestvensky's division alone, could signal his fleet,

"The salvation or the fall of the Empire depends upon the result of this engagement," how much more serious the situation had there been with it the Port Arthur ships, which had handled his vessels somewhat roughly the preceding August.

To an instructed, thoughtful, naval mind in the United States, there is no contingency affecting the country, as interested in the navy, so menacing as the fear of popular clamor influencing an irresolute, or militarily ignorant, administration to divide the battleship force into two divisions, the Atlantic and the Pacific. A determined President, instructed in military matters, doubtless will not yield, but will endeavor by explanation to appease apprehension and quiet outcry. Nevertheless, the danger exists; and always will exist in proportion as the people do not understand the simple principle that an efficient military body depends for its effect in war — and in peace — less upon its position than upon its concentrated force. This does not ignore position, and its value. On the contrary, it is written with a clear immediate recollection of Napoleon's pregnant saying, "War is a business of positions." But the great captain, in the letter in which the phrase occurs, goes on directly to instruct the marshal to whom he is writing so to station the divisions of his corps, for purposes of supply, around a common center, that they can unite rapidly; and can meet the enemy in mass before he can attack any one of them, or move far from his present position against another important French interest.

Concentration indeed, in last analysis, may be

correctly defined as being itself a choice of position; viz.: that the various corps, or ships, shall not be some in one place, and some in others, but all in one place. We Americans have luckily had an object lesson, not at our own expense, but at that of an old friend. There is commonly believed to have been little effective public opinion in Russia at the time the war with Japan was at hand; such as did manifest itself, in the use of dynamite against officials, seems not to have taken into consideration international relations, military or other. But in the councils of the Empire, however constituted, and whatever the weight of the military element, there was shown in act an absolute disregard of principles so simple, so obvious, and so continually enforced by precept and experience, that the fact would be incomprehensible, had not we all seen, in civil as in military life, that the soundest principles, perfectly well known, fail, more frequently than not, to sustain conduct against prepossession or inclination. That communications dominate strategy, and that the communications of Japan in a continental war would be by sea, were clear as daylight. That the whole navy of Russia, united on the scene, would be sufficient, and half of it probably insufficient, certainly hazardous, was equally plain. Yet, ship by ship, half was assembled in the Far East, until Japan saw that this process of division had been carried as far as suited her interests and declared war; after which of course no Russian battleship could go forward alone.

From the military point of view the absurdity of

the procedure is clear; but for national safety it has to be equally clear to statesmen and to people. An outside observer, with some little acquired knowledge of the workings of men's minds, needs small imagination to hear the arguments at the Russian council board. "Things are looking squally in the East," says one; "the fleet ought to be increased." "Increased," says another, "you may say so. All the ships we have ought to be sent, and together, the instant they can be got ready." "Oh but," rejoins a third, "consider how exposed our Baltic shores would be, in case war against us should be declared by Great Britain, which already has an understanding with Japan." The obvious reply, that, in case Great Britain did declare war, the only thing to be done with the Baltic fleet would be to snuggle it close inside of the guns of Cronstadt, would probably be made; if it was, it was not heeded. In a representative government would doubtless have been heard the further remark, "The feeling in our coast towns, at seeing no ship left for their protection, would be so strong, that I doubt if the party could carry the next election." Against this there is no provision, except popular understanding; operative perhaps in the interior, where there is no occasion for fright.

The most instructive feature of this Russian mistake, inexcusable in a government not browbeaten by political turmoil, is that it was made in time of peace, in the face of conditions threatening war. In fact, as is often the case, when war came it was already too late to remedy adequately the blunders or neglects of peace. More than twenty years ago the present writer had occasion to quote emphatically the words of a French author, " Naval Strategy " — naval strategic considerations — " is as necessary in peace as in war." In 1904, nearly a decade had elapsed since Japan had been despoiled of much of her gains in her war with China. Since then Russia had been pursuing a course of steady aggression, in furtherance of her own aims, and contrary to what Japan considered her " vital interests and national honor." It is not necessary to pronounce between the views of the two parties to see that the action of Russia was militarily preposterous, unless her fleet grew in proportion to that of Japan, and of her own purposes, and was kept in hand; that is, kept concentrated. It would have mattered little whether, being united, the outbreak of war found it in the Baltic, or in Vladivostok. That it could come, as did Rozhestvensky, but in double his force, would have been a fact no less emphatic when in the Baltic than in the farther East.

It is precisely the same, in application as well as in principle, with the Atlantic and Pacific coasts of the United States. Both are exposed. Neither need be more exposed than the other; for, in virtue of our geographical position relatively to the other great Powers of the world, it is not the momentary location of the fleet, but its simple existence, adequate in numbers and efficiency, and concentrated in force, which protects both coasts. Any invader from the one side or the other must depend upon sea communications to support his army *throughout the war;*

not merely for the three months needed to bring the United States fleet from one side to the other. But, if the war begin with the fleet divided between the two oceans, one half may be overmatched and destroyed, as was that of Port Arthur; and the second on coming prove unequal to restore the situation, as befell Rozhestvensky. That is to say, Concentration protects both coasts, Division exposes both. IT IS OF VITAL CONSEQUENCE TO THE NATION OF THE UNITED STATES, THAT ITS PEOPLE, CONTEMPLATING THE RUSSO-JAPANESE NAVAL WAR, SUBSTITUTE THEREIN, IN THEIR APPREHENSION, ATLANTIC FOR BALTIC, AND PACIFIC FOR PORT ARTHUR. So they will comprehend as well as apprehend.

30. Rozhestvensky at Tsushima [1]

[THE Russian fleet under Rozhestvensky left Libau October 15, 1904; reached Madagascar January 1, 1905, the day of the surrender of Port Arthur; and entered the Korea or Tsushima Straits on the morning of May 26. A part of the auxiliaries had been left in the mouth of the Yangtse River, but the hospital and repair ships and those laden with naval stores were with the fleet. According to testimony at the court martial of Admiral Rozhestvensky, the battleships entered the straits with coal for three thousand miles, though the distance from the Saddle Islands to Vladivostok was but nine hundred. — EDITOR.]

Criticism here is another case of inferring intentions from actions; but, when the various parts of Rozhestvensky's conduct are taken together, the inference is nearly irresistible that the exaggerated estimate of the influence of an inferior fleet in being possessed his imagination. Besides the excessive coal stowage, he took with him a train of transports, a notorious source of tactical embarrassment in battle, though doubtless equally a source of refitment, if he got them to Vladivostok; and there is no evidence of any attempt at advanced scouting on his own part, or of driving off, as he might have done,

[1] "Naval Strategy," pp. 416–420.

the Japanese scouts which showed up; the result being that Togo knew all about his dispositions, and he knew nothing about Togo's until he saw the enemy's main body.

Now I say, that, while all this was bad management in the face of the enemy, and in so far bad tactics, the bad tactics issued from an error of strategy; and the error in strategy was due to the lack of unity of conception, of that exclusiveness of purpose, which is the essence of strategy, and which subordinates, adjusts, all other factors and considerations to the one exclusive aim. While writing these pages, I came across a few lines by one of the first of German philosophical historians, Ranke, in one of his greatest works, " England in the Seventeenth Century." They apply to policy, but policy is twin brother to strategy. Permit me to quote them:

" Why did William III get the better of James II in Ireland? Because he always kept his one great idea before his eyes, amid the many perplexing circumstances which surrounded him. The decision which he displayed at every moment rested upon the fact that he had *only one end,* and that the one *imposed by the course of things.*"

Apply this to Rozhestvensky. The one end imposed on him by the course of things was the destruction of the Japanese fleet, which comprised every armored vessel Japan could possibly muster for that war. Togo's signal[1] before the battle

---

[1] "The rise or fall of the Empire depends upon to-day's battle. Let every man do his utmost." — EDITOR.

recognized this one end, and there was no reason why his opponent should not have recognized it equally. To reach Vladivostok was only a means to that end; an object most important, because, if

SCENE OF NAVAL WAR
JAPAN AND RUSSIA

attained, it would put the Russians in the best possible condition for battle. But this by no means superseded the one necessary aim, — battle. More, it did not even postpone that aim, as a matter of immediate consideration and preparation; for, though escape through to Vladivostok might be possible, it was not certain. It was not even probable, under all the conditions. Therefore, while every forethought and care should have been to effect escape, if possible, they should have been accompanied with the clear decision that, should battle be forced, the fighting should have been qualified by no thought of escape, and the fleet, like a ship cleared for action, should have been stripped of all fleet encumbrances from the moment of leaving the Saddles. A fleet is half beaten already when it goes into battle with one eye upon something else than fighting.

If Rozhestvensky had recognized these facts, in their due importance and proportion, and had been convinced that battle was his one aim, and that there was at least a very real possibility that he could not postpone it till after Vladivostok, it seems to me he must have reasoned thus: I must have coal enough to reach Vladivostok, on a reasonable calculation of the distance, and of the expenditures of the ships; both which were known. To this amount add a fair margin of safety. This total should be carried for the purpose of escape, if feasible; with perhaps an addition sufficient to last during battle, with funnels pierced, which was a likely accident. Again, there is for each ship a draft of water which best meets her maneuvering needs. The chances are that the enemy will await us either in the narrower part of the sea, or near his navy yards. As there is one position, that in the Straits of Korea, which favors both these objects, it is there I will probably have to fight, if at all. Therefore, as far as possible, the coal carried by the fleet on starting should be such that consumption up to the moment of reaching the straits will put them in their best tactical trim. The coal supply needed to reach Vladivostok is thus adjusted to the exigencies of battle.

Then as regards the transports. For the moment, on this last fateful stretch, they are absolutely of no consequence as affecting results. The adjustment of them, to the end of the battle, is to dismiss them out of mind and presence. If beaten, the loss of them will not be of the slightest consequence to Russia; if successful, they can be summoned from an appointed rendezvous, and escorted to a destination under such protection as may then seem expedient. An Austrian officer has suggested that if the whole body had weighed together, and at night had separated, the supply vessels proceeding under convoy by the east of Japan might have escaped notice; or, if seen, this report might have perplexed Togo, rather than enlightened him. Upon the suggestion I make no comment, other than that it would have been one way of counting out the supply ships.

The imminency of the occasion should have drawn, and did draw, all Japan's fighting force to the Straits of Korea, an element for Rozhestvensky's consideration. According to Semenoff the auxiliary steamers *Terek* and *Kuban* were sent off the east coast expressly to draw attention, but met no one, and their presence was unknown to the Japanese.

I am not disposed to question, or to doubt, that *if* the Russian squadron had escaped Togo, and *if* the separated supply train had been intercepted, it would have been very embarrassing to the ships of war refitting at Vladivostok. Nor do I question that, in case of such escape, the coal remaining in consequence of the deck loads taken would have been of much value for future operations. The more real and the greater those distracting considerations, like those of William III in Ireland, the more do they throw into relief the greatness, as well as the necesssity, of subordinating them to the one thing needful, namely, to be ready to the utmost on the day of battle. They illustrate, too, how misleading is the disposition to compromise, to concede something all around; to straddle the two horses, escape and battle.

Rozhestvensky's course was a compromise, a mix-up of escape and fighting; a strategic blunder to begin with, in not concentrating attention on the one needful thing clearly indicated by the course of events, and hence resulting necessarily in a series of blunders, which comprehensively may be called tactical. They all hang together, as the results of a frame of mind; the overloading with coal, the increased danger of fire therefrom, the submersion of the armor belts, the loss of speed and tactical capacity, the neglect of scouting, the company of the transports, — each of which is a tactical error, — all proceed from the failure to observe that the one governing consideration of strategy, in this war, was a naval battle under the most favorable conditions. It is the repetition of the mistakes of the Port Arthur division. When it becomes clearly imminent that one may have to fight under conditions less favorable than one would desire, conditions are changed; but there is no change of the principles involved. Vladivostok reached, the principle would have required the utmost preparation the yard offered, in the least possible time, so as to be the most fit possible to fight. At the Saddles, the same fitness required the dismissal from influence upon conduct of all thought of Vladivostok, and of supplies there, so far as such thought might modify the preparation for probable battle. It seems very probable that the defective conceptions deducible from Rozhestvensky's conduct were emphasized and reinforced by the heavy preoccupations about supplies, necessarily incidental to his anxious outward voyage. His mind and *morale* had got a twist, a permanent set, from which they could not recover.

PART III
NAVAL AND NATIONAL POLICIES

PART III: NAVAL AND NATIONAL POLICIES

31. EXPANSION AND OVER-SEA BASES [1]

The Annexation of Hawaii

[As the date indicates, the essay was written at the time of the Revolution in Hawaii, six years before its annexation. The part of the essay preceding points out the predominant interest of the United States in the Islands owing to their control of our trade routes and naval approaches, and refers to the benefit to the world from British colonial expansion. — EDITOR.]

But if a plea of the world's welfare seem suspiciously like a cloak for national self-interest, let the latter be accepted frankly as the adequate motive which it assuredly is. Let us not shrink from pitting a broad self-interest against the narrow self-interest to which some would restrict us. The demands of our three great seaboards, the Atlantic, the Gulf, and the Pacific, — each for itself, and all for the strength that comes from drawing closer the ties between them, — are calling for the extension, through the Isthmian Canal, of that broad sea common along which, and along which alone, in

---

[1] "The Interest of America in Sea Power," Hawaii and Our Future Sea Power (1893), pp. 51–54.

all the ages prosperity has moved. Land carriage, always restricted and therefore always slow, toils enviously but hopelessly behind, vainly seeking to replace and supplant the royal highway of nature's own making. Corporate interests, vigorous in that power of concentration which is the strength of armies and of minorities, may here withstand for a while the ill-organized strivings of the multitude, only dimly conscious of its wants; yet the latter, however temporarily opposed and baffled, is sure at last, like the blind forces of nature, to overwhelm all that stand in the way of its necessary progress. So the Isthmian Canal is an inevitable part in the future of the United States; yet one that cannot be separated from other necessary incidents of a policy dependent upon it, whose details cannot be foreseen exactly. But because the precise steps that hereafter may be opportune or necessary cannot yet be foretold certainly, is not a reason the less, but a reason the more, for establishing a principle of action which may serve to guide as opportunities arise. Let us start from the fundamental truth, warranted by history, that the control of the seas, and especially along the great lines drawn by national interest or national commerce, is the chief among the merely material elements in the power and prosperity of nations. It is so because the sea is the world's great medium of circulation. From this necessarily follows the principle that, as subsidiary to such control, it is imperative to take possession, when it can be done righteously, of such maritime positions as contribute to secure command. If this principle be adopted, there will be no hesitation about taking the positions — and they are many — upon the approaches to the Isthmus, whose interests incline them to seek us. It has its application also to the present case of Hawaii.

There is, however, one caution to be given from the military point of view, beyond the need of which the world has not yet passed. Military positions, fortified posts, by land or by sea, however strong or admirably situated, do not confer control by themselves alone. People often say that such an island or harbor will give control of such a body of water. It is an utter, deplorable, ruinous mistake. The phrase indeed may be used by some only loosely, without forgetting other implied conditions of adequate protection and adequate navies; but the confidence of our own nation in its native strength, and its indifference to the defense of its ports and the sufficiency of its fleet, give reason to fear that the full consequences of a forward step may not be weighed soberly. Napoleon, who knew better, once talked this way. "The islands of San Pietro, Corfu, and Malta," he wrote, "will make us masters of the whole Mediterranean." Vain boast! Within one year Corfu, in two years Malta, were rent away from the state that could not support them by its ships. Nay, more: had Bonaparte not taken the latter stronghold out of the hands of its degenerate but innocuous government, that citadel of the Mediterranean would perhaps — would probably — never have passed into those of his chief enemy. There is here also a lesson for us.

32. Application of the Monroe Doctrine [1]

Anglo-American Community of Interests

THE writer has too often already discussed, directly or incidentally, the strategic situation which finds its center in Panama to repeat the same here; but one or two remarks about the Monroe doctrine may be not out of place. Accepting as probably durable the new conditions, which have so largely modified the nation's external policy in the direction of expansion, there is in them nothing to diminish, but rather to intensify, the purpose that there shall be no intrusion of the European political system upon territory whence military effect upon the Isthmus of Panama can be readily exerted. For instance, should a change anticipated by some occur, and Holland enter the German Empire, it will be advantageous that it should even now be understood, as it then would be necessary for us to say, that our consent could not be given to Curaçao forming part of that incorporation. The Isthmus of Panama — in addition to its special importance to us as a link between our Pacific and Atlantic coasts — sums up in itself that one of the two great lines of communication between the Atlantic and the farther East which especially concerns us, and we can no more consent to such a transfer of a fortress

1 "The Problem of Asia" (1900), pp. 133–144.

in the Caribbean, than we would ourselves have thought of acquiring Port Mahon, in the Mediterranean, as a result of our successful war with Spain.

Consideration of interests such as these must be dispassionate upon the one side and upon the other; and a perfectly candid reception must be accorded to the views and the necessities of those with whom we thus deal. During the process of deliberation not merely must preconceptions be discarded, but sentiment itself should be laid aside, to resume its sway only after unbiassed judgment has done its work. The present question of Asia, the evolution of which has taken days rather than years, may entail among its results no change in old maxims, but it nevertheless calls for a review of them in the light of present facts. If from this no difference of attitude results, the confirmed resolve of sober second thought will in itself alone be a national gain. This new Eastern question has greatly affected the importance of communications, enhancing that of the shorter routes, reversing political and military — as distinguished from mercantile — conditions, and bringing again into the foreground of interest the Mediterranean, thus reinvested with its ancient pre-eminence. For the same reason the Caribbean Sea, because of its effect upon the Isthmus of Panama, attains a position it has never before held, emphasizing the application to it of the Monroe doctrine. The Pacific has advanced manifold in consequence to the United States, not only as an opening market, but as a means of transit, and also because our new possessions there, by

giving increased opportunities, entail correspond-
ingly heavier burdens of national responsibility.
The isthmian canals, present and to come,— Suez
and Panama, — summarize and locally accentuate
the essential character of these changes, of which
they are at once an exponent and a factor. It will
be no light matter that man shall have shifted the
Strait of Magellan to the Isthmus of Panama, and
the Cape of Good Hope to the head of the Mediterranean.

The correlative of these new conditions is the
comparative isolation, and the dwindled consequence, of the southern extremes of Africa and
America, which now lie far apart from the changed
direction imposed upon the world's policies. The
regions there situated will have small effect upon
the great lines of travel, and must derive such importance as may remain to them from their intrinsic
productive value. Does there, then, remain sound
reason of national interest for pressing the Monroe
doctrine to the extent of guaranteeing our support
to American states which love us not, and whose
geographical position, south of the valley of the
Amazon, lies outside of effective influence upon the
American isthmus? Does the disposition to do so
arise from sound policy, or from sentiment, or from
mere habit? And, if from either, do the facts
justify retaining a burden of responsibility which
may embarrass our effective action in fields of
greater national consequence — just as South Africa
may prove a drain upon Great Britain's necessary
force about Suez? In short, while the principles

upon which the Monroe doctrine reposes are not
only unimpaired, but fortified, by recent changes,
is it not possible that the application of them may
require modification, intensifying their force in one
quarter, diminishing it in another?

Not the least striking and important of the conditions brought about by the two contemporary
events — the downfall of the Spanish colonial empire and the precipitation of the crisis in eastern
Asia — has been the drawing closer together of the
two great English-speaking nationalities. Despite
recalcitrant objections here and there by unwilling
elements on both sides, the fact remains concrete
and apparent, endued with essential life, and consequent inevitable growth, by virtue of a clearly
recognized community of interest, present and
future. It is no mere sentimental phase, though
sentiment, long quietly growing, had sufficiently
matured to contribute its powerful influence at the
opportune moment; but here, as ever, there was
first the material, — identity of interest, — and not
till afterwards the spiritual, — reciprocity of feeling, — aroused to mutual recognition by the causes
and motives of the Spanish war. That war, and
the occurrences attendant, proclaimed emphatically
that the two countries, in their ideals of duty to the
suffering and oppressed, stood together, indeed, but
in comparative isolation from the sympathies of
the rest of the world.[1]

---

[1] "The writer has been assured, by an authority in which he entirely trusts, that to a proposition made to Great Britain (at the time of
the Spanish-American War) to enter into a combination to constrain the
use of our power, — as Japan was five years ago constrained by the joint

The significance of this fact has been accentuated by the precision with which in the United States the preponderance of intelligence has discerned, and amid many superficially confusing details has kept in mind, as the reasonable guide to its sympathies, that the war in the Transvaal is simply a belated revival of the issue on which our own Revolution was fought, viz., that when representation is denied, taxation is violent oppression. The principle is common to Great Britain and to us, woven into the web of all her history, despite the momentary aberration which led to our revolt. The twofold incident — the two wars and the sympathies aroused, because in both each nation recognized community of principle and of ideals — indicates another great approximation to the unity of mankind; which will arrive in good time, but which is not to be hurried by force or by the impatience of dreamers. The outcome of the civil war in the United States, the unification of Italy, the new German Empire, the growing strength of the idea of Imperial Federation in Great Britain, all illustrate the tendency of humanity to aggregate into greater groups, which in the instances cited have resulted in political combination more or less formal and clearly defined. To the impulse and establishment of each of these steps in advance, war has played a principal part. War it was which preserved our Union. War it was which completed the political unity of Italy,

action of Russia, France, and Germany, — the reply was not only a passive refusal to enter into such combination, but an assurance of active resistance to it, if attempted." — Mahan, "The Problem of Asia" (1900), p. 187. — EDITOR.

and brought the Germans into that accord of sentiment and of recognized interest upon which rest the
foundations and the continuance of their empire.
War it is which has but now quickened the spirit of
sympathy between Great Britain and her colonies,
and given to Imperial Federation an acceleration
into concrete action which could not otherwise have
been imparted; and it needed the stress of war, the
threat of outside interference with a sister nation
in its mission of benevolence, to quicken into positive
action the sympathy of Great Britain with the United
States, and to dispose the latter to welcome gladly
and to return cordially the invaluable support thus
offered.

War is assuredly a very great evil; not the greatest, but among the greatest which afflict humanity.
Yet let it be recognized at this moment, when the
word " Arbitration " has hold of popular imagination, more perhaps by the melody of its associations,
— like the " Mesopotamia " of the preacher, — than
by virtue of a reasonable consideration of both sides
of the question, of which it represents only one, that
within two years two wars have arisen, the righteous
object of either of which has been unattainable by
milder methods. When the United States went to
war with Spain, four hundred thousand of the
latter's colonial subjects had lost their lives by the
slow misery of starvation, inflicted by a measure —
Reconcentration — which was intended, but had
proved inadequate, to suppress an insurrection in-
cited by centuries of oppression and by repeated
broken pledges. The justification of that war rests

upon our right to interfere on grounds of simple humanity, and upon the demonstrated inability of Spain to rule her distant colonies by methods unharmful to the governed. It was impossible to accept renewed promises, not necessarily through distrust of their honesty, but because political incapacity to give just and good administration had been proved by repeated failures.

The justification of Great Britain's war with the Transvaal rests upon a like right of interference — to relieve oppression — and upon the broad general principle for which our colonial ancestors fought the mother-country over a century ago, that " taxation without representation is tyranny." Great Britain, indeed, did not demand the franchise for her misgoverned subjects, domiciled abroad; she only suggested it as a means whereby they might, in return for producing nine tenths of the revenue, obtain fair treatment from the state which was denying it to them. But be it remembered, not only that a cardinal principle upon which English and American liberty rests was being violated, but that at the time when the foreigners were encouraged to enter the Transvaal franchise was attainable by law in five years, while before the five years had expired the law was changed, and the privilege withdrawn by *ex post facto* act.

In each of these wars one of the two nations which speak the English tongue has taken a part, and in each the one engaged has had outspoken sympathy from the other, and from the other alone. The fact has been less evident in the Transvaal war, partly because the issue has been less clear, or less clearly put, chiefly because many foreign-born citizens of the United States still carry with them the prepossessions of their birthplace, rather than those which should arise from perception of their country's interest.

Nevertheless, the foundations stand sure. We have begun to know each other, in community of interest and of traditions, in ideals of equality and of law. As the realization of this spreads, the two states, in their various communities, will more and more closely draw together in the unity of spirit, and all the surer that they eschew the bondage of the letter of alliance.

33. CHANGES IN THE UNITED STATES AND JAPAN [1]

THE occidentalization of Japan, in methods although not in national spirit, — which changes much more slowly, — has been fully demonstrated to an astonished world by the war of 1894 with China. It is one of the incidents of the closing nineteenth century. To this achievement in the military sphere, in the practice of war which Napoleon called the science of barbarians, must be added the development of civil institutions that has resulted in the concession to Japan of all international dignity and privilege; and consequently of a control over the administration of justice among foreigners within her borders, not heretofore obtained by any other Oriental State. It has thus become evident that the weight of Japan in the international balances depends not upon the quality of her achievement, which has been shown to be excellent, but upon the gross amount of her power. Moreover, while in wealth and population, with the resources dependent upon them, she may be deficient, — though rapidly growing, — her geographical position relatively to the Eastern center of interest, and her advantage of insularity, go far to compensate such defect. These confer upon her as a factor in the Eastern

[1] "Retrospect and Prospect" (1902), pp. 15-17.

problem an influence resembling in kind, if not equaling in degree, that which Great Britain has held and still holds in the international relations centering around Europe, the Atlantic, and the Mediterranean.

Yet the change in Japan, significant as it is and influential upon the great problem of the Pacific and Asia, is less remarkable and less important than that which has occurred in the United States. If in the Orient a nation may be said to have been born in a day, even so the event is less sudden and less revolutionary than the conversion of spirit and of ideals — the new birth — which has come over our own country. In this are evident a rapidity and a thoroughness which bespeak impulse from an external source rather than any conscious set process of deliberation, of self-determination within, such as has been that of Japan in her recognition and adoption of material improvements forced upon her attention in other peoples. No man or group of men can pretend to have guided and governed our people in the adoption of a new policy, the acceptance of which has been rather instinctive — I would prefer to say inspired — than reasoned. There is just this difference between Japan and ourselves, the two most changed of peoples within the last half-century. She has adopted other methods; we have received another purpose. The one conversion is material, the other spiritual. When we talk about expansion we are in the realm of ideas. The material addition of expansion — the acreage, if I may so say — is trivial compared with our previous possessions, or with the annexations by European states within a few years. The material profit otherwise, the national gain to us, is at best doubtful. What the nation has gained in expansion is a regenerating idea, an uplifting of the heart, a seed of future beneficent activity, a going out of self into the world to communicate the gift it has so bountifully received.

34. OUR INTERESTS IN THE PACIFIC [1]

[THE preceding pages of the essay explain the dependence of the " Open Door " policy on an international balance of power in the Pacific, and the modification of this balance owing to the growth of the German Navy and the increasing European tension. — EDITOR.]

The result is to leave the two chief Pacific nations, the United States and Japan, whose are the only two great navies that have coastlines on that ocean, to represent there the balance of power. This is the best security for international peace; because it represents, not a bargain, but a fact, readily ascertainable. Those two navies are more easily able than any other to maintain there a concentration of force; and it may even be questioned whether sound military policy may not make the Pacific rather than the Atlantic the station for the United States battle fleet. For the balance of naval power in Europe, which compels the retention of the British and German fleets in the North Sea, protects the Atlantic coast of the United States, — and the Monroe Doctrine, — to a degree to which nothing in Pacific conditions corresponds. Under existing circumstances, neither Germany nor Great Britain can

[1] "The Interest of America in International Conditions," The Open Door (1910), pp. 198–202.

afford, even did they desire, to infringe the external policy of the United States represented in the Monroe Doctrine.

With Japan in the Pacific, and in her attitude towards the Open Door, the case is very different from that of European or American Powers. Her nearness to China, Manchuria, Korea, gives the natural commercial advantages that short and rapid transportation always confers. Labor with her is still cheap, another advantage in open competition; but the very fact of these near natural markets, and her interest in them, cannot but breed that sense of proprietorship which, in dealing with ill-organized states, easily glides into the attempt at political control that ultimately means control by force. Hence the frequent reports, true or untrue, that such advantage is sought and accomplished. Whether true or not, these illustrate what nations continually seek, when opportunity offers or can be made. This is in strict line with that which we call Protection; but with the difference that Protection is exercised within the sphere commonly recognized as legitimate, either by International Law or by the policy of competing states. The mingled weakness and perverseness of Chinese negotiators invite such attempt, and endanger the Open Door; give rise to continual suspicion that undue influence resting upon force is affecting equality of treatment, or is establishing a basis for inequality in the future. There can be no question that the general recent attitude of Russia and Japan, however laudably meant, does arouse such suspicions.

Then again, the American possession, the Hawaiian Islands, are predominantly Japanese in labor population; a condition which, as the outcome of little more than a generation, warrants the jealousy of Japanese immigration on the part of the Pacific coast. Finally, the population of that coast is relatively scanty, and its communications with the East, though rapid for express trains, are slow for the immense traffic of men and stores which war implies and requires. That is, the power of the country east of the Rocky Mountains has far to go, and with poor conveyance, in order to reinforce the Western Coast; the exact opposite of our advantage of rapid maritime access to the Panama Canal. In the absence of the fleet, invasion may be easy. Harm may be retrieved in measure by the arrival of the fleet later; but under present world conditions the Pacific coast seems incomparably the more exposed of the three great divisions of the American shore line — the Atlantic, the Gulf, and the Pacific.

35. THE GERMAN STATE AND ITS MENACE [1]

THE prototype of modern Germany is to be found rather in the Roman Empire, to which in a certain sense the present German Empire may be said to be — if not heir — at least historically affiliated. The Holy Roman Empire merged into that somewhat extenuated figment attached to the Austrian Hapsburgs, which finally deceased at the opening of the nineteenth century; but the idea itself survived, and was influential in determining the form and name which the existing powerful Germanic unity has assumed. To this unity the national German character contributes an element not unlike that of antiquity, in the subordination of the individual to the state. As a matter of national characteristic, this differs radically from the more modern conception of the freedom and rights of the individual, exemplified chiefly in England and the United States. It is possible to accept the latter as the superior ideal, as a higher stage of advance, as ultimately more fruitful of political progress, yet at the same time to recognize the great immediate advantage of the massed action which subordinates the interests of the individual, sinks the unit in the whole, in order to promote the interests of the community. It may be noted incidentally, without

[1] "The Interest of America in International Conditions" (1910), pp. 38-46.

further insistence just here, that the Japanese Empire, which in a different field from the German is manifesting the same restless need for self-assertion and expansion, comes to its present with the same inheritance from its past, of the submergence of the individual in the mass. It was equally the characteristic of Sparta among the city states of ancient Greece, and gave to her among them the preponderance she for a time possessed. As an exhibition of social development, it is generally anterior and inferior to that in which the rights of the individual are more fully recognized; but as an element of mere force, whether in economics or in international policies, it is superior.

The two contrasted conceptions, the claims of the individual and the claims of the state, are familiar to all students of history. The two undoubtedly must coexist everywhere, and have to be reconciled; but the nature of the adjustment, in the clear predominance of the one or the other, constitutes a difference which in effect upon the particular community is fundamental. In international relations, between states representing the opposing ideas, it reproduces the contrast between the simple discipline of an army and the complicated disseminated activities of the people, industrial, agricultural, and commercial. It repeats the struggle of the many minor mercantile firms against a single great combination. In either field, whatever the ultimate issue, — and in the end the many will prevail, — the immediate result is that preponderant concentrated force has its way for a period which may thus

be one of great and needless distress; and it not
only has its way, but it takes its way, because, whatever progress the world has made, the stage has not
been reached when men or states willingly subordinate their own interests to even a reasonable
regard for that of others. It is not necessary to
indulge in pessimistic apprehension, or to deny
that there is a real progress of the moral forces
lumped under the name of " public opinion." This
unquestionably tells for much more than it once did;
but still the old predatory instinct, that he should
take who has the power, survives, in industry and
commerce, as well as in war, and moral force is not
sufficient to determine issues unless supported by
physical. Governments are corporations, and corporations have not souls. Governments moreover
are trustees, not principals; and as such must put
first the lawful interests of their wards, their own
people.

It matters little what may be the particular intentions now cherished by the German government.
The fact upon which the contemporary world needs
to fasten its attention is that it is confronted by the
simple existence of a power such as is that of the
German Empire; reinforced necessarily by that of
Austria-Hungary, because, whatever her internal
troubles and external ambitions, Austria is bound
to Germany by nearness, by inferior power, and by
interests, partly common to the two states, as surely
as the moon is bound to the earth and with it constitutes a single group in the planetary system.
Over against this stands for the moment a number

of states, Russia, Italy, France, Great Britain. The recent action of Russia has demonstrated her international weakness, the internal causes of which are evident even to the most careless observer. Italy still belongs to the Triple Alliance, of which Germany and Austria are the other members; but the inclination of Italy towards England, springing from past sympathies, and as a state necessarily naval, because partly insular, partly peninsular, is known, as is also her recent drawing towards France as compared with former estrangement. Also, in the Balkan regions and in the Adriatic Sea there is more than divergence between the interest of Italy and the ambitions of Austria, — supported by Germany, — as shown in the late annexations and their antecedents. An Austrian journal, which foreshadowed the annexations with singular acumen, has written recently,[1] "We most urgently need a fleet so strong that it can rule the Northern Adriatic basin," — in which lies the Italian Venice, as well as the Austrian Trieste, — "support the operations of our land army, protect our chief commercial ports against hostile maritime undertakings, and prevent us from being throttled at the Strait of Otranto. To do this, the fleet must at least attain the approximate strength of our probable enemy. If we lag behind in developing our naval programme, Italy will so outrun us that we can never overtake her. Here more than elsewhere to stand still is to recede; but to recede would be to renounce the historical mission of Austria." The Austrian *Dread-*

[1] *The Mail*, April 20, 1910.

noughts are proceeding, and the above throws an interesting side light upon the equipoise of the Triple Alliance. In the Algeciras Conference, concerning the affairs of Morocco, Italy did not sustain Germany; Austria only did so.

Analyzing thus the present international relations of Europe, we find on the one side the recently constituted Triple *Entente,* France, Great Britain, and Russia; on the other the Triple Alliance, Austria-Hungary, Germany, and Italy, of thirty years' standing. The sympathies of Italy, as distinguished from the pressure of conditions upon her, and from her formal association, are doubtful; and the essentials of the situation seem to be summed up in the Triple *Entente* opposed by the two mid-Europe military monarchies.

The Bulwark of British Sea Power [1]

[The intervening pages show that exposure on their land frontiers would weaken the aid that could be given Great Britain by her allies in continental Europe. — EDITOR.]

These conclusions, if reasonable, not only emphasize the paramount importance in world politics of the British navy, but they show also that there are only two naval states which can afford to help Great Britain with naval force, because they alone have no land frontiers which march with those of Germany. These states are Japan and the United States. In looking to the future, it becomes

[1] "The Interest of America in International Conditions" (1910), pp. 161–164

for them a question whether it will be to their interest, whether they can afford, to exchange the naval supremacy of Great Britain for that of Germany; for this alternative may arise. Those two states and Germany cannot, as matters now stand, touch one another, except on the open sea; whereas the character of the British Empire is such that it has everywhere sea frontiers, is everywhere assailable where local naval superiority does not exist, as for instance in Australia, and other Eastern possessions. The United States has upon Great Britain the further check of Canada, open to land attack.

A German navy, supreme by the fall of Great Britain, with a supreme German army able to spare readily a large expeditionary force for over-sea operations, is one of the possibilities of the future. Great Britain for long periods, in the Seven Years War and Napoleonic struggle, 1756–1815, has been able to do, and has done, just this; not because she has had a supreme army, but because, thanks to her insular situation, her naval supremacy covered effectually both the home positions and the expedition. The future ability of Germany thus to act is emphasized to the point of probability by the budgetary difficulties of Great Britain, by the general disorganization of Russia, and by the arrest of population in France. Though vastly the richer nation, the people of Great Britain, for the very reason of greater wealth long enjoyed, are not habituated to the economical endurance of the German; nor can the habits of individual liberty in England or

America accept, unless under duress, the heavy yoke of organization, of regulation of individual action, which constitutes the power of Germany among modern states.

The rivalry between Germany and Great Britain to-day is the danger point, not only of European politics, but of world politics as well.

36. Advantages of Insular Position [1]

Great Britain and the Continental Powers

EVERY war has two aspects, the defensive and the offensive, to each of which there is a corresponding factor of activity. There is something to gain, the offensive; there is something to lose, the defensive. The ears of men, especially of the uninstructed, are more readily and sympathetically open to the demands of the latter. It appeals to the conservatism which is dominant in the well-to-do, and to the widespread timidity which hesitates to take any risk for the sake of a probable though uncertain gain. The sentiment is entirely respectable in itself, and more than respectable when its power is exercised against breach of the peace for other than the gravest motives — for any mere lucre of gain. But its limitations must be understood. A sound defensive scheme, sustaining the bases of the national force, is the foundation upon which war rests; but who lays a foundation without intending a superstructure? The offensive element in warfare is the superstructure, the end and aim for which the defensive exists, and apart from which it is to all purposes of war worse than useless. When war has been accepted as necessary, success means

---

[1] "Retrospect and Prospect," Considerations Governing the Disposition of Navies (1902), pp. 151–170.

nothing short of victory; and victory must be sought by offensive measures, and by them only can be ensured. " Being in, bear it, that the opposer may be ware of thee." No mere defensive attitude or action avails to such end. Whatever the particular mode of offensive action adopted, whether it be direct military attack, or the national exhaustion of the opponent by cutting off the sources of national well-being, whatsoever method may be chosen, offense, injury, weakening of the foe, to annihilation if need be, must be the guiding purpose of the belligerent. Success will certainly attend him who drives his adversary into the position of the defensive and keeps him there.

Offense therefore dominates, but it does not exclude. The necessity for defense remains obligatory, though subordinate. The two are complementary. It is only in the reversal of *rôles,* by which priority of importance is assigned to the defensive, that ultimate defeat is involved. Nor is this all. Though opposed in idea and separable in method of action, circumstances not infrequently have permitted the union of the two in a single general plan of campaign, which protects at the same time that it attacks. " Fitz James's blade was sword and shield." Of this the system of blockades by the British Navy during the Napoleonic wars was a marked example. Thrust up against the ports of France, and lining her coasts, they covered — shielded — the operations of their own commerce and cruisers in every sea; while at the same time, crossing swords, as it were, with the fleets within,

ever on guard, ready to attack, should the enemy
give an opening by quitting the shelter of his ports,
they frustrated his efforts at a combination of his
squadrons by which alone he could hope to reverse
conditions. All this was defensive; but the same
operation cut the sinews of the enemy's power by
depriving him of sea-borne commerce, and promoted the reduction of his colonies. Both these
were measures of offense; and both, it may be added,
were directed upon the national communications, the
sources of national well-being. The means was one,
the effect twofold. . . .

[It is shown that, in the case of insular states,
offense and defense are often closely combined,
home security depending on control of the sea
assured by offensive action of the national fleet. —
EDITOR.]

An insular state, which alone can be purely maritime, therefore contemplates war from a position of
antecedent probable superiority from the twofold
concentration of its policy; defense and offense being
closely identified, and energy, if exerted judiciously,
being fixed upon the increase of naval force to the
clear subordination of that more narrowly styled
military. The conditions tend to minimize the
division of effort between offensive and defensive
purpose, and, by greater comparative development
of the fleet, to supply a larger margin of disposable
numbers in order to constitute a mobile superiority
at a particular point of the general field. Such a
decisive local superiority at the critical point of
action is the chief end of the military art, alike in

tactics and strategy.   Hence it is clear that an insular state, if attentive to the conditions that should
dictate its policy, is inevitably led to possess a superiority in that particular kind of force, the
mobility of which enables it most readily to project
its power to the more distant quarters of the earth,
and also to change its point of application at will
with unequalled rapidity.

The general considerations that have been advanced concern all the great European nations, in
so far as they look outside their own continent, and
to maritime expansion, for the extension of national
influence and power; but the effect upon the action
of each differs necessarily according to their several
conditions.   The problem of sea-defense, for instance, relates primarily to the protection of the
national commerce everywhere, and specifically as
it draws near the home ports; serious attack upon
the coast, or upon the ports themselves, being a
secondary consideration, because little likely to befall a nation able to extend its power far enough to
sea to protect its merchant ships.   From this point
of view the position of Germany is embarrassed at
once by the fact that she has, as regards the world
at large, but one coast-line.   To and from this all
her sea commerce must go; either passing the English Channel, flanked for three hundred miles by
France on the one side and England on the other,
or else going north about by the Orkneys, a most
inconvenient circuit, and obtaining but imperfect
shelter from recourse to this deflected route.   Holland, in her ancient wars with England, when the

two were fairly matched in point of numbers, had dire experience of this false position, though her navy was little inferior in numbers to that of her opponent. This is another exemplification of the truth that distance is a factor equivalent to a certain number of ships. Sea-defense for Germany, in case of war with France or England, means established naval predominance at least in the North Sea; nor can it be considered complete unless extended through the Channel and as far as Great Britain will have to project hers into the Atlantic. This is Germany's initial disadvantage of position, to be overcome only by adequate superiority of numbers; and it receives little compensation from the security of her Baltic trade, and the facility for closing that sea to her enemies. In fact, Great Britain, whose North Sea trade is but one-fourth of her total, lies to Germany as Ireland does to Great Britain, flanking both routes to the Atlantic; but the great development of the British sea-coast, its numerous ports and ample internal communications, strengthen that element of sea defense which consists in abundant access to harbors of refuge.

For the Baltic Powers, which comprise all the maritime States east of Germany, the commercial drawback of the Orkney route is a little less than for Hamburg and Bremen, in that the exit from the Baltic is nearly equidistant from the north and south extremities of England; nevertheless the excess in distance over the Channel route remains very considerable. The initial naval disadvantage is in no wise diminished. For all the communities east of the Straits of Dover it remains true that in war commerce is paralyzed, and all the resultant consequences of impaired national strength entailed, unless decisive control of the North Sea is established. That effected, there is security for commerce by the northern passage; but this alone is mere defense. Offense, exerted anywhere on the globe, requires a surplusage of force, over that required to hold the North Sea, sufficient to extend and maintain itself west of the British Islands. In case of war with either of the Channel Powers, this means, as between the two opponents, that the eastern belligerent has to guard a long line of communications, and maintain distant positions, against an antagonist resting on a central position, with interior lines, able to strike at choice at either wing of the enemy's extended front. The relation which the English Channel, with its branch the Irish Sea, bears to the North Sea and the Atlantic — that of an interior position — is the same which the Mediterranean bears to the Atlantic and the Indian Sea; nor is it merely fanciful to trace in the passage round the north of Scotland an analogy to that by the Cape of Good Hope. It is a reproduction in miniature. The conditions are similar, the scale different. What the one is to a war whose scene is the north of Europe, the other is to operations by European Powers in Eastern Asia.

To protract such a situation is intolerable to the purse and *morale* of the belligerent who has the disadvantage of position. This of course leads us straight back to the fundamental principles of all naval war, namely, that defense is ensured only by offense, and that the one decisive objective of the offensive is the enemy's organized force, his battle fleet. Therefore, in the event of a war between one of the Channel Powers, and one or more of those to the eastward, the control of the North Sea must be at once decided. For the eastern State it is a matter of obvious immediate necessity, of commercial self-preservation. For the western State the offensive motive is equally imperative; but for Great Britain there is defensive need as well. Her Empire imposes such a development of naval force as makes it economically impracticable to maintain an army as large as those of the Continent. Security against invasion depends therefore upon the fleet. Postponing more distant interests, she must here concentrate an indisputable superiority. It is, however, inconceivable that against any one Power Great Britain should not be able here to exert from the first a preponderance which would effectually cover all her remoter possessions. Only an economical decadence, which would of itself destroy her position among nations, could bring her so to forego the initial advantage she has, in the fact that for her offense and defense meet and are fulfilled in one factor, the command of the sea. History has conclusively demonstrated the inability of a state with even a single continental frontier to compete in naval development with one that is insular, although of smaller population and resources. A coalition of Powers may indeed affect the balance. As a rule, however, a single state against a coalition holds the interior position, the concentrated force; and while calculation should rightly take account of possibilities, it should beware of permitting imagination too free sway in presenting its pictures. Were the eastern Powers to combine they might prevent Great Britain's use of the North Sea for the safe passage of her merchant shipping; but even so she would but lose commercially the whole of a trade, the greater part of which disappears by the mere fact of war. Invasion is not possible, unless her fleet can be wholly disabled from appearing in that sea. From her geographical position, she still holds her gates open to the outer world, which maintains three fourths of her commerce in peace.

37. Bearing of Political Developments on Naval Policy and Strategy [1]

THE external activities of Europe, noted a dozen years ago and before, have now to a certain extent been again superseded by rivalries within Europe itself. Those rivalries, however, are the result of their previous external activities, and in the last analysis they depend upon German commercial development. This has stimulated the German Empire to a prodigious naval programme, which affects the whole of Europe and may affect the United States. In 1897 I summed up two conspicuous European conditions as being the equilibrium then existing between France and Germany, with their respective allies, and the withdrawal of Great Britain from active association with the affairs of the Continent. At that date the Triple Alliance, Austria, Germany, Italy, stood against the Dual Alliance, France and Russia; Great Britain apart from both, but with elements of antagonism against Russia and France, and not against the German monarchies or Italy. These antagonisms arose wholly from conditions external to Europe, — in India against Russia, and in Africa against France. Later, the paralysis of Russia, through her defeat by Japan, and through her internal troubles, left France alone

1 "Naval Strategy" (1911), pp. 104–112.

for a time; during which Germany, thus assured against land attack, was better able to devote much money to the fleet, as the protector of her growing commerce. The results have been a projected huge German navy, and a German altercation with France relative to Moroccan affairs; incidents which have aroused Great Britain to a sense of naval danger, and have propelled her to the understandings — whatever they amount to — with France and Russia, which we now know as the Triple *Entente*. In short, Great Britain has abandoned the isolation of twenty years ago, stands joined to the Dual Alliance, and it becomes a Triple *Entente*.

To the United States this means that Great Britain, once our chief opponent in matters covered by the Monroe Doctrine, but later by the logic of events drawn to recede from that opposition, so that she practically backed us against Europe in 1898, and subsequently conceded the Panama arrangement known as the Hay-Pauncefote Treaty, cannot at present count for as much as she did in naval questions throughout the world. It means to the United States and to Japan that Great Britain has too much at stake at home to side with the one or the other, granting she so wished, except as bound by treaty, which implies reciprocal obligations. Between her and Japan such specific obligations exist. They do not in the case of the United States; and the question whether the two countries are disposed to support one another, and, if so, to what extent, or what the attitude of Great Britain would be in case of difficulty between Japan and the

United States, are questions directly affecting naval strategy.[1]

Great Britain does indeed for the moment hold Germany so far in check that the German Empire also can do no more than look after its European interests; but should a naval disaster befall Great Britain, leaving Germany master of the naval situation, the world would see again a predominant fleet backed by a predominant army, and that in the hands, not of a state satiated with colonial possessions, as Great Britain is, but of one whose late entry into world conditions leaves her without any such possessions at all of any great value. The habit of mind is narrow which fails to see that a navy such as Germany is now building will be efficacious for other ends than those immediately proposed. The existence of such a fleet is a constant factor in contemporary politics; the part which it shall play depending upon circumstances not always to be foreseen. Although the colonial ambitions of Germany are held in abeyance for the moment, the wish cannot but exist to expand her territory by foreign acquisitions, to establish external bases for the support of commercial or political interests, to build up such kindred communities as now help to constitute the British Empire, homes for emigrants, markets for industries, sources of supplies of raw materials, needed by those industries.

[1] Since this was written, a new Treaty of Alliance between Great Britain and Japan, operative for ten years, has been signed — July 13, 1911. By its terms either Power will be released from its military obligation to the other, as against a third with which it may have a treaty of general arbitration, such as that framed between Great Britain and the United States.

All such conditions and ambitions are incidents with which Strategy, comprehensively considered, has to deal. By the successive enunciations of the Monroe Doctrine the United States stands committed to the position that no particle of American soil shall pass into the hands of a non-American State other than the present possessor. No successful war between foreign states, no purchase, no exchange, no merger, such as the not impossible one of Holland with Germany, is allowed as valid cause for such transfer. This is a very large contract; the only guarantee of which is an adequate navy, however the term "adequate" be defined. Adequacy often depends not only upon existing balances of power, such, for instance, as that by which the British and German navies now affect one another, which for the moment secures the observance of the Doctrine. Account must be taken also of evident policies which threaten to disturb such balances, such as the official announcement by Germany of her purpose to create a "fleet of such strength that, even for the mightiest naval power, a war with Germany would involve such risks as to jeopardize its own supremacy." This means, at least, that Great Britain hereafter shall not venture, as in 1898, to back the United States against European interference; nor to support France in Morocco; nor to carry out as against Germany her alliance with Japan. It is a matter of very distinct consequence in naval strategy that Great Britain, after years of contention with the United States, essentially opposed to the claims of the Monroe Doctrine, should at last have come to substantial coincidence with the American point of view, even though she is not committed to a formal announcement to that effect.[1] Such relations between states are primarily the concern of the statesman, a matter of international policies; but they are also among the data which the strategist, naval as well as land, has to consider, because they are among the elements which determine the constitution and size of the national fleet.

I here quote with approval a statement of the French Captain Darrieus:

"Among the complex problems to which the idea of strategy gives rise there is none more important than that of the constitution of the fleet; and every project which takes no account of the foreign relations of a great nation, nor of the material limit fixed by its resources, rests upon a weak and unstable base."

I repeat also the quotation from Von der Goltz: "We must have a *national* strategy, a *national* tactics." I cannot too entirely repudiate any casual word of mine, reflecting the tone which once was so traditional in the navy that it might be called professional, — that "political questions belong rather to the statesman than to the military man." I find these words in my old lectures, but I very soon learned better, from my best military friend, Jomini; and I believe that no printed book of mine endorses the opinion that external politics are of no professional concern to military men.

[1] Since these words were written such formal announcement has been made by a member of the British Cabinet, Sir Edward Grey, the Secretary for Foreign Affairs, on May 23, 1911. *The Mail*, May 24, 1911.

It was in accordance with this changed opinion that in 1895, and again in 1897, I summed up European conditions as I conceived them to be; pointing out that the distinguishing feature at that time was substantial equilibrium on the Continent, constituting what is called the Balance of Power; and, in connection with the calm thus resulting, an immense colonizing movement, in which substantially all the great Powers were concerned. This I indicated as worthy of the notice of naval strategists, because there were parts of the American continents which for various reasons might attract upon themselves this movement, in disregard of the Monroe Doctrine.

Since then the scene has shifted greatly, the distinctive feature of the change being the growth of Germany in industrial, commercial, and naval power, — all three; while at the same time maintaining her military pre-eminence, although that has been somewhat qualified by the improvement of the French army, just as the growth of the German navy has qualified British superiority at sea. Coincident with this German development has been the decline of Russia, owing to causes generally understood; the stationariness of France in population, while Germany has increased fifty per cent; and the very close drawing together of Germany and Austria, for reasons of much more controlling power than the mere treaty which binds them. The result is that to-day central Europe, that is, Austria and Germany, form a substantially united body, extending from water to water, from North Sea to Adriatic, wielding a mili-

tary power against which, on the land, no combination in Europe can stand. The Balance of Power
no longer exists; that is, if my estimate is correct of
the conditions and dispersion which characterize the
other nations relatively to this central mass.

This situation, coinciding with British trade jealousies of the new German industries, and with the
German naval programme, have forced Great Britain out of the isolation which the Balance of Power
permitted her. Her *ententes* are an attempt to
correct the disturbance of the balance; but, while
they tend in that direction, they are not adequate
to the full result desired. The balance remains
uneven; and consequently European attention is
concentrated upon European conditions, instead of
upon the colonizing movements of twenty years ago.
Germany even has formally disavowed such colonizing ambitions, by the mouth of her ambassador
to the United States, confirmed by her minister of
foreign affairs, although a dozen years ago they
were conspicuous. Concerning these colonizing
movements, indeed, it might be said that they have
reached a moment of quiet, of equilibrium, while
internally Europe is essentially disquieted, as various
incidents have shown.

The important point to us here is the growing
power of the German Empire, in which the efficiency
of the State as an organic body is so greatly superior to that of Great Britain, and may prove to
be to that of the United States. The two English-
speaking countries have wealth vastly superior, each
separately, to that of Germany; much more if acting

together.   But in neither is the efficiency of the Government for handling the resources comparable to that of Germany; and there is no apparent chance or recognized inducement for them to work together, as Germany and Austria now work in Europe.   The consequence is that Germany may deal with each in succession much more effectively than either is now willing to consider; Europe being powerless to affect the issue so long as Austria stands by Germany, as she thoroughly understands that she has every motive to do.

It is this line of reasoning which shows the power of the German navy to be a matter of prime importance to the United States.   The power to control Germany does not exist in Europe, except in the British navy; and if social and political conditions in Great Britain develop as they now promise, the British navy will probably decline in relative strength, so that it will not venture to withstand the German on any broad lines of policy, but only in the narrowest sense of immediate British interests. Even this condition may disappear, for it seems as if the national life of Great Britain were waning at the same time that that of Germany is waxing.   The truth is, Germany, by traditions of two centuries, inherits now a system of state control, not only highly developed but with a people accustomed to it, — a great element of force; and this at the time when control of the individual by the community — that is, by the state — is increasingly the note of the times.   Germany has in this matter a large start. Japan has much the same.

When it is remembered that the United States, like Great Britain and like Japan, can be approached only by sea, we can scarcely fail to see that upon the sea primarily must be found our power to secure our own borders and to sustain our external policy, of which at the present moment there are two principal elements; namely, the Monroe Doctrine and the Open Door. Of the Monroe Doctrine President Taft, in his first message to Congress, has said that it has advanced sensibly towards general acceptance; and that maintenance of its positions in the future need cause less anxiety than it has in the past. Admitting this, and disregarding the fact that the respect conceded to it by Europe depends in part at least upon European rivalries modifying European ability to intervene, — a condition which may change as suddenly as has the power of Russia within the decade, — it remains obvious that the policy of the Open Door requires naval power quite as really and little less directly than the Monroe Doctrine. For the scene of the Open Door contention is the Pacific; the gateway to the Pacific for the United States is the Isthmus; the communications to the Isthmus are by way of the Gulf of Mexico and the Caribbean Sea. The interest of that maritime region therefore is even greater now than it was when I first undertook the strategic study of it, over twenty years ago. Its importance to the Monroe Doctrine and to general commercial interests remains, even if modified.

At the date of my first attempt to make this study of the Caribbean, and to formulate certain principles relative to Naval Strategy, there scarcely could be said to exist any defined public consciousness of European and American interest in sea power, and in the methods of its application which form the study of Strategy. The most striking illustration of this insensibility to the sea was to be found in Bismarck, who in a constructive sense was the greatest European statesman of that day. After the war with France and the acquisition of Alsace and Lorraine, he spoke of Germany as a state satiated with territorial expansion. In the matter of external policy she had reached the limits of his ambitions for her; and his mind thenceforth was set on internal development, which should harmonize the body politic and ensure Germany the unity and power which he had won for her. His scheme of external relations did not stretch beyond Europe. He was then too old to change to different conceptions, although he did not neglect to follow the demand of the people as their industry and commerce developed.

The contrast between the condition of indifference to the sea which he illustrated and that which now exists is striking; and the German Empire, which owes to him above all men its modern greatness, offers the most conspicuous illustration of the change. The new great navies of the world since 1887 are the German, the Japanese, and the American. Every state in Europe is now awake to the fact that the immediate coming interests of the world, which are therefore its own national interest, must be in the other continents. Europe in its relatively settled conditions offers really the base of operations for enterprises and decisive events, the scene of which will be in countries where political or economical backwardness must give place to advances which will be almost revolutionary in kind. This can scarcely be accomplished without unsettlements, the composing of which will depend upon force. Such force by a European state — with the single exception of Russia, and possibly, in a less degree, of Austria — can be exerted only through a navy.

38. Seizure of Private Property at Sea [1]

THE essence of the question involved in the seizure of " private property " at sea is transportation; and with three such conspicuous instances [2] within a century its effectiveness is historically demonstrated. The belligerent state, in the exercise of a right as yet conceded by international law, says in substance to its adversary, " I forbid your citizens the maritime transportation of their commercial property. Articles of whatever character, including the vessels which carry them, violating this lawful order will be seized and condemned." Seizure is made contingent upon movement; otherwise the property is merely bidden to stay at home, where it will be safe. All this is in strict conformity with the execution of law under common conditions; and the practice is now regulated with a precision and system consonant to other legal adjudication, the growth of centuries of jurisprudence directed to this particular subject. Its general tendency I have indicated by certain specific instances. It is efficient to the ends of war, more or less, according to circumstances; and by distributing the burden over the whole community affected it tends to peace, as ex-

[1] "Some Neglected Aspects of War" (1907), pp. 171–191.
[2] The Napoleonic Wars, the War of 1812, and the American Civil War. For the effect of commerce warfare in these struggles, see pp. 91–99. — Editor.

emption from capture could not do. If the suffering of war could be made to fall only on the combatants actually in the field, the rest of the nation being protected from harm and loss by the assured ability to pursue their usual avocations undisturbed, the selfishness of men would more readily resort to violence to carry their ends.

In support of the widespread effects of interruption to transportation, I gladly quote one of the recent contendents for immunity of " private property " from maritime capture. Having on one page maintained the ineffectiveness of the seizure, because individual losses never force a nation to make peace, he concludes his article by saying:

" The question interests directly and vitally thousands of people in every country. It is of vital importance to those who go down to the sea in ships, and those who occupy their business in great waters. It appeals not only to every shipowner, but also to every merchant whose goods are shipped upon the sea, to every farmer whose grain is sent abroad, to every manufacturer who sells to a foreign market, and to every banker who is dependent upon the prosperity of his countrymen."

I can do little to enhance this vivid presentation by an opponent; yet if we add to his list the butchers, the bakers, the tailors, shoemakers, grocers, whose customers economize; the men who drive drays to and from shipping, and find their occupation gone; the railroads, as the great common carriers, whose freights fall off; the stockholders whose dividends shrink; we shall by no means have exhausted the far-reaching influence of this intermeddling with transportation. It is a belligerent measure which touches every member of the hostile community, and, by thus distributing the evils of war, as insurance distributes the burden of other losses, it brings them home to every man, fostering in each a disposition to peace.

It doubtless will not have escaped readers familiar with the subject of maritime prize that so far I have not distinguished between the interruption of transportation by blockade and that by seizure on the high seas. The first, it may be said, is not yet in question; the second only is challenged. My reason has been that the underlying military principle — and, as I claim, justification — is the same in both; and, as we are dealing with a question of war, the military principle is of equal consideration with any other, if not superior. The effect produced is in character the same in both. In efficacy, they differ, and their comparative values in this respect are a legitimate subject for discussion. In principle and method, however, they are identical; both aim at the stoppage of transportation, as a means of destroying the resources of the enemy, and both are enforced by the seizure and condemnation of " private property " transgressing the orders.

This community of operation is so evident that, historically, the advocates of exemption of private property from confiscation in the one case have demanded, or at the least suggested, that blockade as a military measure cannot be instituted against commerce — that it can be resorted to only as against contraband, or where a port is "invested" by land as well as by sea. This was Napoleon's contention in the Berlin Decree; and it is worthy of grave attention that, under the pressure of momentary expediency, the United States more than once, between 1800 and 1812, advanced the same view. This I have shown in my history of the War of 1812.[1] Had this opinion then prevailed, the grinding blockade of the War of Secession could not have been applied. If we may imagine the United States and the Confederate States parties to a Hague Conference, we can conceive the impassioned advocacy of restricted blockade by the one, and the stubborn refusal of the other. This carries a grave warning to test seeming expediency in retaining or yielding a prescriptive right. There is no moral issue, if my previous argument is correct; unless it be moral, and I think it is, to resort to pecuniary pressure rather than to bloodshed to enforce a belligerent contention. As regards expediency, however, each nation should carefully weigh the effects upon itself, upon its rivals, and upon the general future of the community of states, before abandoning a principle of far-reaching consequence, and in operation often beneficent in restraining or shortening war.

It has been urged that conditions have so changed, through the numerous alternatives to sea transport now available, that the former efficacy can no longer be predicted. There might be occasional local suffering, but for communities at large the streams of supply are so many that the particular result of

[1] Vol. I, pp. 146–148.

general popular distress will not be attained to any decisive degree. Has this argument really been well weighed? None, of course, will dispute that certain conditions have been much modified, and for the better. Steam not only has increased rapidity of land transit for persons and goods; it has induced the multiplication of roads, and enforced the maintenance of them in good condition. Thanks to such maintenance, we are vastly less at the mercy of the seasons than we once were, and communities now have several lines of communication open where formerly they were dependent upon one. Nevertheless, for obvious reasons of cheapness and of facility, water transport sustains its ascendancy. It may carry somewhat less proportionately than in old times; but, unless we succeed in exploiting the air, water remains, and always must remain, the great medium of transportation. The open sea is a road which needs neither building nor repairs. Compared with its boundless expanse, two lines of rails afford small accommodation — a circumstance which narrowly limits their capacity for freight.

[It is shown that water transportation still plays an immense part in commerce, even in the case of inland watercourses in competition with railroads, and that any interruption of commerce throws a heavy burden on the nation involved. — Editor.]

Such derangement of an established system of sea transportation is more searching, as well as more easy, when the shipping involved has to pass close by an enemy's shores; and still more if the ports of possible arrival are few. This is conspicuously the case of Germany and the Baltic States relatively to Great Britain, and would be of Great Britain were Ireland independent and hostile. The striking development of German mercantile tonnage is significant of the growing grandeur, influence, and ambitions of the empire. Its exposure, in case of war with Great Britain, and only in less degree with France, would account, were other reasons wanting, for the importunate demand for naval expansion. Other reasons are not wanting; but in the development of her merchant shipping Germany, to use a threadbare phrase, has given a hostage to Fortune. Except by the measure advocated, and here opposed, of exempting from capture merchant vessels of a belligerent, with their cargoes, as being " private property," Germany is bound over to keep the peace, unless occasion of national safety — vital interests — or honor drive her, or unless she equip a navy adequate to so great a task as protecting fully the carrying trade she has laboriously created. The exposure of this trade is not merely a matter of German interest, nor yet of British. It is of international concern, a circumstance making for peace.

The retort is foreseen: How stands a nation to which the native mercantile shipping, carrying trade, is a distinctly minor interest, and therefore does not largely affect the question of transportation? This being maintained by neutrals, the accretion of national wealth by circulation may go on little impaired by hostilities. The first most obvious reply is that such is a distinctly specialized case in a general problem, and that its occurrence and continuance are dependent upon circumstances which frequently vary. It lacks the elements of permanence, and its present must therefore be regarded with an eye to the past and future. A half-century ago the mercantile marine of the United States was, and for nearly a century before had been, a close second to that of Great Britain; to-day it is practically non-existent, except for coasting-trade. On the other hand, during the earlier period the thriving Hanse towns were nearly the sole representatives of German shipping, which now, issuing from the same harbors, on a strip of coast still narrow, is pressing rapidly forward under the flag of the empire to take the place vacated by the Americans.

With such a reversal of conditions in two prominent examples, the problem of to-day in any one case is not that of yesterday, and may very well not be that of to-morrow. From decade to decade experience shifts like a weather-cock; the statesman mounted upon it becomes a Mr. Facing-Bothways. The denial of commercial blockade, the American national expediency of 1800, suggested by such eminent jurists as John Marshall and James Madison, would have been ruinous manacles to the nation of 1861–65. A government weighing its policy with reference to the future, having regard to possible as well as actual conditions, would do well before surrendering existing powers — the bird in the hand — to consider rather the geographical position of the country, its relation to maritime routes — the strategy, so to say, of the general permanent situation — and the military principles upon which maritime capture rests. In that light a more accurate estimate will be made of temporary tactical circumstances, to-day's conditions—such, for instance, as set forth by the present Lord Chancellor of Great Britain.[1] In his letter, favoring immunity from capture for " private property," disproportionate stress is laid upon the dangers of Great Britain, the points which make against her; a serious tactical error. The argument from exposure is so highly developed, that the possible enemies whose co-operation is needed to secure the desired immunity for " private " property might well regard the request to assist as spreading the net in the sight of the bird; a vanity which needs not a wise man to detect. On the other hand, the offensive advantage of capture to Great Britain, owing to her situation, is, in my judgment, inadequately appreciated.

The writer has fallen into the mistake which our General Sherman characterized as undue imagination concerning what " the man on the other side of the hill" might do; a quaint version of the first Napoleon's warning against " making a picture to yourself." The picture of Great Britain's dangers is overdrawn; that to her enemies — " the full measure of the mischief we could do to a Continental nation " — is underdrawn. It would seem as if, in his apprehension, " the disastrous consequences [2] which would flow from even slight depredations by commerce destroyers on British shipping " could find no parallel in the results to a

[1] The "Times" of October 14, 1905.
[2] Indirect, I presume.

Continental trade from British cruisers. France or Germany, for example, shut off from the sea, can be supplied by rail from, say, Antwerp or Rotterdam; but it is apparently inconceivable that, in the contingency of a protracted naval war, the same ports might equally supply Great Britain by neutral ships. Alternate sea routes close, apparently automatically; only alternate land routes stay open. Thus undue weight is laid upon defensive motives, where the offensive requires the greater emphasis. The larger merchant tonnage of Great Britain involves a greater defensive element, yes; but are not defensive conditions favorably modified by her greater navy, and by her situation, with all her western ports open to the Atlantic, from Glasgow to Bristol and round to Southampton? And is not the station for such defense identical with the best for offense by maritime capture? The British vessels there occupy also a superior position for coal renewal; the difficulty of which for an enemy, threatening the Atlantic approaches to Great Britain, seems too largely discounted by imaginations preoccupied with hostile commerce destroyers.

The concluding sentence of Lord Loreburn's letter contains a warning familiar to military thought. " Great Britain will gain much from a change long and eagerly *desired* by the great majority of other Powers." The wish of a possible enemy is the beacon which suggests the shoal. The truth is, if the British Navy maintains superiority, it is to the interest of her enemies to have immunity from capture for " private property; " if it falls, it is to their interest to be able to capture. The inference is safe that probable enemies, if such there be, and if they entertain the wish asserted, do not expect shortly to destroy the British Navy.

While unconvinced by the reasoning, it is refreshing to recognize in this letter a clear practical enunciation which sweeps away much sentimental rhetoric. " I urge [immunity for private property] not upon any ground of sentiment or humanity (indeed, no operation of war inflicts less suffering than the capturing of unarmed vessels at sea), but upon the ground that on the balance of argument, coolly weighed, the interests of Great Britain will gain much from the change." I more than doubt the conclusion; but its sobriety contrasts pleasantly with the exuberances, "noble and enlightened action," " crown of glory," and the like, with which it pleases certain of our American advocates to enwreathe this prosaic utilitarian proposition.

A possibility which affects the general question much more seriously than others so far considered, is that of neutral carriers taking the place of a national shipping exposed to capture under present law. This is one phase of a change which has come over the general conditions of carrying trade since the United States became a nation, and since Great Britain, three quarters of a century afterwards, formally repealed her Navigation Acts. The discussion preceding this repeal, together with the coincident Free Trade movement, preceded by but a few years the Treaty of Paris in 1856, and gave an impulse which doubtless facilitated the renounce-

ment in that treaty by Great Britain of the right
to capture enemy's property under a neutral flag.
The concession was in the air, as we say; which
proves only that it was contagious, not that it was
wise. Like many hasty steps, however, once taken
it probably is irreversible.

The effect of this concession has been to legalize,
among the several great states signatory to the
treaty, the carriage of belligerent property by neutral ships, in which previously it had been liable to
seizure. In its later operation, the condemnation
of the enemy's property had not involved the neutral
carrier further than by the delays necessary to take
her into port, adjudicate the question of ownership,
and remove the property, if found to be belligerent.
Such detention, however, was a strong deterrent,
and acted as an impediment to the circulation of
belligerent wealth by neutral means. It tended to
embarrass and impoverish the belligerent; hence the
removal of it is a modification of much importance.
Neutral shipping thus is now free to take a part in
hostilities, which formerly it could only do at the
risk of loss, more or less serious. To carry belligerent property, which under its own flag would be
open to seizure, is to aid the belligerent; is to take
part in the war.

In considering such an amelioration, if it be so
regarded, it is possible to exaggerate its degree. If
a nation cherishes its carrying-trade, does a large
part of its transportation in its own vessels, and is
unable in war to protect them, the benefit of the
innovation will be but partial. Its own shipping,

driven from the sea, is an important element in the total navigation of the world, and the means to replace it will not be at once at hand. Neutrals have their own commerce to maintain, as well as that of the weaker belligerent. They would not undertake the whole of the latter, if they could; and, if they would, they will not at once have the means. Steamships driven off the sea, and for the moment lost to navigation, cannot be replaced as rapidly as the old sailing-vessels. Moreover, neutral merchants have to weigh the chances of hostilities being short, and that the banished shipping of the belligerent may return in its might to the seas with the dawn of peace, making their own a drug on the market. In short, while the belligerent profits from a change which gives him free use of neutral ships, whereas he formerly had only a limited use, a considerable embarrassment remains. The effect is identical in principle and operation with that before indicated, as resulting from blockading a few chief harbors. A certain large fraction of transportation is paralyzed, and the work done by it is thrown upon ports and roads which have not the necessary facilities. It is as though a main trunk line of railroad were seized and held. The general system is deranged, prices rise, embarrassment results, and is propagated throughout the business community. This affects the nation by the suffering of thousands of individuals, and by the consequent reduction of revenue.

It would seem, therefore, that even under modern conditions maritime capture — of " private " property — is a means of importance to the ends of war; that it acts directly upon the individual citizens and upon the financial power of the belligerent, the effect being intensified by indirect influence upon the fears of the sensitive business world. These political and financial consequences bring the practice into exact line with military principle; for, being directed against the resources of the enemy, by interrupting his communications with the outer world, it becomes strictly analogous to operations against the communications of an army with its base — one of the chief objects of strategy. Upon the maintenance of communications the life of an army depends, upon the maintenance of commerce the vitality of a state. Money, credit, is the life of war. Lessen it, and vigor flags; destroy it, and resistance dies. Accepting these conclusions, each state has to weigh the probable bearing upon its own fortunes of the continuance or discontinuance of the practice. From the military point of view the question is not merely, nor chiefly, "What shall our people escape by the abandonment of this time-sanctioned method?" but, "What power to overcome the enemy shall we thereby surrender?" It is a question of balance, beween offense and defense. As Jefferson said, when threatened with a failure of negotiations, "We shall have to begin the irrational process of trying which can do the other most harm." As a summary of war, the sentence is a caricature; but it incidentally embodies Farragut's aphorism, "The best defense is a rapid fire from our own guns." For the success of war, offense is better than defense; and in contemplating this or any other military measure, let there be dismissed at once, as preposterous, the hope that war can be carried on without some one or something being hurt; that the accounts should show credit only and no debit.

For the community of states a broader view should be taken, from the standpoint that whatever tends to make war more effective tends to shorten it and to prevent it.

39. The Moral Aspect of War [1]

THE poet's words, " The Parliament of man, the federation of the world," were much in men's mouths this past summer. There is no denying the beauty of the ideal, but there was apparent also a disposition, in contemplating it, to contemn the slow processes of evolution by which Nature commonly attains her ends, and to impose at once, by convention, the methods that commended themselves to the sanguine. Fruit is not best ripened by premature plucking, nor can the goal be reached by such short cuts. Step by step, in the past, man has ascended by means of the sword, and his more recent gains, as well as present conditions, show that the time has not yet come to kick down the ladder which has so far served him. Three hundred years ago, the people of the land in which the Conference was assembled wrenched with the sword civil and religious peace, and national independence, from the tyranny of Spain. Then began the disintegration of her empire, and the deliverance of peoples from her oppression; but this was completed only last year, and then again by the sword — of the United States.

In the centuries which have since intervened,

1 "Some Neglected Aspects of War," The Peace Conference and the Moral Aspect of War (1899), pp. 45–52.

what has not " justice, with valor armed," when confronted by evil in high places, found itself compelled to effect by resort to the sword? To it was due the birth of the United States, not least among the benefits of which was the stern experience that has made Great Britain no longer the mistress, but the mother, of her dependencies. The control, to good from evil, of the devastating fire of the French Revolution, and of Napoleon, was due to the sword. The long line of illustrious names and deeds, of those who bore it not in vain, has in our times culminated — if indeed the end is even yet nearly reached — in the new birth of the United States by the extirpation of human slavery, and in the downfall, but yesterday, of a colonial empire identified with tyranny. What the sword, and it supremely, tempered only by the stern demands of justice and of conscience, and the loving voice of charity, has done for India and for Egypt, is a tale at once too long and too well known for repetition here. Peace, indeed, is not adequate to all progress; there are resistances that can be overcome only by explosion. What means less violent than war would in a half-year have solved the Caribbean problem, shattered national ideas deep rooted in the prepossessions of a century, and planted the United States in Asia, face to face with the great world problem of the immediate future? What but the War of 1898 rent the veil which prevented the English-speaking communities from seeing eye to eye, and revealed to each the face of a brother? Little wonder that a war which, with comparatively little bloodshed, brought such consequences, was followed by the call for a Peace Conference!

Power, force, is a faculty of national life; one of the talents committed to nations by God. Like every other endowment of a complex organization, it must be held under control of the enlightened intellect and of the upright heart; but no more than any other can it be carelessly or lightly abjured, without incurring the responsibility of one who buries in the earth that which was entrusted to him for use. And this obligation to maintain right, by force if need be, while common to all states, rests peculiarly upon the greater, in proportion to their means. Much is required of those to whom much is given. So viewed, the ability speedily to put forth the nation's power, by adequate organization and other necessary preparation, according to the reasonable demands of the nation's intrinsic strength and of its position in the world, is one of the clear duties involved in the Christian word " watchfulness," — readiness for the call that may come, whether expectedly or not. Until it is demonstrable that no evil exists, or threatens the world, which cannot be obviated without recourse to force, the obligation to readiness must remain; and, where evil is mighty and defiant, the obligation to use force — that is, war — arises. Nor is it possible, antecedently, to bring these conditions and obligations under the letter of precise and codified law, to be administered by a tribunal. The spirit of legalism is marked by blemishes as real as those commonly attributed to " militarism," and not more elevated. The considerations which determine good and evil, right and wrong, in crises of national life, or of the world's history, are questions of equity often too complicated for decision upon mere rules, or even upon principles, of law, international or other. The instances of Bulgaria, of Armenia, and of Cuba, are entirely in point; and it is most probable that the contentions about the future of China will afford further illustration. Even in matters where the interest of nations is concerned, the moral element enters; because each generation in its day is the guardian of those which shall follow it. Like all guardians, therefore, while it has the power to act according to its best judgment, it has no right, for the mere sake of peace, to permit known injustice to be done to its wards.

The present strong feeling in favor of arbitration, throughout the nations of the world, is in itself a subject for congratulation almost unalloyed. It carries indeed a promise, to the certainty of which no paper covenants can pretend; for it influences the conscience by inward conviction, not by external fetter. But it must be remembered that such sentiments, from their very universality and evident laudableness, need correctives, for they bear in themselves a great danger of excess or of precipitancy. Excess is seen in the disposition, far too prevalent, to look upon war not only as an evil, but as an evil unmixed, unnecessary, and therefore always unjustifiable; while precipitancy, to reach results considered desirable, is evidenced by the wish to *impose* arbitration, to prevent recourse to war, by a general pledge previously made. Both frames of mind receive expression in the words of speakers among whom a leading characteristic is lack of measuredness and of proportion. Thus an eminent citizen is reported to have said: " There is no more occasion for two nations to go to war than for two men to settle their difficulties with clubs." Singularly enough, this point of view assumes to represent peculiarly Christian teaching. In so doing, it willfully ignores the truth that Christianity, while it will not force the conscience by other than spiritual arguments, as " compulsory " arbitration might, distinctly recognizes the sword as the resister and remedier of evil in the sphere " of this world."

Arbitration's great opportunity has come in the advancing moral standards of states, whereby the disposition to deliberate wrong-doing has diminished; consequently, the occasions for redressing wrong by force are less frequent to arise. In view of recent events, however, and very especially of notorious, high-handed oppression, initiated since the calling of the Peace Conference,[1] and resolutely continued during its sessions in defiance of the public opinion of the world at large, it is premature to assume that such occasions belong wholly to the past. Much less can it be assumed that there will be no further instances of a community believing, conscientiously and entirely, that honor and duty require of it a certain course, which another community with equal integrity may hold to be incon-

[1] Lest this be misunderstood to be an allusion to the recent measures of Japan in Korea, I renew here the caution that in this article all references to the Peace Conference are to that of 1899.

sistent with the rights and obligations of its own members. It is, for instance, quite possible, especially to one who has recently visited Holland, to conceive that Great Britain and the Boers are alike satisfied of the substantial justice of their respective claims. It is permissible most earnestly to hope that, in disputes between sovereign states, arbitration may find a way to reconcile peace with fidelity to conscience, in the case of both; but if the conviction of conscience remains unshaken, war is better than disobedience, — better than acquiescence in recognized wrong. The great danger of undiscriminating advocacy of arbitration, which threatens even the cause it seeks to maintain, is that it may lead men to tamper with equity, to compromise with unrighteousness, soothing their conscience with the belief that war is so entirely wrong that beside it no other tolerated evil is wrong. Witness Armenia, and witness Crete. War has been avoided; but what of the national consciences that beheld such iniquity and withheld the hand?

40. The Practical Aspect of War [1]

IF it be true, as I have expressed my own conviction, that moral motives are gaining in force the world over, we can have hope of the time when they shall prevail; but it is evident that they must prevail over all nations equally, or with some approach to equality, or else discussion between two disputants will not rest on the same plane. In the difference between the United States and Spain, I suppose the argument of the United States, the moral justification to itself of its proposed action, would be that misgovernment of Cuba, and needless Cuban suffering, had continued so long as to show that Spain was not capable of giving good government to her distant dependency. There was no occasion to question her desire to give it, the honesty either of her assertions or measures to that end; but it was quite apparent that it was not in her to give effect to her efforts. Now, presuming Spain to take that view, it is conceivable (to the imagination) that her rulers might say, " Yes, it is true, we have failed continuously. The Cubans have a moral right to good government, and as we have not been able to give it them, it is right that we should step out." But, assuming Spain unequal to such sublime moral conviction and self-abnegation, what was the United

[1] "Some Neglected Aspects of War," The Hague Conference and the Practical Aspect of War (1907), pp. 75–80, 90–93.

States to do, as a practical matter? What she did was perfectly practical; she used the last argument of nations as international law stands; but, suppose she had gone to arbitration, upon what grounds would the Court proceed? What the solid pre-arranged basis of its decision, should that be that Spain must evacuate Cuba? Is there anything in the present accord of states, styled International Law, that would give such power? And, more pertinent still, are states prepared now to concede to an arbitral Court the power to order them out of territory which in its opinion they misgovern, or which in its opinion they should not retain after conquest? *e. g.*, Schleswig Holstein, Alsace and Lorraine, the Transvaal, Porto Rico and the Philippine Islands?

Or, take another impending and very momentous instance, one fraught with immeasurable issues. If I rightly appreciate conditions, there is, among the English-speaking communities bordering the Pacific, a deep instinctive popular determination, one of those before which rulers have to bow, to exclude, from employment in the sparsely settled territories occupied by them, the concentrated crowded mass of mankind found in Japan and China. More than anything else this sums up the question of the Pacific. Two seas of humanity, on very different levels as to numbers and economical conditions, stand separated only by this artificial dyke of legislation, barring the one from rushing upon and flooding the other. I do not criticize an attitude with which, whether I approve or not, I can sympathize; but as

I look at the legislation, and contrast the material conditions, I wonder at the improvidence of Australasia in trusting that laws, though breathing the utmost popular conviction and purpose, can protect their lands from that which threatens. " Go home," said Franklin to a fellow colonist in the days of unrest in America, " and tell them to get children. That will settle all our difficulties." Fill up your land with men of your own kind, if you wish to keep it for yourselves. The Pacific States of North America are filling up, and, more important, they back solidly upon, and are politically one with, other great communities into which the human tide is pouring apace; yet in them, too, labor may inflict upon its own aims revolutionary defeat, if for supposed local advantage it embarrasses the immigration of its own kind. It is very different for those who are severed from their like by sea, and therefore must stand on their own bottom. All the naval power of the British Empire cannot suffice ultimately to save a remote community which neither breeds men in plenty nor freely imports them.

We speak of these questions now as racial, and the expression is convenient. It is compact, and represents truly one aspect of such situations, which, however, are essentially economical and territorial. In long-settled countries race and territory tend to identity of meaning, but we need scarce a moment's recollection to know that race does not bind as do border lines, nor even they as do economical facts. Economical facts largely brought about the separation of America from Great Britain; economical facts brought about the American Union and continue to bind it. The closer union of the territories which now constitute the British Empire must be found in economical adjustments; the fact of common race is not sufficient thereto. Now, economical influences are of the most purely material order — the order of personal self-interest; in that form at least they appeal to the great majority, for the instructed political economists form but a small proportion of any community. Race, yes; territory — country — yes; the heart thrills, the eyes fill, self-sacrifice seems natural, the moral motive for the moment prevails; but in the long run the hard pressure of economical truth comes down upon these with the tyranny of the despot. There are, indeed, noble leaders not a few, who see in this crushing burden upon their fellow millions an enemy to be confronted and vanquished, not by direct opposition, but by circumvention, relieving his sway by bettering environment, and so giving play to the loftier sentiments. But that these men may so work they need to be, as we say, independent, released from the grip of daily bread; and their very mission, alike in its success and its failures, testifies to the preponderant weight of economical conditions in the social world. . . .

If with wealth, numbers and opportunity, a people still cannot so organize their strength as to hold their own, it is not practical to expect that those to whom wealth and opportunity are lacking, but who have organizing faculty and willingness to fight, will not under the pressure of need enter

upon an inheritance which need will persuade themselves is ethically their due.   What, it may be asked,
is likely to be the reasoning of an intelligent Chinese
or Japanese workman, realizing the relative opportunities of his crowded country and those of Australia and California, and finding himself excluded
by force?   What ethical, what moral, value will he
find in the contention that his people should not
resort to force to claim a share in the better conditions from which force bars him?   How did the
white races respect the policy of isolation in Japan
and China, though it only affected commercial advantages?   I do not in the least pronounce upon the
ethical propriety of exclusion by those in possession
— the right of property, now largely challenged.   I
merely draw attention to the apparent balance of
ethical argument, with the fact of antagonistic
economical conditions; and I say that for such a
situation the only practical arbiter is the physical
force, of which war is merely the occasional political
expression.

In the broad outlook, which embraces not merely
armed collision, but the condition of preparation
and attitude of mind that enable a people to put
forth, on demand, the full measure of their physical
strength, — numerical, financial and military, — to
repel a threatened injury or maintain a national
right, war is the regulator and adjuster of those
movements of the peoples, which in their tendencies
and outcome constitute history.   These are natural
forces, which from their origin and power are self-
existent and independent in relation to man.   His

provision against them is war; the artificial organization of other forces, intrinsically less powerful materially, but with the advantage which intelligent combination and direction confer. By this he can measurably control, guide, delay, or otherwise beneficially modify, results which threaten to be disastrous in their extent, tendency, or suddenness. So regarded war is remedial or preventive.

I apprehend that these two adjectives, drawn from the vocabulary of the healer, embody both the practical and moral justification of war. An ounce of prevention is worth a pound of cure. It will be well that we invoke moral power to help heal the evils of the world, as the physician brings it to bear on the ills of the body; but few are prepared to rely upon it alone. We need material aid as well. The dikes of Holland withstand by direct opposition the natural mission of the North Sea to swallow up the land they protect. The levees of the Mississippi restrain and guide to betterment the course of the mighty current, which but for them would waste its strength to devastate the shores on either hand. These two artificial devices represent a vast expenditure of time, money, and energy; of unproductive labor so-called; but they are cheaper than a flood. The police of our great cities prevent the outburst of crime, the fearful possibilities of which manifest themselves on the happily rare occasions when material prevention has from any cause lapsed. The police bodies are a great expense; but they cost less than a few days of anarchy. Let us not deceive ourselves by fancying that the strong material impulses which drive those masses of men whom we style nations, or races, are to be checked or guided, unless to the argument of a reasonable contention there be given the strong support of organized material power. If the organized disappear, the unorganized will but come into surer and more dreadful collision.

41. Motives for Naval Power [1]

THERE is one further conclusion to be drawn from the war between Japan and Russia, which contradicts a previous general impression that I myself have shared, and possibly in some degree have contributed to diffuse. That impression is, that navies depend upon maritime commerce as the cause and justification of their existence. To a certain extent, of course, this is true; and, just because true to a certain extent, the conclusion is more misleading. Because partly true, it is accepted as unqualifiedly true. Russia has little maritime commerce, at least in her own bottoms; her merchant flag is rarely seen; she has a very defective sea-coast; can in no sense be called a maritime nation. Yet the Russian navy had the decisive part to play in the late war; and the war was unsuccessful, not because the navy was not large enough, but because it was improperly handled. Probably, it also was intrinsically insufficient — bad in quality; poor troops as well as poor generalship. The disastrous result does not contravene the truth that Russia, though with little maritime shipping, was imperatively in need of a navy.

I am not particularly interested here to define the relations of commerce to a navy. It seems reasonable to say that, where merchant shipping exists, it

[1] "Naval Strategy," pp. 445-447.

tends logically to develop the form of protection
which is called naval; but it has become perfectly
evident, by concrete examples, that a navy may be
necessary where there is no shipping.   Russia and
the United States to-day are such instances in point.
More and more it becomes clear, that the functions
of navies are distinctly military and international,
whatever their historical origin in particular cases.
The navy of the United States, for example, took
its rise from purely commercial considerations.   External interests cannot be confined to those of commerce.   They may be political as well as commercial; may be political because commercial, like
the claim to " the open door " in China; may be
political because military, essential to national defense, like the Panama Canal and Hawaii; may be
political because of national prepossessions and
sympathies, race sympathies, such as exist in Europe,
or traditions like the Monroe Doctrine.   The Monroe Doctrine in its beginnings was partly an expression of commercial interest, directed against a
renewal of Spanish monopoly in the colonial system;
it was partly military, defensive against European
aggressions and dangerous propinquity; partly political, in sympathy with communities struggling for
freedom.
    A broad basis of mercantile maritime interests
and shipping will doubtless conduce to naval efficiency, by supplying a reserve of material and personnel.   Also, in representative governments, military interests cannot without loss dispense with the
backing which is supplied by a widely spread, deeply

rooted, civil interest, such as merchant shipping would afford us.

To prepare for war in time of peace is impracticable to commercial representative nations, because the people in general will not give sufficient heed to military necessities, or to international problems, to feel the pressure which induces readiness. All that naval officers can do is to realize to themselves vividly, make it a part of their thought, that a merchant shipping is only one form of the many which the external relations of a country can assume. We have such external questions in the Monroe Doctrine, the Panama Canal, the Hawaiian Islands, the market of China, and, I may add, in the exposure of the Pacific Coast, with its meagre population, insufficiently developed resources, and somewhat turbulent attitude towards Asiatics. The United States, with no aggressive purpose, but merely to sustain avowed policies, for which her people are ready to fight, although unwilling to prepare, needs a navy both numerous and efficient, even if no merchant vessel ever again flies the United States flag. If we hold these truths clearly and comprehensively, as well as with conviction, we may probably affect those who affect legislation. At all events, so to hold will do no harm.

APPENDIX

CHRONOLOGICAL OUTLINE

1840. September 27, Alfred Thayer Mahan born at West Point, New York, son of Professor Dennis Hart Mahan of the U. S. Military Academy.

1854–1856. Student at Columbia College in the City of New York.

1856. September 30, entered the third class, U. S. Naval Academy, as acting midshipman. Appointed from the 10th Congressional District of New York.

1859. June 9, graduated as midshipman.

1859–1861. Frigate *Congress,* Brazil station.

1861. August 31, promoted to lieutenant. Converted steamer *James Adger* for ten days.

1861–1862. Steam corvette *Pocahontas,* in the Potomac flotilla; capture of Port Royal, November 7, 1861; South Atlantic Blockading Squadron.

1862–1863. Naval Academy at Newport, Rhode Island. First lieutenant in the *Macedonian* during the summer practice cruise to England in 1863.

1863–1864. Steam corvette *Seminole,* West Gulf Blockading Squadron.

1864–1865. *James Adger;* staff of Rear Admiral Dahlgren, South Atlantic Blockading Squadron; *James Adger.*

1865–1866. Double-ender *Muscoota.*

1865. June 7, promoted to lieutenant commander.

1866. Ordnance duty, Washington Navy Yard.

1867–1869. Steam sloop *Iroquois,* to Asiatic station, via Cape of Good Hope. Detached in 1869; returned via Rome and Paris.

1869. Commanding gunboat *Aroostook,* Asiatic station.

1870–1871. Navy yard, New York.

1871. *Worcester,* home station.

1872. Promoted to commander. Receiving ship, New York.

1873–1874. Commanding side-wheel steamer *Wasp* in the Rio de la Plata.

1875–1876. Navy yard, Boston.

1877–1880. Naval Academy, Annapolis.

1880–1883. Navy yard, New York.

1883–1885. Commanding steam sloop *Wachusett,* South Pacific Squadron.

1885. Assigned to Naval War College, as lecturer on naval history and strategy.

1886–1889. President of Naval War College.

1889–1892. Special duty, Bureau of Navigation. Member of commission to choose site for navy yard in Puget Sound.

1892–1893. President of Naval War College.

1893–1895. Commanding cruiser *Chicago,* flagship of Rear Admiral Erben, European station.

1895–1896. Special duty at the Naval War College.

1896. November 17, retired as captain on his own application after forty years' service.

1896–1912. Special duty in connection with Naval War College.

1898. Member of Naval War Board during Spanish War.

1899. Delegate to Hague Peace Conference.

1906. June 29, rear admiral on the retired list.

1914. December 1, died at the Naval Hospital, Washington.

ACADEMIC HONORS

D.C.L., Oxford, 1894; LL.D., Cambridge, 1894; LL.D., Harvard, 1895; LL.D., Yale, 1897; LL.D., Columbia, 1900; LL.D., Magill, 1909; President of the American Historical Association, 1902.

PUBLISHED WORKS

1883. " The Gulf and Inland Waters."

1890. " The Influence of Sea Power upon History, 1660–1783."

1892. " The Influence of Sea Power upon the French Revolution and Empire, 1793–1812." Two volumes.
" The Life of Admiral Farragut."

1897. " The Life of Nelson: the Embodiment of the Sea Power of Great Britain." Two volumes.
" The Interest of America in Sea Power, Present and Future."

1899. " Lessons of the War with Spain."

1900. " The Problem of Asia, and its Effect upon International Policies."
" The Story of the War with South Africa, 1899–1900."

1901. " Types of Naval Officers, Drawn from the History of the British Navy."

1902. " Retrospect and Prospect: Studies in International Relations, Naval and Political."

1905. " Sea Power in its Relations to the War of 1812." Two volumes.

1907. " Some Neglected Aspects of War."
" From Sail to Steam: Recollections of a Naval Life."

1908. " Naval Administration and Warfare."

1909. " The Harvest Within: Thoughts on the Life of a Christian."

1910. " The Interest of America in International Conditions."

1911. " Naval Strategy, Compared and Contrasted with the Principles and Practice of Military Operations on Land."

1912. " Armaments and Arbitration: the Place of Force in International Relations."

1913. " The Major Operations of the Navies in the War of American Independence."

UNCOLLECTED ESSAYS

(For a more extended list, see W. D. Puleston, "Life of Mahan,"
p. 363.

"Reflections, Historical and Other, Suggested by the Battle of the Sea of Japan," *U. S. Naval Institute*, June, 1906; reprinted in *Journal of the Royal United Service Institution*, November, 1906.

"The Battleship of All Big Guns," *World's Work*, January, 1911.

"Misrepresenting Mr. Roosevelt," *Outlook*, June 17, 1911.

"Importance of Command of the Sea," *Scientific American*, December 9, 1911.

"Was Panama a Chapter of National Dishonor?" *North American Review*, October, 1912.

"Japan among Nations," *Living Age*, August 2, 1913.

"Twentieth Century Christianity," *North American Review*, April, 1914.

"Macdonough at Plattsburg," *North American Review*, August, 1914.

"The Panama Canal and the Distribution of the Fleet," *North American Review*, September, 1914.

REFERENCES

The standard biography of Mahan is by Captain W. D. Puleston, U.S.N. (Yale University Press, 1939). Of value also are an earlier biography by C. C. Taylor (1920) and a collection of letters from Mahan to Samuel A'Court Ashe (Duke University Library Publications, 1931). Aside from book reviews, the more important articles on Mahan are as follows:

"Mahan's Counsels to the United States," G. S. Clarke, *Nineteenth Century*, February, 1898.

"Mahan on Sea Power," S. G. W. Benjamin, *New York Times Book Review*, January 18, 1902.

"La Maîtrise de la Mer," Auguste Moireau, *Revue des Deux Mondes*, October, 1902.

"Some American Historians," Professor H. Morse Stephens, *World's Work*, July, 1902.

"Lee at Appomattox and Other Papers," Charles Francis Adams, 1903, p. 356 ff.

"The Writings of Mahan," *New York Nation*, December 10, 1914.

"A Great Public Servant," Theodore Roosevelt, *Outlook*, January 13, 1915. See also *Outlook*, December 9, 1914.

"Alfred Thayer Mahan — In Memoriam," *United States Naval Institute*, January–February, 1915.

"The Influence of America's Greatest Naval Strategist on the War in Europe," *Current Opinion*, February, 1915. (Taken from Paris *Figaro*.)

"Naval History: Mahan and His Successors," *Military Historian and Economist*, January, 1918.

"Scrapping Mahan," W. O. Stevens, *Yale Review*, April, 1923.

"Incendiary Mahan," L. M. Hacker, *Scribner's Magazine*, April, 1934.

"Mahan, Naval Philosopher," W. D. Puleston, *Scribner's Magazine*, November, 1934.

"Mahan's 'The Problem of Asia'; the Future in Retrospect," Tyler Dennett, *Foreign Affairs*, April, 1935.

"Mahan and the Present War," H. C. Ferraby, *Nineteenth Century and After*, April, 1940.

"A Re-Examination of Mahan's Concept of Sea Power," W. D. Puleston, *U. S. Naval Institute Proceedings*, September, 1940.

INDEX

A CATALOG OF SELECTED
DOVER BOOKS
IN ALL FIELDS OF INTEREST

A CATALOG OF SELECTED DOVER
BOOKS IN ALL FIELDS OF INTEREST

CONCERNING THE SPIRITUAL IN ART, Wassily Kandinsky. Pioneering work by father of abstract art. Thoughts on color theory, nature of art. Analysis of earlier masters. 12 illustrations. 80pp. of text. 5⅜ x 8½. 23411-8 Pa. $4.95

ANIMALS: 1,419 Copyright-Free Illustrations of Mammals, Birds, Fish, Insects, etc., Jim Harter (ed.). Clear wood engravings present, in extremely lifelike poses, over 1,000 species of animals. One of the most extensive pictorial sourcebooks of its kind. Captions. Index. 284pp. 9 x 12. 23766-4 Pa. $14.95

CELTIC ART: The Methods of Construction, George Bain. Simple geometric techniques for making Celtic interlacements, spirals, Kells-type initials, animals, humans, etc. Over 500 illustrations. 160pp. 9 x 12. (USO) 22923-8 Pa. $9.95

AN ATLAS OF ANATOMY FOR ARTISTS, Fritz Schider. Most thorough reference work on art anatomy in the world. Hundreds of illustrations, including selections from works by Vesalius, Leonardo, Goya, Ingres, Michelangelo, others. 593 illustrations. 192pp. 7⅛ x 10¼. 20241-0 Pa. $9.95

CELTIC HAND STROKE-BY-STROKE (Irish Half-Uncial from "The Book of Kells"): An Arthur Baker Calligraphy Manual, Arthur Baker. Complete guide to creating each letter of the alphabet in distinctive Celtic manner. Covers hand position, strokes, pens, inks, paper, more. Illustrated. 48pp. 8¼ x 11. 24336-2 Pa. $3.95

EASY ORIGAMI, John Montroll. Charming collection of 32 projects (hat, cup, pelican, piano, swan, many more) specially designed for the novice origami hobbyist. Clearly illustrated easy-to-follow instructions insure that even beginning papercrafters will achieve successful results. 48pp. 8¼ x 11. 27298-2 Pa. $3.50

THE COMPLETE BOOK OF BIRDHOUSE CONSTRUCTION FOR WOODWORKERS, Scott D. Campbell. Detailed instructions, illustrations, tables. Also data on bird habitat and instinct patterns. Bibliography. 3 tables. 63 illustrations in 15 figures. 48pp. 5¼ x 8½. 24407-5 Pa. $2.50

BLOOMINGDALE'S ILLUSTRATED 1886 CATALOG: Fashions, Dry Goods and Housewares, Bloomingdale Brothers. Famed merchants' extremely rare catalog depicting about 1,700 products: clothing, housewares, firearms, dry goods, jewelry, more. Invaluable for dating, identifying vintage items. Also, copyright-free graphics for artists, designers. Co-published with Henry Ford Museum & Greenfield Village. 160pp. 8¼ x 11. 25780-0 Pa. $10.95

HISTORIC COSTUME IN PICTURES, Braun & Schneider. Over 1,450 costumed figures in clearly detailed engravings–from dawn of civilization to end of 19th century. Captions. Many folk costumes. 256pp. 8⅜ x 11¾. 23150-X Pa. $12.95

STICKLEY CRAFTSMAN FURNITURE CATALOGS, Gustav Stickley and L. & J. G. Stickley. Beautiful, functional furniture in two authentic catalogs from 1910. 594 illustrations, including 277 photos, show settles, rockers, armchairs, reclining chairs, bookcases, desks, tables. 183pp. 6½ x 9¼. 23838-5 Pa. $11.95

AMERICAN LOCOMOTIVES IN HISTORIC PHOTOGRAPHS: 1858 to 1949, Ron Ziel (ed.). A rare collection of 126 meticulously detailed official photographs, called "builder portraits," of American locomotives that majestically chronicle the rise of steam locomotive power in America. Introduction. Detailed captions. xi + 129pp. 9 x 12. 27393-8 Pa. $13.95

AMERICA'S LIGHTHOUSES: An Illustrated History, Francis Ross Holland, Jr. Delightfully written, profusely illustrated fact-filled survey of over 200 American lighthouses since 1716. History, anecdotes, technological advances, more. 240pp. 8 x 10¾. 25576-X Pa. $12.95

TOWARDS A NEW ARCHITECTURE, Le Corbusier. Pioneering manifesto by founder of "International School." Technical and aesthetic theories, views of industry, economics, relation of form to function, "mass-production split" and much more. Profusely illustrated. 320pp. 6⅛ x 9¼. (USO) 25023-7 Pa. $9.95

HOW THE OTHER HALF LIVES, Jacob Riis. Famous journalistic record, exposing poverty and degradation of New York slums around 1900, by major social reformer. 100 striking and influential photographs. 233pp. 10 x 7⅞. 22012-5 Pa. $11.95

FRUIT KEY AND TWIG KEY TO TREES AND SHRUBS, William M. Harlow. One of the handiest and most widely used identification aids. Fruit key covers 120 deciduous and evergreen species; twig key 160 deciduous species. Easily used. Over 300 photographs. 126pp. 5⅜ x 8½. 20511-8 Pa. $3.95

COMMON BIRD SONGS, Dr. Donald J. Borror. Songs of 60 most common U.S. birds: robins, sparrows, cardinals, bluejays, finches, more–arranged in order of increasing complexity. Up to 9 variations of songs of each species. Cassette and manual 99911-4 $8.95

ORCHIDS AS HOUSE PLANTS, Rebecca Tyson Northen. Grow cattleyas and many other kinds of orchids–in a window, in a case, or under artificial light. 63 illustrations. 148pp. 5⅜ x 8½. 23261-1 Pa. $5.95

MONSTER MAZES, Dave Phillips. Masterful mazes at four levels of difficulty. Avoid deadly perils and evil creatures to find magical treasures. Solutions for all 32 exciting illustrated puzzles. 48pp. 8¼ x 11. 26005-4 Pa. $2.95

MOZART'S DON GIOVANNI (DOVER OPERA LIBRETTO SERIES), Wolfgang Amadeus Mozart. Introduced and translated by Ellen H. Bleiler. Standard Italian libretto, with complete English translation. Convenient and thoroughly portable–an ideal companion for reading along with a recording or the performance itself. Introduction. List of characters. Plot summary. 121pp. 5¼ x 8½. 24944-1 Pa. $3.95

TECHNICAL MANUAL AND DICTIONARY OF CLASSICAL BALLET, Gail Grant. Defines, explains, comments on steps, movements, poses and concepts. 15-page pictorial section. Basic book for student, viewer. 127pp. 5⅜ x 8½. 21843-0 Pa. $4.95

BRASS INSTRUMENTS: Their History and Development, Anthony Baines. Authoritative, updated survey of the evolution of trumpets, trombones, bugles, cornets, French horns, tubas and other brass wind instruments. Over 140 illustrations and 48 music examples. Corrected and updated by author. New preface. Bibliography. 320pp. 5⅜ x 8½. 27574-4 Pa. $9.95

HOLLYWOOD GLAMOR PORTRAITS, John Kobal (ed.). 145 photos from 1926-49. Harlow, Gable, Bogart, Bacall; 94 stars in all. Full background on photographers, technical aspects. 160pp. 8⅜ x 11¼. 23352-9 Pa. $12.95

MAX AND MORITZ, Wilhelm Busch. Great humor classic in both German and English. Also 10 other works: "Cat and Mouse," "Plisch and Plumm," etc. 216pp. 5⅜ x 8½. 20181-3 Pa. $6.95

THE RAVEN AND OTHER FAVORITE POEMS, Edgar Allan Poe. Over 40 of the author's most memorable poems: "The Bells," "Ulalume," "Israfel," "To Helen," "The Conqueror Worm," "Eldorado," "Annabel Lee," many more. Alphabetic lists of titles and first lines. 64pp. 5 3/16 x 8¼. 26685-0 Pa. $1.00

PERSONAL MEMOIRS OF U. S. GRANT, Ulysses Simpson Grant. Intelligent, deeply moving firsthand account of Civil War campaigns, considered by many the finest military memoirs ever written. Includes letters, historic photographs, maps and more. 528pp. 6⅛ x 9¼. 28587-1 Pa. $12.95

AMULETS AND SUPERSTITIONS, E. A. Wallis Budge. Comprehensive discourse on origin, powers of amulets in many ancient cultures: Arab, Persian Babylonian, Assyrian, Egyptian, Gnostic, Hebrew, Phoenician, Syriac, etc. Covers cross, swastika, crucifix, seals, rings, stones, etc. 584pp. 5⅜ x 8½. 23573-4 Pa. $15.95

RUSSIAN STORIES/PYCCKNE PACCKA3bl: A Dual-Language Book, edited by Gleb Struve. Twelve tales by such masters as Chekhov, Tolstoy, Dostoevsky, Pushkin, others. Excellent word-for-word English translations on facing pages, plus teaching and study aids, Russian/English vocabulary, biographical/critical introductions, more. 416pp. 5⅜ x 8½. 26244-8 Pa. $9.95

PHILADELPHIA THEN AND NOW: 60 Sites Photographed in the Past and Present, Kenneth Finkel and Susan Oyama. Rare photographs of City Hall, Logan Square, Independence Hall, Betsy Ross House, other landmarks juxtaposed with contemporary views. Captures changing face of historic city. Introduction. Captions. 128pp. 8¼ x 11. 25790-8 Pa. $9.95

AIA ARCHITECTURAL GUIDE TO NASSAU AND SUFFOLK COUNTIES, LONG ISLAND, The American Institute of Architects, Long Island Chapter, and the Society for the Preservation of Long Island Antiquities. Comprehensive, well-researched and generously illustrated volume brings to life over three centuries of Long Island's great architectural heritage. More than 240 photographs with authoritative, extensively detailed captions. 176pp. 8¼ x 11. 26946-9 Pa. $14.95

NORTH AMERICAN INDIAN LIFE: Customs and Traditions of 23 Tribes, Elsie Clews Parsons (ed.). 27 fictionalized essays by noted anthropologists examine religion, customs, government, additional facets of life among the Winnebago, Crow, Zuni, Eskimo, other tribes. 480pp. 6⅛ x 9¼. 27377-6 Pa. $10.95

FRANK LLOYD WRIGHT'S HOLLYHOCK HOUSE, Donald Hoffmann. Lavishly illustrated, carefully documented study of one of Wright's most controversial residential designs. Over 120 photographs, floor plans, elevations, etc. Detailed perceptive text by noted Wright scholar. Index. 128pp. 9¼ x 10¾. 27133-1 Pa. $11.95

THE MALE AND FEMALE FIGURE IN MOTION: 60 Classic Photographic Sequences, Eadweard Muybridge. 60 true-action photographs of men and women walking, running, climbing, bending, turning, etc., reproduced from rare 19th-century masterpiece. vi + 121pp. 9 x 12. 24745-7 Pa. $10.95

1001 QUESTIONS ANSWERED ABOUT THE SEASHORE, N. J. Berrill and Jacquelyn Berrill. Queries answered about dolphins, sea snails, sponges, starfish, fishes, shore birds, many others. Covers appearance, breeding, growth, feeding, much more. 305pp. 5¼ x 8¼. 23366-9 Pa. $9.95

GUIDE TO OWL WATCHING IN NORTH AMERICA, Donald S. Heintzelman. Superb guide offers complete data and descriptions of 19 species: barn owl, screech owl, snowy owl, many more. Expert coverage of owl-watching equipment, conservation, migrations and invasions, etc. Guide to observing sites. 84 illustrations. xiii + 193pp. 5⅜ x 8½. 27344-X Pa. $8.95

MEDICINAL AND OTHER USES OF NORTH AMERICAN PLANTS: A Historical Survey with Special Reference to the Eastern Indian Tribes, Charlotte Erichsen-Brown. Chronological historical citations document 500 years of usage of plants, trees, shrubs native to eastern Canada, northeastern U.S. Also complete identifying information. 343 illustrations. 544pp. 6½ x 9¼. 25951-X Pa. $12.95

STORYBOOK MAZES, Dave Phillips. 23 stories and mazes on two-page spreads: Wizard of Oz, Treasure Island, Robin Hood, etc. Solutions. 64pp. 8¼ x 11. 23628-5 Pa. $2.95

NEGRO FOLK MUSIC, U.S.A., Harold Courlander. Noted folklorist's scholarly yet readable analysis of rich and varied musical tradition. Includes authentic versions of over 40 folk songs. Valuable bibliography and discography. xi + 324pp. 5⅜ x 8½. 27350-4 Pa. $9.95

MOVIE-STAR PORTRAITS OF THE FORTIES, John Kobal (ed.). 163 glamor, studio photos of 106 stars of the 1940s: Rita Hayworth, Ava Gardner, Marlon Brando, Clark Gable, many more. 176pp. 8⅜ x 11¼. 23546-7 Pa. $14.95

BENCHLEY LOST AND FOUND, Robert Benchley. Finest humor from early 30s, about pet peeves, child psychologists, post office and others. Mostly unavailable elsewhere. 73 illustrations by Peter Arno and others. 183pp. 5⅜ x 8½. 22410-4 Pa. $6.95

YEKL and THE IMPORTED BRIDEGROOM AND OTHER STORIES OF YIDDISH NEW YORK, Abraham Cahan. Film Hester Street based on Yekl (1896). Novel, other stories among first about Jewish immigrants on N.Y.'s East Side. 240pp. 5⅜ x 8½. 22427-9 Pa. $6.95

SELECTED POEMS, Walt Whitman. Generous sampling from *Leaves of Grass.* Twenty-four poems include "I Hear America Singing," "Song of the Open Road," "I Sing the Body Electric," "When Lilacs Last in the Dooryard Bloom'd," "O Captain! My Captain!"–all reprinted from an authoritative edition. Lists of titles and first lines. 128pp. 5³⁄₁₆ x 8¼. 26878-0 Pa. $1.00

MY BONDAGE AND MY FREEDOM, Frederick Douglass. Born a slave, Douglass became outspoken force in antislavery movement. The best of Douglass' autobiographies. Graphic description of slave life. 464pp. 5⅜ x 8½. 22457-0 Pa. $8.95

FOLLOWING THE EQUATOR: A Journey Around the World, Mark Twain. Fascinating humorous account of 1897 voyage to Hawaii, Australia, India, New Zealand, etc. Ironic, bemused reports on peoples, customs, climate, flora and fauna, politics, much more. 197 illustrations. 720pp. 5⅜ x 8½. 26113-1 Pa. $15.95

THE PEOPLE CALLED SHAKERS, Edward D. Andrews. Definitive study of Shakers: origins, beliefs, practices, dances, social organization, furniture and crafts, etc. 33 illustrations. 351pp. 5⅜ x 8½. 21081-2 Pa. $8.95

THE MYTHS OF GREECE AND ROME, H. A. Guerber. A classic of mythology, generously illustrated, long prized for its simple, graphic, accurate retelling of the principal myths of Greece and Rome, and for its commentary on their origins and significance. With 64 illustrations by Michelangelo, Raphael, Titian, Rubens, Canova, Bernini and others. 480pp. 5⅜ x 8½. 27584-1 Pa. $9.95

PSYCHOLOGY OF MUSIC, Carl E. Seashore. Classic work discusses music as a medium from psychological viewpoint. Clear treatment of physical acoustics, auditory apparatus, sound perception, development of musical skills, nature of musical feeling, host of other topics. 88 figures. 408pp. 5⅜ x 8½. 21851-1 Pa. $11.95

THE PHILOSOPHY OF HISTORY, Georg W. Hegel. Great classic of Western thought develops concept that history is not chance but rational process, the evolution of freedom. 457pp. 5⅜ x 8½. 20112-0 Pa. $9.95

THE BOOK OF TEA, Kakuzo Okakura. Minor classic of the Orient: entertaining, charming explanation, interpretation of traditional Japanese culture in terms of tea ceremony. 94pp. 5⅜ x 8½. 20070-1 Pa. $3.95

LIFE IN ANCIENT EGYPT, Adolf Erman. Fullest, most thorough, detailed older account with much not in more recent books, domestic life, religion, magic, medicine, commerce, much more. Many illustrations reproduce tomb paintings, carvings, hieroglyphs, etc. 597pp. 5⅜ x 8½. 22632-8 Pa. $12.95

SUNDIALS, Their Theory and Construction, Albert Waugh. Far and away the best, most thorough coverage of ideas, mathematics concerned, types, construction, adjusting anywhere. Simple, nontechnical treatment allows even children to build several of these dials. Over 100 illustrations. 230pp. 5⅜ x 8½. 22947-5 Pa. $8.95

DYNAMICS OF FLUIDS IN POROUS MEDIA, Jacob Bear. For advanced students of ground water hydrology, soil mechanics and physics, drainage and irrigation engineering, and more. 335 illustrations. Exercises, with answers. 784pp. 6⅛ x 9¼. 65675-6 Pa. $19.95

SONGS OF EXPERIENCE: Facsimile Reproduction with 26 Plates in Full Color, William Blake. 26 full-color plates from a rare 1826 edition. Includes "TheTyger," "London," "Holy Thursday," and other poems. Printed text of poems. 48pp. 5¼ x 7. 24636-1 Pa. $4.95

OLD-TIME VIGNETTES IN FULL COLOR, Carol Belanger Grafton (ed.). Over 390 charming, often sentimental illustrations, selected from archives of Victorian graphics—pretty women posing, children playing, food, flowers, kittens and puppies, smiling cherubs, birds and butterflies, much more. All copyright-free. 48pp. 9¼ x 12¼. 27269-9 Pa. $7.95

PERSPECTIVE FOR ARTISTS, Rex Vicat Cole. Depth, perspective of sky and sea, shadows, much more, not usually covered. 391 diagrams, 81 reproductions of drawings and paintings. 279pp. 5⅜ x 8½. 22487-2 Pa. $7.95

DRAWING THE LIVING FIGURE, Joseph Sheppard. Innovative approach to artistic anatomy focuses on specifics of surface anatomy, rather than muscles and bones. Over 170 drawings of live models in front, back and side views, and in widely varying poses. Accompanying diagrams. 177 illustrations. Introduction. Index. 144pp. 8⅜ x11¼. 26723-7 Pa. $8.95

GOTHIC AND OLD ENGLISH ALPHABETS: 100 Complete Fonts, Dan X. Solo. Add power, elegance to posters, signs, other graphics with 100 stunning copyright-free alphabets: Blackstone, Dolbey, Germania, 97 more–including many lower-case, numerals, punctuation marks. 104pp. 8⅛ x 11. 24695-7 Pa. $8.95

HOW TO DO BEADWORK, Mary White. Fundamental book on craft from simple projects to five-bead chains and woven works. 106 illustrations. 142pp. 5⅜ x 8. 20697-1 Pa. $5.95

THE BOOK OF WOOD CARVING, Charles Marshall Sayers. Finest book for beginners discusses fundamentals and offers 34 designs. "Absolutely first rate . . . well thought out and well executed."–E. J. Tangerman. 118pp. 7¾ x 10⅝. 23654-4 Pa. $7.95

ILLUSTRATED CATALOG OF CIVIL WAR MILITARY GOODS: Union Army Weapons, Insignia, Uniform Accessories, and Other Equipment, Schuyler, Hartley, and Graham. Rare, profusely illustrated 1846 catalog includes Union Army uniform and dress regulations, arms and ammunition, coats, insignia, flags, swords, rifles, etc. 226 illustrations. 160pp. 9 x 12. 24939-5 Pa. $10.95

WOMEN'S FASHIONS OF THE EARLY 1900s: An Unabridged Republication of "New York Fashions, 1909," National Cloak & Suit Co. Rare catalog of mail-order fashions documents women's and children's clothing styles shortly after the turn of the century. Captions offer full descriptions, prices. Invaluable resource for fashion, costume historians. Approximately 725 illustrations. 128pp. 8⅜ x 11¼. 27276-1 Pa. $11.95

THE 1912 AND 1915 GUSTAV STICKLEY FURNITURE CATALOGS, Gustav Stickley. With over 200 detailed illustrations and descriptions, these two catalogs are essential reading and reference materials and identification guides for Stickley furniture. Captions cite materials, dimensions and prices. 112pp. 6½ x 9¼. 26676-1 Pa. $9.95

EARLY AMERICAN LOCOMOTIVES, John H. White, Jr. Finest locomotive engravings from early 19th century: historical (1804–74), main-line (after 1870), special, foreign, etc. 147 plates. 142pp. 11⅜ x 8¼. 22772-3 Pa. $10.95

THE TALL SHIPS OF TODAY IN PHOTOGRAPHS, Frank O. Braynard. Lavishly illustrated tribute to nearly 100 majestic contemporary sailing vessels: Amerigo Vespucci, Clearwater, Constitution, Eagle, Mayflower, Sea Cloud, Victory, many more. Authoritative captions provide statistics, background on each ship. 190 black-and-white photographs and illustrations. Introduction. 128pp. 8⅞ x 11¾. 27163-3 Pa. $14.95

EARLY NINETEENTH-CENTURY CRAFTS AND TRADES, Peter Stockham (ed.). Extremely rare 1807 volume describes to youngsters the crafts and trades of the day: brickmaker, weaver, dressmaker, bookbinder, ropemaker, saddler, many more. Quaint prose, charming illustrations for each craft. 20 black-and-white line illustrations. 192pp. 4⅝ x 6. 27293-1 Pa. $4.95

VICTORIAN FASHIONS AND COSTUMES FROM HARPER'S BAZAR, 1867–1898, Stella Blum (ed.). Day costumes, evening wear, sports clothes, shoes, hats, other accessories in over 1,000 detailed engravings. 320pp. 9⅜ x 12¼. 22990-4 Pa. $15.95

GUSTAV STICKLEY, THE CRAFTSMAN, Mary Ann Smith. Superb study surveys broad scope of Stickley's achievement, especially in architecture. Design philosophy, rise and fall of the Craftsman empire, descriptions and floor plans for many Craftsman houses, more. 86 black-and-white halftones. 31 line illustrations. Introduction 208pp. 6½ x 9¼. 27210-9 Pa. $9.95

THE LONG ISLAND RAIL ROAD IN EARLY PHOTOGRAPHS, Ron Ziel. Over 220 rare photos, informative text document origin (1844) and development of rail service on Long Island. Vintage views of early trains, locomotives, stations, passengers, crews, much more. Captions. 8⅞ x 11¾. 26301-0 Pa. $13.95

THE BOOK OF OLD SHIPS: From Egyptian Galleys to Clipper Ships, Henry B. Culver. Superb, authoritative history of sailing vessels, with 80 magnificent line illustrations. Galley, bark, caravel, longship, whaler, many more. Detailed, informative text on each vessel by noted naval historian. Introduction. 256pp. 5⅜ x 8½. 27332-6 Pa. $7.95

TEN BOOKS ON ARCHITECTURE, Vitruvius. The most important book ever written on architecture. Early Roman aesthetics, technology, classical orders, site selection, all other aspects. Morgan translation. 331pp. 5⅜ x 8½. 20645-9 Pa. $8.95

THE HUMAN FIGURE IN MOTION, Eadweard Muybridge. More than 4,500 stopped-action photos, in action series, showing undraped men, women, children jumping, lying down, throwing, sitting, wrestling, carrying, etc. 390pp. 7⅞ x 10⅝. 20204-6 Clothbd. $27.95

TREES OF THE EASTERN AND CENTRAL UNITED STATES AND CANADA, William M. Harlow. Best one-volume guide to 140 trees. Full descriptions, woodlore, range, etc. Over 600 illustrations. Handy size. 288pp. 4½ x 6⅜. 20395-6 Pa. $6.95

SONGS OF WESTERN BIRDS, Dr. Donald J. Borror. Complete song and call repertoire of 60 western species, including flycatchers, juncoes, cactus wrens, many more–includes fully illustrated booklet. Cassette and manual 99913-0 $8.95

GROWING AND USING HERBS AND SPICES, Milo Miloradovich. Versatile handbook provides all the information needed for cultivation and use of all the herbs and spices available in North America. 4 illustrations. Index. Glossary. 236pp. 5⅜ x 8½. 25058-X Pa. $7.95

BIG BOOK OF MAZES AND LABYRINTHS, Walter Shepherd. 50 mazes and labyrinths in all–classical, solid, ripple, and more–in one great volume. Perfect inexpensive puzzler for clever youngsters. Full solutions. 112pp. 8⅛ x 11. 22951-3 Pa. $4.95

CATALOG OF DOVER BOOKS

ANATOMY: A Complete Guide for Artists, Joseph Sheppard. A master of figure drawing shows artists how to render human anatomy convincingly. Over 460 illustrations. 224pp. 8⅜ x 11¼. 27279-6 Pa. $11.95

MEDIEVAL CALLIGRAPHY: Its History and Technique, Marc Drogin. Spirited history, comprehensive instruction manual covers 13 styles (ca. 4th century thru 15th). Excellent photographs; directions for duplicating medieval techniques with modern tools. 224pp. 8⅜ x 11¼. 26142-5 Pa. $12.95

DRIED FLOWERS: How to Prepare Them, Sarah Whitlock and Martha Rankin. Complete instructions on how to use silica gel, meal and borax, perlite aggregate, sand and borax, glycerine and water to create attractive permanent flower arrangements. 12 illustrations. 32pp. 5⅜ x 8½. 21802-3 Pa. $1.00

EASY-TO-MAKE BIRD FEEDERS FOR WOODWORKERS, Scott D. Campbell. Detailed, simple-to-use guide for designing, constructing, caring for and using feeders. Text, illustrations for 12 classic and contemporary designs. 96pp. 5⅜ x 8½. 25847-5 Pa. $3.95

SCOTTISH WONDER TALES FROM MYTH AND LEGEND, Donald A. Mackenzie. 16 lively tales tell of giants rumbling down mountainsides, of a magic wand that turns stone pillars into warriors, of gods and goddesses, evil hags, powerful forces and more. 240pp. 5⅜ x 8½. 29677-6 Pa. $6.95

THE HISTORY OF UNDERCLOTHES, C. Willett Cunnington and Phyllis Cunnington. Fascinating, well-documented survey covering six centuries of English undergarments, enhanced with over 100 illustrations: 12th-century laced-up bodice, footed long drawers (1795), 19th-century bustles, 19th-century corsets for men, Victorian "bust improvers," much more. 272pp. 5⅜ x 8¼. 27124-2 Pa. $9.95

ARTS AND CRAFTS FURNITURE: The Complete Brooks Catalog of 1912, Brooks Manufacturing Co. Photos and detailed descriptions of more than 150 now very collectible furniture designs from the Arts and Crafts movement depict davenports, settees, buffets, desks, tables, chairs, bedsteads, dressers and more, all built of solid, quarter-sawed oak. Invaluable for students and enthusiasts of antiques, Americana and the decorative arts. 80pp. 6½ x 9¼. 27471-3 Pa. $8.95

HOW WE INVENTED THE AIRPLANE: An Illustrated History, Orville Wright. Fascinating firsthand account covers early experiments, construction of planes and motors, first flights, much more. Introduction and commentary by Fred C. Kelly. 76 photographs. 96pp. 8¼ x 11. 25662-6 Pa. $8.95

THE ARTS OF THE SAILOR: Knotting, Splicing and Ropework, Hervey Garrett Smith. Indispensable shipboard reference covers tools, basic knots and useful hitches; handsewing and canvas work, more. Over 100 illustrations. Delightful reading for sea lovers. 256pp. 5⅜ x 8½. 26440-8 Pa. $8.95

FRANK LLOYD WRIGHT'S FALLINGWATER: The House and Its History, Second, Revised Edition, Donald Hoffmann. A total revision–both in text and illustrations–of the standard document on Fallingwater, the boldest, most personal architectural statement of Wright's mature years, updated with valuable new material from the recently opened Frank Lloyd Wright Archives. "Fascinating"–*The New York Times*. 116 illustrations. 128pp. 9¼ x 10¾. 27430-6 Pa. $12.95

AUTOBIOGRAPHY: The Story of My Experiments with Truth, Mohandas K. Gandhi. Boyhood, legal studies, purification, the growth of the Satyagraha (nonviolent protest) movement. Critical, inspiring work of the man responsible for the freedom of India. 480pp. 5⅜ x 8½. (USO) 24593-4 Pa. $8.95

CELTIC MYTHS AND LEGENDS, T. W. Rolleston. Masterful retelling of Irish and Welsh stories and tales. Cuchulain, King Arthur, Deirdre, the Grail, many more. First paperback edition. 58 full-page illustrations. 512pp. 5⅜ x 8½. 26507-2 Pa. $9.95

THE PRINCIPLES OF PSYCHOLOGY, William James. Famous long course complete, unabridged. Stream of thought, time perception, memory, experimental methods; great work decades ahead of its time. 94 figures. 1,391pp. 5⅜ x 8½. 2-vol. set.
Vol. I: 20381-6 Pa. $13.95
Vol. II: 20382-4 Pa. $14.95

THE WORLD AS WILL AND REPRESENTATION, Arthur Schopenhauer. Definitive English translation of Schopenhauer's life work, correcting more than 1,000 errors, omissions in earlier translations. Translated by E. F. J. Payne. Total of 1,269pp. 5⅜ x 8½. 2-vol. set.
Vol. 1: 21761-2 Pa. $12.95
Vol. 2: 21762-0 Pa. $12.95

MAGIC AND MYSTERY IN TIBET, Madame Alexandra David-Neel. Experiences among lamas, magicians, sages, sorcerers, Bonpa wizards. A true psychic discovery. 32 illustrations. 321pp. 5⅜ x 8½. (USO) 22682-4 Pa. $9.95

THE EGYPTIAN BOOK OF THE DEAD, E. A. Wallis Budge. Complete reproduction of Ani's papyrus, finest ever found. Full hieroglyphic text, interlinear transliteration, word-for-word translation, smooth translation. 533pp. 6½ x 9¼.
21866-X Pa. $11.95

MATHEMATICS FOR THE NONMATHEMATICIAN, Morris Kline. Detailed, college-level treatment of mathematics in cultural and historical context, with numerous exercises. Recommended Reading Lists. Tables. Numerous figures. 641pp. 5⅜ x 8½.
24823-2 Pa. $11.95

THEORY OF WING SECTIONS: Including a Summary of Airfoil Data, Ira H. Abbott and A. E. von Doenhoff. Concise compilation of subsonic aerodynamic characteristics of NACA wing sections, plus description of theory. 350pp. of tables. 693pp. 5⅜ x 8½. 60586-8 Pa. $14.95

THE RIME OF THE ANCIENT MARINER, Gustave Doré, S. T. Coleridge. Doré's finest work; 34 plates capture moods, subtleties of poem. Flawless full-size reproductions printed on facing pages with authoritative text of poem. "Beautiful. Simply beautiful."–*Publisher's Weekly.* 77pp. 9¼ x 12. 22305-1 Pa. $7.95

NORTH AMERICAN INDIAN DESIGNS FOR ARTISTS AND CRAFTSPEOPLE, Eva Wilson. Over 360 authentic copyright-free designs adapted from Navajo blankets, Hopi pottery, Sioux buffalo hides, more. Geometrics, symbolic figures, plant and animal motifs, etc. 128pp. 8⅜ x 11. (EUK) 25341-4 Pa. $8.95

SCULPTURE: Principles and Practice, Louis Slobodkin. Step-by-step approach to clay, plaster, metals, stone; classical and modern. 253 drawings, photos. 255pp. 8⅛ x 11.
22960-2 Pa. $11.95

THE INFLUENCE OF SEA POWER UPON HISTORY, 1660–1783, A. T. Mahan. Influential classic of naval history and tactics still used as text in war colleges. First paperback edition. 4 maps. 24 battle plans. 640pp. 5⅜ x 8½.   25509-3 Pa. $14.95

THE STORY OF THE TITANIC AS TOLD BY ITS SURVIVORS, Jack Winocour (ed.). What it was really like. Panic, despair, shocking inefficiency, and a little heroism. More thrilling than any fictional account. 26 illustrations. 320pp. 5⅜ x 8½.
20610-6 Pa. $8.95

FAIRY AND FOLK TALES OF THE IRISH PEASANTRY, William Butler Yeats (ed.). Treasury of 64 tales from the twilight world of Celtic myth and legend: "The Soul Cages," "The Kildare Pooka," "King O'Toole and his Goose," many more. Introduction and Notes by W. B. Yeats. 352pp. 5⅜ x 8½.   26941-8 Pa. $8.95

BUDDHIST MAHAYANA TEXTS, E. B. Cowell and Others (eds.). Superb, accurate translations of basic documents in Mahayana Buddhism, highly important in history of religions. The Buddha-karita of Asvaghosha, Larger Sukhavativyuha, more. 448pp. 5⅜ x 8½.   25552-2 Pa. $12.95

ONE TWO THREE . . . INFINITY: Facts and Speculations of Science, George Gamow. Great physicist's fascinating, readable overview of contemporary science: number theory, relativity, fourth dimension, entropy, genes, atomic structure, much more. 128 illustrations. Index. 352pp. 5⅜ x 8½.   25664-2 Pa. $8.95

ENGINEERING IN HISTORY, Richard Shelton Kirby, et al. Broad, nontechnical survey of history's major technological advances: birth of Greek science, industrial revolution, electricity and applied science, 20th-century automation, much more. 181 illustrations. ". . . excellent . . ."–*Isis.* Bibliography. vii + 530pp. 5⅜ x 8¼.
26412-2 Pa. $14.95

DALÍ ON MODERN ART: The Cuckolds of Antiquated Modern Art, Salvador Dalí. Influential painter skewers modern art and its practitioners. Outrageous evaluations of Picasso, Cézanne, Turner, more. 15 renderings of paintings discussed. 44 calligraphic decorations by Dalí. 96pp. 5⅜ x 8½. (USO)   29220-7 Pa. $4.95

ANTIQUE PLAYING CARDS: A Pictorial History, Henry René D'Allemagne. Over 900 elaborate, decorative images from rare playing cards (14th–20th centuries): Bacchus, death, dancing dogs, hunting scenes, royal coats of arms, players cheating, much more. 96pp. 9¼ x 12¼.   29265-7 Pa. $12.95

MAKING FURNITURE MASTERPIECES: 30 Projects with Measured Drawings, Franklin H. Gottshall. Step-by-step instructions, illustrations for constructing handsome, useful pieces, among them a Sheraton desk, Chippendale chair, Spanish desk, Queen Anne table and a William and Mary dressing mirror. 224pp. 8⅛ x 11¼.
29338-6 Pa. $13.95

THE FOSSIL BOOK: A Record of Prehistoric Life, Patricia V. Rich et al. Profusely illustrated definitive guide covers everything from single-celled organisms and dinosaurs to birds and mammals and the interplay between climate and man. Over 1,500 illustrations. 760pp. 7½ x 10⅛.   29371-8 Pa. $29.95

Prices subject to change without notice.

Available at your book dealer or write for free catalog to Dept. GI, Dover Publications, Inc., 31 East 2nd St., Mineola, N.Y. 11501. Dover publishes more than 500 books each year on science, elementary and advanced mathematics, biology, music, art, literary history, social sciences and other areas.